Why Is This a Question?

Everything about the
origins & oddities of language
you never thought to ask

Paul Anthony Jones

Elliott&Thompson

First published 2022 by
Elliott and Thompson Limited
2 John Street
London WC1N 2ES
www.eandtbooks.com

This paperback edition published in 2023

ISBN: 978-1-78396-702-5

9 8 7 6 5 4 3 2 1

A catalogue record for this book is available from
the British Library.

Typesetting: Marie Doherty
Printed by CPI Group (UK) Ltd, Croydon, CR0 4YY

For my mam and dad

Every fact of every language, in the view of the linguistic student, calls for his investigation, since only in the light of all can any be completely understood. To assemble, arrange, and explain the whole body of linguistic phenomena, so as thoroughly to comprehend them, in each separate part and under all aspects, is his endeavour.

William Dwight Whitney,
Language and the Study of Language (1867)

Contents

Preface

Everyone is interested in language. I honestly believe that. It's one of the few things that connects us all – every culture on Earth has a language – and it takes only a glimmer of introspection to find what we say and why we say it interesting.

I noticed this recently, sitting in a pub one Saturday afternoon with a non-linguist friend of mine. He had spotted something I had recently posted on Twitter: the letter A is a tiny millennia-old drawing of an ox's head, snout upwards, and if you trace its history back through time, you'll find it comes from an Egyptian hieroglyph, ☒. (The full story behind that comes on page 128.)

'Is that really true?' he asked. I get that a lot on Twitter – it's almost as if there's a lot of disinformation on there.

'Yeah,' I replied. 'Snout at the top, horns at the bottom. Quite a lot of our letters come from hieroglyphs, actually.'

'Really? That's amazing.'

'I know, right?' I beamed. I was breaking through to the hardest of non-linguistic hearts. 'Like, M looks the way it does because it comes from the hieroglyph for water, which was a sort of wavy, zigzaggy line.' I drew a jagged line of MMMMs in the air with my finger.

'Wow.' A pause. 'That's honestly amazing.' He looked down at his phone, at the picture I'd tweeted showing the letter A's gradual evolution from two-horned ox to two-legged triangle. Another pause. 'It's your round, by the way.'

Admittedly, yes, it was a short-lived moment of introspection, quickly brought to an end by an empty pint glass. But, hey, I'll take it. Confirmation of my theory that there really is something about this that unites us all in shared curiosity.

Personally, it's been over twenty years since I first became fascinated by the science of language. In an English class on my first day at college, I still remember the slow realisation that this was an English lesson, but not as I knew it. Shakespeare and Steinbeck remained steadfastly on their shelves, and in their place out came syntax trees, truth tables, conversational transcriptions, diagrams of the brain, Old English, Middle English and the phonetic alphabet. I was hooked. I didn't know then that this would end up being such a big part of my life, of course, and I'd probably not have believed you if you'd told me that it would. But within a few short years I was a postgraduate student of linguistics, looking to follow that well-trodden path into research and academia.

But by the end of that course, I realised something was afoot. In short, I had hated it.

Not the subject, you understand, nor the brilliant, accomplished people I was working with. The problem was a wholesale one. It seemed to me that here was this magnificent subject – the most fascinating subject in the world – being preserved like a museum piece, behind glass and under lock and key, never to be touched or meddled with, and only ever to be shown to the people who had the time or inclination to enter the museum in the first place. I found myself wanting to tell everyone about everything, and how there's so much more to the study of English – or, rather, to language itself – than most of us will ever learn from school. And yet the opposite seemed to be the norm. It felt secretive and cliquish, not open and collaborative, and I felt increasingly at odds with it.

On my last day, in a final meeting with one of my tutors, I took the plunge. I told her I wasn't going to take my studies further as planned, and was going to gamble that prospective career in academia, go back to waiting tables, and try to build a career for myself doing what I had, in truth, always promised myself I would do. I was going to write. Away from classrooms and campuses, I was going to write about language, for as many people as possible.

'A gentleman scholar?!' she exclaimed, excellently failing to hide her horror. I guess she meant that as a slight. I think I took it as a badge of honour.

And now, here we are. It's over a decade since I started writing purely for fun about The Most Fascinating Subject in the World™, and in that time I've written books and countless articles, given I don't know how many talks and interviews, and found myself tweeting and blogging to a lively online audience as @HaggardHawks. Along the way, I like to think I've edged open those museum doors and made all of this a little more accessible to everyone – no matter their background or expertise, no matter how casual or professional their interest in language, and no matter their (in)ability to read Latin and Greek. This book feels a little like the culmination of that.

It's been a long time coming; I think I've been mentally drafting and redrafting this for about eight years. Back then, I wrote a blog about the origin of the number *eleven*, and why both it and *twelve* aren't listed among our teens. (A more robust version of that story is explained on page 109.) I kept thinking as I wrote it that this was one of those questions we would probably never think to ask, yet as soon as we did, we'd want to know the answer. I filed that thought away, along with the idea to answer several more ponderables like it in a book one day. *Why Is This a Question?* is now that book.

The chapters that follow answer twenty questions such as this, ranging from the basics of our language – defining our words and languages themselves – through to some of the more infamous quirks of the English language, and finally casting a more philosophical eye over the inner workings of language and human communication. It's an immense topic, in retrospect, and without a doubt this has been the toughest writing challenge I've ever taken on. I've always said that distilling any academic subject for a mass audience is a little like walking a tightrope: you don't want to talk down to people who have an understanding of it already, but you don't want to lean too far the other way and talk over the heads of everyone who does not. Every sentence here has had to walk that line, and I can only hope my balancing act has worked. From an academic point of view, I hope too that some of the decisions I've made to keep technical jargon, symbols and academic conventions to a minimum are the right ones. And from an armchair linguist's point of view, I hope that despite all the theories, models, studies and experiments, this doesn't feel too much like a dusty old textbook. A guidebook to a dusty old museum, though – that, I would take.

Introduction

What Is the English Language?

*Viewed freely, the English language is the accretion and
growth of every dialect, race, and range of time, and is the culling
and composition of all. From this point of view, it stands for
Language in the largest sense, and is really the greatest of studies.*

Walt Whitman, 'Slang in America' (1885)

A few miles from Germany's border with Denmark lies a grassy
patchwork of low-lying hills and lakes called the Angeln
peninsula. That name, *Angeln*, is popularly said to refer to the
fish-hook-shaped angle at which this broad crook of land juts out
from the European mainland to form the westernmost arm of the
Baltic Sea. Angeln itself forms one of the northernmost tips of one
of Germany's northernmost states, Schleswig-Holstein, and to this
growing list of superlatives we can add one more: this unassuming
corner of Europe has inadvertently given its name to a language now
spoken by one-quarter of the people on Earth.

Angeln was the homeland and namesake of the Angles, one
of the ancient peoples whose arrival in Britain kick-started the

development of the English language. England itself is literally 'Angle-land', and what you're reading here is 'Angle-ish'. But what's on this page bears little resemblance to anything the Angles themselves would have known and used some fifteen centuries ago. The story of how their language became our language is the story of the English language itself.

So let's set the scene. The Angles originally occupied much of the territory spanning the modern Danish border. To their north were the Jutes, while to the south dwelled the Saxons, the Frisians, the Franks and countless other tribal groups dotted across the western heartland of Europe. These were all descendants of an even earlier wave of migrants from the Ukrainian steppes, who began settling across Europe and Asia in the third millennium BCE. We're so far back in history at this point that this early migration was probably sparked by the domestication of horses, a landmark achievement that allowed the burden of long-distance travel to be shared with animals for the first time. No longer bound to lands accessible only on foot, people could now journey much more widely – and, as they did so, these ancient wanderers brought with them their equally ancient language.

No record of that language survives, but just as long-dead creatures can be reassembled from their fossilised remains, historical linguists have been able to reconstruct much of it by unearthing evidence from the languages we use today. Similarities between different languages in the present often point to a common ancestor in the past, and as more of these family parallels are discovered, a more detailed ancestral picture can be drawn.

Through this kind of research, we now know with some certainty how this ancient protolanguage might have sounded and operated, what many of its words might have been, and we can even pinpoint where it first emerged: by combining linguistic evidence with more tangible evidence from archaeology and anthropology, we can retrace its speakers' steps back across Europe to the northern and eastern shores of the Black Sea, where they and their language first emerged around 6,500 years ago. As their culture advanced and the world opened up as a consequence, these Bronze Age peoples migrated and eventually came to inhabit a vast region extending from the fringes and islands of western Europe to the Indian subcontinent. The language they spoke, ultimately, has come to be known as Proto-Indo-European.

With groups of its speakers now scattered so widely, contact between them naturally diminished. That isolation meant any quirks or local differences in the way each individual group happened to speak were not heard or adopted elsewhere. Over the next 3,000 years or so these differences gradually grew more numerous and accentuated, until the entire Proto-Indo-European language had broken up into a patchwork of regional dialects – each with its own unique local features – spoken everywhere from the beaches of Spain to the Arctic coasts of Russia and the banks of the Ganges. As they continued to diverge, these dialects became sufficiently distinct to be no longer understood by outsiders. Far from being merely different forms of the same mutual language, they had become the foundations of an entirely new set of languages.

In this way, almost every language now spoken across this vast stretch of the globe is a living descendant of this one ancestral proto-language. Through the Indo-European family tree, English is related not only to its nearest geographical neighbours, including Welsh and Irish, but to the likes of Spanish and Italian, Polish and Albanian,

Urdu and Afghan Pashto. Our linguistic ancestors wandered so far, in fact, that you could travel to the foothills of the Himalayas today and hear local Nepali speakers using such familiar-sounding words as *naam* ('name'), *musa* ('mouse'), *patha* ('path') and *dryagana* ('dragon').

In the area of Europe the Angles came to occupy, Proto-Indo-European initially devolved into a dialect known as Proto-Germanic. But by the first century BCE, this too had begun to break apart as scattered groups of its speakers developed increasingly distinct tongues. On the islands of Denmark and the coasts of Norway and Sweden, a new set of North Germanic dialects emerged; their descendants today include modern-day Danish, Norwegian and Swedish. In central Poland, an East Germanic branch arose, although its offspring (including the languages once spoken by the Goths and the Vandals) are now extinct. And in Germany, the Netherlands and mainland Denmark, a family of West Germanic dialects developed among the major players in our story – the Angles, Saxons and Jutes. Their descendants include German, Dutch, Flemish and Luxembourgish, and had history played out differently it's likely these would have remained the only major West Germanic languages still in existence. But at this point in our story, all that changed.

In the mid-fifth century CE, many Angles, Saxons and Jutes started to abandon their homes on the mainland and cross the sea to Britain. Quite what compelled them to do so is unclear. The Saxons had been raiding British coasts for 200 years before they began to settle there permanently, so it's possible their growing knowledge of the island prompted the move. Threats to agriculture, like droughts or flooding, might have proved a factor too, as medieval historians later recorded that Angeln was eventually abandoned altogether. But according to the most famous version of this story, the first Germanic settlers arrived in England for one very good and very simple reason: they were invited.

Britain at that time was only home to around 2 million people (though more conservative estimates put that figure closer to 500,000). Most of these were Celtic Britons, whose ancestors would have been among the islands' earliest inhabitants. Further north were the Picts and Scots, and for a time Britain was home to a considerable Roman population too, following the emperor Claudius' invasion in 43 CE. The Romans had introduced Latin, but outside the law and the military, the day-to-day language of many Britons had remained their native Celtic tongue, Common Brittonic. Had the Angles and Saxons never arrived, it's probable this would have formed the basis of what you're currently reading.

By the fifth century, however, the Romans were gone. With their empire dwindling and Rome besieged, the troops keeping Britain under Roman rule were now needed closer to home, leaving the cities they had founded to fend for themselves. In the face of recurrent (and, apparently, naked) raids from the north, many quickly began to struggle.

> No sooner were they [the Romans] gone than the Picts and Scots . . . hastily landed . . . inspired with the same avidity for blood, and all more eager to shroud their villainous faces in bushy hair than to cover with decent clothing those parts of their body which required it.
>
> St Gildas, *On the Ruin and Conquest of Britain* (*c.* 510)

In desperation, the de facto leader of the Britons, Vortigern, sent word to the Continent that mercenaries were needed to bolster his defences, and offered Kent's Isle of Thanet as payment for all those who came to his assistance. Three shipfuls of fighters, led by two Jutish brothers, Hengist and Horsa, landed at nearby Ebbsfleet in 449. In the months that followed, they clashed repeatedly with the Picts and Scots, reportedly successfully defending the Britons' interests every single time.

As ever more mercenaries arrived, however, the territory Vortigern had initially offered proved inadequate, and many new arrivals began settling much more widely across the island – with some even bringing their families and possessions with them to start new lives in Britain. This gradual encroachment proved understandably unwelcome to the Britons, and relations between the two sides soured. The situation reached a tipping point in 455, when both Horsa and one of Vortigern's sons, Catigern, were killed in fighting near the village of Aylesford in Kent. In response, Catigern's brother Vortimer raised an army and for a time succeeded in pushing the Anglo-Saxons back to the North Sea coast. But Hengist retaliated, boosting his own forces by inviting even more of his countrymen to come and take advantage of 'the richness of the land' and 'the worthlessness of the Britons'. By the end of the decade, he had established himself as ruler of the now Jutish kingdom of Kent. Further north and west, more and more Germanic settlers were arriving on British soil. The Anglo-Saxon invasion had begun.

In a final attempt to offset further bloodshed, a summit was arranged in 472, at which it was hoped a peaceful compromise could be brokered. All those in attendance agreed to arrive unarmed as a show of good will, but midway through proceedings that promise was broken. Drawing swords from inside their robes, the Anglo-Saxons launched a surprise attack on the Britons, killing all except Vortigern and one of his earls. This single act of duplicitousness – the so-called Treachery of the Long Knives – effectively ended Celtic rule in Britain and left a vacuum of power the Anglo-Saxons were quick to fill.

Vortigern's short-sightedness in effectively inviting a superior fighting force to the table has since become the stuff of legend, with much of this blood-spattered tale now considered a myth concocted later to make the founding of Anglo-Saxon England a more dramatic affair. Whether true or not, by the turn of the century, the Celtic hold on Britain was undoubtedly weakening. The Angles now controlled much of northern and eastern England; the Saxons ruled over the Midlands and south, and the Jutes maintained their south-east corner, alongside a second territory at Hampshire. For their part, the Britons made several attempts to reclaim their lands, but none had lasting success and many simply merged into the Anglo-Saxon way of life. Others retreated as their power and status dwindled, drifting westwards into Wales and Cornwall, northwards into Cumbria and the Borderlands, and southwards, across the Channel to Brittany. It is this retreat that remains at least partly responsible for the strongholds of Celtic language and culture that endure here today.

With the Anglo-Saxons now in charge of their 'Angle-land', the West Germanic language they had brought with them naturally became the principal language of ancient Britain. But with its speakers now cut off from their continental cousins, local differences again began to emerge that soon formed the foundations of an entirely new 'Anglish' language. The success of the Anglo-Saxon invasion therefore marks the beginning of our language's history – but, even by this point, the language of early England would scarcely have resembled anything on this page.

For one thing, the earliest Old English texts were written in runes, not the Latin alphabet we use today. Initially, English maintained many of the complex grammatical features of its Germanic ancestor too, dividing its words into genders, and using an intricate system of word endings to flag the grammatical roles of the words in its sentences. When it comes to the development of our language, the Anglo-Saxon invasion might have placed the pieces on the board, but the game itself was just beginning.

So what happened? Where did our runic letters go? Why did the Latin alphabet replace them? And what happened to our gendered vocabulary? It is questions such as these, which are so seldom asked, that this book seeks to answer – but to do so addresses only one part of the story.

Yes, English no longer classifies its words into genders – but why do so many other languages continue to do so? Yes, our alphabet has long since replaced our Germanic ancestors' runes – but where did these two different writing systems come from in the first place? Take a further step back from questions like these, and you might find yourself contemplating the true nuts and bolts of language. Why do different languages exist at all? Why do the letters you're reading here look the way they do? How do they communicate what we want them to? As you read this sentence, how are you understanding what these seemingly arbitrary symbols mean? And, while we're on the topic, what even is a question? Or a language? Or, for that matter, a word?

Q. 1

What Is a Word?

*Our use of words is generally inaccurate
and seldom completely correct, but our
meaning is recognised none the less.*

St. Augustine, *Confessions* (c. 397–8)

Have you ever been asked what a word means, but found yourself utterly unable to explain it? I can still remember the look of panic on my schoolteacher's face when a boy in my class asked her what *grace* was (and why Mary was so full of it). And then there was the friend of mine whose endlessly curious three-year-old asked him what *depth* meant while he was filling her paddling pool during a lazy summer barbecue, and in doing so instantly bamboozled every adult in earshot. Some words, it seems, are just difficult to define. We know what they mean, and can use them without a second thought – but try putting that meaning into words and it's hard not to resort to little more than a string of synonyms. 'Depth? Well, it's just *depth*, isn't it? Like . . . *deepness*.'

When it comes to defining our indefinables, one of the great ironies of language is that the word *word* is one of them. It might not seem as though it should prompt the same navel-gazing as something like *grace*, and if someone were to ask you what a *word* was you'd probably be able to give them a fair idea. ('A *word*? Well, it's a word, isn't it? Like . . . a little bit of language.') But in practice, words are surprisingly difficult to pin down, and practically every test or definition devised to do so quickly comes unstuck.

One common explanation is that words are everything found between spaces in writing. That's certainly how word-counting computer programs operate, and a glance over this page might make it seem a reliable yardstick. But how would you count the first word in the previous sentence, *that's*? Is that one word or two?

Another way of defining it is that when extra material is added to a sentence, additional words will always fall between, not inside, those already there. So *The owl and the pussycat went to sea* could become *The wise owl fledglings and even the aloof pussycat quickly went back to the sea*. We'd certainly never find ourselves talking about an *o-wise-wl* or a *puss-aloof-ycat*, but any definition assuming words can never be infixed like this is *abso-bloody-lutely* flawed.*

Broad rules of thumb such as these are clearly little use here. A much better starting point is that simple definition from earlier: a *word* is just a little bit of language. As throwaway as that might seem, at first glance it makes sense. We recognise *at, first* and *glance*

---

* The emphatic insertion of one word inside another is called tmesis; when it happens specifically with profanity, it's known as expletive infixation. Although it is often explained using examples such as *fan-bloody-tastic* or *in-fucking-credible*, in rhetorical terms tmesis can also refer to the emphatic division of the two halves of a pair of words, often for humour as much as emphasis, as in 'Stop your chit and your chat!' or 'I want no hanky, nor panky!'

as words, and can read them here as individual 'bits' of language. But it's explaining precisely what these 'bits' are that proves difficult, because as it stands that definition could easily be misinterpreted. After all, individual letters are just bits of language too, as are individual sounds, punctuation marks, nonsense jumbles of characters, and even whole sentences and paragraphs. To exclude everything that *isn't* a word, while including everything that *is*, we're clearly going to need some firmer ground rules.

Some are certainly more difficult to explain than others, but all words have a meaning. Adding that requirement immediately cuts out a lot of this excess noise, as letters and sounds have no meaning at all on their own, and sentences and paragraphs go too far the other way – blending multiple smaller units into larger, more meaningful wholes. Calling a word a single *meaningful* unit of language certainly feels like a more reliable definition, but there's still a problem: in language, not everything that has a meaning is a word.

owl	*owls*
pussycat	*pussycats*
dog	*dogs*
house	*houses*
word	*words*

In English, we typically add an *–s* onto the end of a noun to create its plural – changing one *word* into many *words*, one *dog* into multiple *dogs*, and a detached *house* into a row of *houses*. We'd scarcely think of that *–s* as a word in its own right, yet to be capable of creating this kind of change it must have some kind of meaning. Put another way, if a *dog* is a canine animal, and *dogs* means 'more than one canine animal', then surely –*s* must be the part that means 'more than one'. So wouldn't that make –*s* too a single, meaningful unit of language?

The problem is that –*s* is not a word, but a morpheme. Morphemes are the smallest possible meaning-bearing components of a language; the meaning they carry (like the 'more than one' meaning of –*s*) is called a sememe. By definition, morphemes can't be broken down into anything smaller that likewise has any kind of meaningful content. So while the –*s* of *dogs* is a morpheme, the meaningless *d*– is not.

Confusingly, that definition means many words count as morphemes too. *Dog* can be broken down only into its individual sounds, 'd', 'o' and 'g', and because they have no meaning on their own, it is a morpheme as well. *Dogs*, on the other hand, can be split apart – into its singular root, *dog* ('canine animal'), plus the plural tag –*s* ('more than one'). So, while one *dog* is a morpheme, multiple *dogs* are not. That overlap can make morphemes a tricky concept to grasp, but this distinction is an important one: whatever definition of a *word* we end up with, it will have to include the likes of both *dog* and *dogs*, while excluding the likes of –*s*. Dig a little deeper, however, and we have a neat way of doing just that.

Morphemes play a hugely important role in how our language operates. As well as changing singular words into plurals (*dog*, *dogs*), we can use the likes of –*ing* and –*ed* to change the tense of verbs (giving us *talking* and *talked* from *talk*), and use –*er* and –*est* to expand on our adjectives (making *quicker* and *quickest* out of *quick*). These are known as inflectional morphemes, as they work solely to alter the grammar of whatever root they attach to. Conversely, so-called derivational morphemes work to change the meaning of their roots, and thereby create entirely new words. We can use *–less* to form words implying an absence of something, like *faultless* or *timeless*, or tag *anti–* onto a word to create its opposite, such as *antihero* or *anticlimax*.

Unlike the words they connect to, however, on their own the likes of *–s* and *anti–* are lost. Attached to nothing, they mean nothing. You could no more draw someone's attention to a pack of dogs by shouting '*–s!*' than you could label yourself '*anti–*' without there being something to be *anti–* against. These are bound morphemes – fragments of language whose sememes come to the surface only when they are 'bound' to other things. The opposite, like *dog* and *house*, are free morphemes, which need no such support. And when it comes to defining a word, this freedom is crucial.

The linguist Leonard Bloomfield defined a *word* as a 'minimum free form' – a single unit of language, smaller than a phrase or a sentence, that is capable of maintaining its meaning on its own. The likes of *dog* and *dogs*, *owl* and *pussycat*, *linguist* and *definition* all pass that test, but on their own, *–s* and *anti–* fail it. Demanding a word not only have a meaning but be *independently* meaningful therefore excludes bound morphemes, like *–s*, while including everything we can use them to create. It's an ingenious solution. But where does that leave these?

doghouse	*coffee shop*
hotplate	*ice cream*
greenhouse	*walking stick*
downstairs	*toy factory*
blackbird	*golf ball*
loudspeaker	*post office*

When two or more words come together like this, they form a compound. Despite their twofold structure, compound words represent single concepts; if they didn't, there'd be no difference between a *loudspeaker* and a *loud speaker*.

But while *loudspeaker* and all the other words on the left here are classed as closed or 'univerbated' compounds, united as a single word, those on the right are open compounds, divided by a space.* These too are single concepts, as you cannot drop the *golf* from *golf ball* any more than you could claim a *house* and a *doghouse* are the same thing. Open compounds are therefore single, independently meaningful units of language built from single, independently meaningful units of language. We can't split them up, because their meaning relies on both their halves working together. So effectively, we're back where we started: is *coffee shop* one word or two? Fortunately, Bloomfield foresaw this problem and devised another ingenious solution. Unfortunately, this time he leads us into increasingly murky water.

---

* It's often just convention, legibility or personal preference that dictates whether a compound is open or closed. Without its space, *postoffice* is arguably too much of a jumble to function intelligibly as a single word – though the same was doubtless once thought of compounds such as *matchbox* and *hairstyle*, so perhaps *post office* will follow suit in the future. It's by no means uncommon for words to migrate from open to closed over time, often as their familiarity increases. After all, *today* and *tomorrow* were both once two words, as were the first *mailboxes* and *newspapers*, and anyone who has lived through the internet age will have seen the first *web sites*, *e-mails* and *voice mails* become *websites*, *emails* and *voicemails*. Even today some compounds remain in a state of flux, and happily exist in both forms: you're just as likely to see a sign for a *car park* as you are for a *carpark*.

As anyone who has ever studied poetry or Shakespeare will know, all words have a natural pattern of stressed and unstressed syllables. *Pattern* is stressed on its first syllable: PA-*ttern*. *Solution* on its second: *so*-LU-*tion*. Some longer words have multiple stressed syllables: IN-*di*-VID-*u-al*. Yet all words have just one primary stress – that is, one syllable accented above all others. So while both the first and third syllables of *individual* are stressed, IN-*di*-VID-*u-al*, only the third syllable receives the primary stress: IN-*di*-VID-*u-al*.

In English, unlike other languages, this stress is unpredictable and can fall in different places in different words. But that inconsistency allows it to play a crucial role in how we interpret the words we hear. Written down, a word such as *conduct*, for instance, is ambiguous, yet read aloud, we can shift its stress back and forth to differentiate between a person's behaviour (CON-*duct*) and the act of leading an orchestra (*con*-DUCT). In compounds, this disambiguating effect is even more obvious. Because *greenhouse* works as a single unit, it has just one primary stress: GREEN-*house*. Were its two halves just to happen to fall side by side in a sentence (*He lives in the green house opposite the red house*), they would operate independently, and so both be stressed: GREEN HOUSE. It's a subtle difference, but in practice it's enough for us to distinguish a glass structure for growing plants from a house that just happens to be green. It's also why you can go *downstairs* without necessarily going *down stairs*, and why you wouldn't need a *loudspeaker* to listen to a *loud speaker*. And it's why only the first of these two statements is true:

A crow is a black bird.
A crow is a blackbird.

Open compounds operate as single units too, and so have just one primary stress. Alter or reassign that stress, and their pairing will no longer function as a single unit but as a two-word phrase. A ball for playing golf is a GOLF *ball* (open compound), but a grand party for the members of a golf club is a GOLF BALL (two-word phrase). A staff for aiding a walker is a WAL-*king stick*, but a WAL-*king* STICK is a pole that's sprouted legs and ambled away. And while a child could play perfectly safely with a TOY FAC-*tory*, they would seldom be left unattended inside a TOY *fac-tory*. Try saying this sentence aloud too:

My French teacher is Swedish.

You probably read *French teacher* as an open compound there, and understood that sentence as referring to a teacher of French who just happens to come from Sweden. Stress precisely the same pair of words as a two-word phrase, however, and you'll have a much more factually questionable statement about a teacher from France who is also somehow from Sweden.

Taking stress into account like this proves that open compounds behave just as all our other words, and have one primary stress. As a result, we need to ensure they are included under our definition – but relying on stress alone to decide what's in and what's out is problematic, as not all our compound words are quite so keen to follow the rules. How do you say *ice cream*, for instance? Some people stress its first syllable: ICE *cream*. Others stress its second: *ice* CREAM. Some stress both: ICE CREAM. Some people might even switch between the three in different contexts. Under Bloomfield's stress rules, this would make *ice cream* a word to some people, a two-word phrase to others, and sometimes a word and sometimes a phrase to everybody else. That's not a particularly satisfactory conclusion, admittedly. How can we define what a *word* is if we can't all agree what is and isn't as a word in the first place?

Perhaps, then, we need to rethink our approach. As soon as we're forced to consider the stress patterns of individual words, our focus shifts from written language to spoken language. Speech predates writing, of course, as our evolutionary ancestors were talking to one another long before they thought to put pen to paper (or stylus to clay, as the case may be). Rather than bogging ourselves down in the problems posed by letters and spaces on a page, why not take our language back to its roots and consider a word as primarily a set of sounds? The sounds 'd', 'o' and 'g' (or phonetically, /d/, /ɒ/ and /g/) together form the word *dog*, /dɒg/, which carries the meaning 'canine animal'. String together the seven sounds in /kɒfɪ ʃɒp/, and you'll have the single meaningful compound word *coffee shop*, with its one primary stress, regardless of whether it is written open or closed.

Drawing this line in the linguistic sand gives us this definition: a *word* is a single independently meaningful unit of language, consisting of a sound or series of sounds, that can be represented as a series of written characters. Focusing on sound first and considering spelling only as an afterthought avoids the issues presented by compound words, while leaving bound morphemes and everything else to one side. Does that solve our problem? In basic terms, yes – if you're looking for an answer to the question in the title of this chapter, then something along these lines is probably the closest you will come to defining a word in any kind of watertight way. But in broader terms, no – even at this late stage, there are innumerable problems here.

At the beginning of this chapter, we touched on whether *that's* constitutes one word or two. We still haven't answered that question, for the very good reason it's all but impossible to do so conclusively. The same goes for contractions such as *dontcha*, *shoulda*, *gotcha* and *imma*, which operate as single word-like units in speech, despite being built from multiple individual words smashed together. Consider this too: now we know how bound morphemes work, would *anti-dog* qualify as a word? How about if someone were to comment on how *coffee-shopless* their neighbourhood was? You'd doubtless know what they meant, but is that a word?

Here's a sobering thought as well: at no point here have we stepped outside the cosy confines of English to consider how this definition might fare in other languages. German is well known for its capacity to string multiple elements together to form single word-like units with multifaceted meanings. In 1999, the official Association for the German Language nominated *Rindfleischetikettierungsüberwachungsaufgabenübertragungsgesetz* as one of its Words of the Year.* Is that a single word, or a conjoined collection of individual words? We'll come on to other languages in more detail later, but even without their input we're still in a quagmire here. There is, however, some good news: in the grand scheme of things, none of this really matters.

As much as we might think of the study of language as being the study of words, when it comes to examining and comparing

---

* This sixty-three-letter behemoth refers to a law concerning the labelling of beef; when it was introduced to the state legislature of Mecklenburg–Western Pomerania, the minister responsible for it felt obliged to apologise. The occurrence led to *Rindfleischetikettierungsüberwachungsaufgabenübertragungsgesetz* earning both a place for itself in the *Guinness Book of Records*, and on the shortlist for the 1999 German Word of the Year. Perhaps understandably, it lost out to *das Millennium*.

languages, the word *word* just isn't a particularly useful one. The reason we've ended up discussing the likes of morphemes and sememes here is because labels like these are of much greater value to language study than anything as vacuous and temperamental as *word*. Sure, when we don't need to be quite so academically rigorous, having a word like *word* to throw around is immensely useful. It lets us talk about the *words* on a page, jot down a few *words*, have a few *words* with someone, learn and translate *words* into a different language, and count the number of *words* in an assignment or essay. Up to the end of this sentence, you'll have read 3,025 of them in this chapter, and as something with which to casually divide up our written world, *word* works just fine. When it comes to trying to pin down its meaning more precisely, however, perhaps we shouldn't be too surprised that something we use so loosely defies all our attempts to define it.

Q. 2

What Is a Language?

Language is the most massive and inclusive art we know, a
mountainous and anonymous work of unconscious generations.

Edward Sapir, *Language* (1921)

In 2018, a team of researchers studying orangutans in the forests of Indonesia made a remarkable discovery. They had devised an experiment in which one of the team would be disguised as a threat – draping themselves with a blanket of tiger stripes, for instance – and crawl on all fours across the jungle floor, beneath where a mother orangutan and her young were sitting in the branches. Understandably, in most cases the mothers reacted swiftly, raised an alarm and retreated further into the treetops. But, sometimes, they waited. In fact, sometimes as much as twenty minutes would go by before the mother finally produced her alarm call, long after the test was over and the threat had disappeared.

At first, the researchers were baffled as to why some of the mothers appeared to be acting at such a delay, but the reason eventually became clear. Far from being lax or inattentive, they were teaching.

By waiting until it had moved on, the mothers could demonstrate to their young how to report a threat without risking attracting its attention while it was there. Effectively, their calls were not meant to mean 'There is a danger' but rather 'If you ever again see what we saw earlier, this is the sound to make.' True enough, it was found to be the mothers with the eldest offspring – who would naturally be better acclimatised to life in the jungle – that tended to delay the longest, while those with the youngest offspring seemed justifiably more concerned with escaping to safety.

It was a groundbreaking discovery. The fact that the mothers were able to assess the risk of a situation then decide its potential as a teaching opportunity was remarkable enough, but this experiment had also proved orangutans are capable of something called displaced reference – the ability to communicate about something not actually present at the moment of communication.

Displacement is a fundamental aspect of human language. Without it, we would never be able to tell stories or recall anecdotes, talk about the past or the future, and our conversations would be forever confined to a world of only immediately visible and experienceable things. In order to understand this story, for instance, you would have to have an orangutan alongside you right now as a live reference point – hardly the most practical foundation for a system of communication. Yet in nature, displaced reference is rare.* When you

---

* It was long believed honeybees were the only creatures capable of exhibiting displacement besides humans, as their 'waggle-dances' are used to inform other bees of the location of new sources of nectar. Studies have since found ants might use a similar technique to recruit others from their colony to retrieve food too large to carry on their own, and there is evidence ravens can inform one another of larger finds too.

hear birds chirruping in the trees, it's fair to say they're not discussing last week's weather, or what they hope will be on the bird table tomorrow. They're responding purely to the here and now – establishing territories, searching for mates, seeing off rivals, forming social bonds and reporting predators. Finding evidence of displacement in any wild creature was therefore a significant discovery. Finding it in one of our evolutionary cousins, however, had profound implications on the origin and development of our language, and our understanding of language itself in the natural world.

In the 1960s the linguist Charles Hockett included displaced reference on a list of what he called the design features of language. In all, he identified more than a dozen phenomena such as this that he considered collectively unique to human communication. So as well as our ability to talk about displaced things, our language can be defined by its learnability – our capacity to acquire new languages alongside those we already know. We can pass language on to other people thanks to a feature he called traditional transmission. What you're currently reading is an example of reflexiveness – our ability to use language to talk about language. Prevarication is what allows us to concoct stories and tell untruths. And because the production of language is deliberate, it exhibits specialisation: it is an intentional act, not merely the by-product of some other process, as when a dog's panting just happens to communicate to its owner that it's hot.

Perhaps the most basic feature on Hockett's checklist was the so-called vocal–auditory channel of human language – the two-way, back-and-forth arrangement by which one person speaks and another person hears. That channel in turn exhibits interchangeability: the listener can easily swap places with the speaker. And while the speaker can project sound in any direction, the listener can identify where that sound is coming from and shift to receive it more clearly thanks to a dual feature Hockett called broadcast transmission and directional reception.

The tendency of speech to fade instantly after it is produced is its transitoriness. Its capacity to carry meaning is its semanticity. A speaker can hear themselves talk thanks to something called total feedback. Arbitrariness means there is no sensible connection between the sounds we make and the meanings we attach to them: what we call *dogs*, *trees* and *walnuts* could just as easily be *cats*, *clouds* and *footstools*, as they're all fundamentally random labels. The fact each is comprised of individual sounds ('d', 'o', 'g') is called discreteness. And as those sounds have no meaning on their own, language operates around a two-tier framework called double articulation: our near endless supply of meaningful words is built from a limited supply of meaningless sounds.

Many of these features are found in other forms of natural communication – not just orangutan calls, but birdsong, whalesong, and the nectar dances of honeybees. (Some, like double articulation, are even true of music.) Find yourself a system that ticks all sixteen of Hockett's boxes, however, and by definition you will have human language.

As thorough as Hockett's checklist might be, it's fair to say his is hardly the most succinct of definitions. Instead, we can much more concisely say that language is a structured, speech-based system of communication.

We say it is *structured* because rules govern how it operates, and when those rules aren't followed, intelligible language isn't produced. The dos and don'ts of grammar form much of this basic rulebook, as without them there'd be no standard way of saying what we want to say and we'd all end up doing our own thing, forever unable to understand one another. These rules become so ingrained that we can use and apply them without a second thought, even to words we've never encountered before. If you were to discover the word *shring* were a noun, for instance, your inbuilt rulebook would instantly deduce that if you had a *shring* and I had a *shring*, we would together have two *shrings*. Discover it were a verb, however, and you would instead figure out that if you were to *shring* and I were to *shring*, we would both be *shringing*, and tomorrow we would have *shringed* (or even *shrung*).

But some rules are more subtle and are never taught to us as overtly as the rules of grammar, leaving us largely unaware we know them at all. Phonotactics is the branch of language that concerns what sounds and sound combinations are permissible in a language, and which are not. We largely piece this information together ourselves based on evidence from the so-called ambient language that surrounds us from the moment we're born – so although *shring* is not an English word, you'll know instinctively that it *could* be, while something like *ngrish* could not. You never had to be told that English doesn't use the 'ng' sound at the beginning of its words (while some languages, such as Albanian and Cantonese, do) but you'll nevertheless know that to be the case, based on a lifetime of linguistic evidence, not one word of which began *ng–*. Gaining an intuitive feel for what sounds right and wrong is a skill we develop astonishingly early: studies have suggested infants as young as nine months are already so attuned to the sounds of their family's mother tongue that they can filter out unfamiliar sounds from other languages.*

---

* In a 1993 study, six-month- and nine-month-old infants from a mix of English-speaking and Dutch-speaking families were read lists of words in both

We say that language is *speech-based* as it was from our ancestors' vocalisations that it first developed some 100,000 years or so ago. It took written language only a mere 95,000 years to catch up, and even more recently we've added the likes of sign language and Braille to our inventory when our other senses are impaired. But such visual and tactile forms of language are only optional extras, not universals, and language remains a predominantly speech-driven process.

We can call language *a system of communication* because no matter how it is transmitted, the passing-on of information is its fundamental purpose. Language and communication are not the same, however, as language is only one form of communication alongside all the other sensory techniques living things use to send messages to one another. The territorial sprays of cats and the signal-sending clouds of pheromones released by insects can at least be *likened* to language, but such scent-based communication is mercifully not an inbuilt quality of language itself, leaving us perfectly capable of communicating without the need to release foul smells. At least, not intentionally.

When we talk about language as a whole, however, we mean something different from *a* language. That distinction was unpicked more than a century ago, by one of the founders of modern linguistics, Ferdinand de Saussure. In a revolutionary series of lectures in

---

languages, including many words breaking the phonotactic rules of their family's mother tongue. The six-month-olds were found to show no preference for either list, but the nine-month-olds were found to pay closer attention to the words from their mother tongue than those that were foreign to them. Presumably our ability to recognise the sounds of our mother tongue is a faculty that usually develops sometime between these two ages.

the early 1900s, Saussure separated language itself (which he gave the French name *langage*) from the individual languages we use to talk to one another (the *langue*) and the personal, idiosyncratic language produced by an individual (the *parole*, the French word for speech). According to Saussure, language as a whole, or *langage*, is partly characterised by our ability to invent words and give them meanings – or, in his terms, *signifiers* and *signifieds*. When enough of these signifying pairs become established among a group of people, a language, or *langue*, is created. But this vast mutually understood system of words and meanings is abstract, confined invisibly to the minds and voices of its speakers. Only when they talk to one another or write things down – that is, produce their *parole* – does the *langue* become anything tangible, and capable of being heard, read, circulated and studied. Neither half, therefore, can exist without the other: without the *langue* there would be no language to produce, yet without the *parole*, the langue would remain unspoken, and utterly undetectable.

We might not think along quite the same philosophical lines as Saussure, of course, but his concept of a *langue* nevertheless mirrors what we would call a language: a single system of communication mutually understood and maintained by a group of people. In other words, if language itself is our capacity to communicate, then *a* language is one of the means by which we do just that.

We can identify individual languages using three common features. Each one has a grammar, comprising the rules that hold it together, including those of its syntax, which dictates the order of the words in its sentences. Those words comprise its lexicon, or vocabulary. And that in turn is built from a set of speech sounds, or phonemes, that make up its phonological system. So just as written letters (D, O, G) form an alphabet, spoken phonemes ('d', 'o', 'g') form a language's phonology.

A grammar, a lexicon and a phonology might be common to all known languages, but not every language showcases them in quite the same way. English is popularly said to have the world's biggest vocabulary, while you could learn all 137 words of the Toki Pona language in an afternoon. Our hundreds of thousands of words are all built from around forty-five different phonemes (depending on your accent), while by some counts the entire Hawaiian language uses only thirteen, and the Taa language of Botswana has well over a hundred. And English syntax typically follows a strict subject–verb–object or SVO order: *I* (subject) *eat* (verb) *pizza* (object). In Japanese, however, the equivalent sentence would be *I pizza eat* (SOV), while in Irish, it would be *Eat I pizza* (VSO). In Malagasy, *Eat pizza I* (VOS). In the Urarina language of Peru, *Pizza eat I* (OVS). In Venezuela's Warao language – and in less than 1 per cent of the world's languages overall – it would be *Pizza I eat* (OSV). And in the Warlpiri language of Australia, it could be literally anything, as it has no fixed word order whatsoever.

Aside from some basic common ground then, languages exhibit enormous differences. Yet there's often just as much variation within individual languages themselves. The rules and structures that hold our languages together are not so strict as to impose precisely the same form of a language on everyone who uses them, so that despite ostensibly sharing the same language, different people often produce noticeably different forms of it. And it is this variation that gives us our dialects.

Essentially, a dialect is a distinct form of a language that somehow differs from the standard in terms of those three features: grammar, vocabulary and phonology. It's easy to presume dialects are purely geographical language features, and we're certainly used to the idea of a language changing from one place to the next. But dialects can be distinguished by other factors too, such as age, race, class, gender and even occupation. Minderico is a near-extinct dialect of Portuguese once used solely by textile workers. Pitmatic is a dwindling dialect of English used exclusively by mineworkers in the coalfields of north-east England. Australia's Yanyuwa language has separate dialects for its male and female speakers. And because it was initially taught in segregated boys' and girls' schools, Irish Sign Language developed distinct male and female dialects in the mid-1900s. But if a language is a system of communication used mutually by a group of people, how is a dialect any different? Put another way, how can we tell if what we're dealing with is a dialect, like Minderico, or a language in its own right, like Portuguese?

This decision is usually based on a concept called mutual intelligibility. If two people can communicate perfectly well, despite any noticeable differences, they would be said to speak different dialects of the same language. If they cannot understand one another, they would be speaking different languages. We can always learn a new language alongside one we already know, of course, but without this prior learning there will always be a barrier between a language we are familiar with and one we are not. A different dialect, by definition, should never cause a problem.

As neat as this rule may seem, however, in reality the situation is rarely quite so clear cut.

> *Jeg drikker vand, men du drikker kaffe.*
> *Jeg drikker vann, men du drikker kaffe.*
> *Jag dricker vatten, men du dricker kaffe.*

To an unaccustomed eye or ear, these three sentences (meaning 'I am drinking water, but you are drinking coffee') might look as though they come from different dialects, given their similarities. In fact, each is written in something we would unquestionably think of as a language – the first is in Danish, the second in Norwegian, and the third in Swedish. The long and interconnected histories of these three languages have left them remarkably similar to one another today, to the extent that a Dane, a Norwegian and a Swede could hold a conversation together relatively easily, with each speaking their mother tongue. Under our rule of mutual intelligibility, however, these could easily be classed as overlapping dialects rather than individual languages. And 4,000 miles away in China, we find the complete opposite.

China is a hugely diverse nation, home to more than 300 different languages. Many of these are mutually unintelligible, yet almost all share the same writing system, first introduced under the Qing Dynasty more than 2,000 years ago. Give or take a handful of outliers here and there, the widespread use of this standard system today means the majority of China's languages now look all but identical in print, despite their often striking dissimilarities. The written character for 'plant', for instance, 植物, is *zhíwù* in Mandarin, *zik mat* in Cantonese, *zeq veq* in Wu, *chhut-vut* in Hakka, *sit-but* in Min Nan, and has countless other variations elsewhere.

Since the early 1900s, successive governments in China have attempted to resolve this inconsistency by promoting not just a common writing system but a single unifying language, based primarily on the Beijing dialect of Mandarin. Some three-quarters of the population now claim some knowledge of this Standard Chinese language – but the success of its rollout has effectively relegated all the country's other languages to the status of its dialects. These 'dialects', however, including Cantonese and Min Nan, are in reality wildly distinct languages, often much more different from one another than Danish, Norwegian and Swedish.

Inconsistencies such as these are found all over the world. A Moroccan Arabic speaker would struggle to converse fluently with fellow Arabic speakers from Somalia, Lebanon or Yemen, despite each ostensibly speaking a regional variation of the same language. In Azerbaijan, meanwhile, the local Azeri language is so similar to nearby Turkish that unsubtitled Turkish soap operas are among the country's most popular television programmes.* Clearly, mutual intelligibility is not quite the hard and fast rule it might have seemed. So what is it that earns some systems of communication the title *language*, while others remain *dialects*? Oddly, the answer has less to do with language itself, and more with how we divide up the world around us.

The reason Standard Chinese came to be based on Beijing Mandarin is because Beijing had become the seat of power in China by the time a standardised language was being formulated. Before then, the prestige dialect had been that of China's southern capital, Nanjing, and had power not shifted northwards in the eighteenth

---

* A popular anecdote highlighting at least one difference between Azeri and Turkish concerns the former Turkish prime minister, Süleyman Demirel, who visited Azerbaijan shortly after independence in 1993. At a press conference in Baku, the Azerbaijani president Heydar Aliyev flatteringly referred to Demirel as 'one of the most renowned businessmen of the Turkish world', using the local Azeri word *pezevenk* to mean essentially a great businessman. However, in Turkish, *pezevenk* means 'whoremonger', allegedly leading Demirel to reply diplomatically, 'Mr Aliyev, you are no less a pezevenk than I.'

and nineteenth centuries, this would doubtless have formed the standard instead. The foundations of one of the world's most widely spoken languages were therefore laid down not on a dialect picked for any practical reason, such as ease of learning or grammatical straight-forwardness, but because it just so happened to be the language of the capital and its corridors of power. And when it comes to what we think of as our 'languages', time and again we find arbitrary and politicised decisions just like this one.

What we called Danish just a few paragraphs ago, for instance, is really Copenhagen Danish – a regional dialect that rose to become the national standard by default, after the introduction of the print-ing press circulated the capital's language nationwide. In Albania, after the Second World War, the country's strict communist govern-ment capriciously made its Tosk dialect the new national standard, and simply ousted the previous standard, Elbasan, in the process. And when the rival city states of Italy coalesced as a single nation in the 1800s, the newly unified government selected Florentine Tuscan as the national language because it had been the language of Dante and Machiavelli and so had a certain literary cachet. As a consequence, the likes of Venetian, Neapolitan, Sicilian, Lombard and Piedmontese all effectively came to be seen as regional dialects of the national standard – while what we now think of as just 'Italian' was spoken by only 2 per cent of the population when it was first imposed nationwide.*

---

* It's misleading to think of all the regional languages of Italy as dialects, as some are so distinct that they belong to different branches of the linguistic family tree and are entirely unrelated. Piedmontese, for instance, is a so-called Gallo-Italic language, sharing closer family ties to French and Catalan than to standard Italian. Italian itself has also been so heavily influenced by many of the

Conversely, rather than a country elevating one of its dialects to the status of a language, a region can sometimes be elevated to the status of a country and take its dialect along for the ride. In recent decades, this has been particularly noticeable in the south-east corner of Europe. The official language of Yugoslavia, for instance, was Serbo-Croatian, but when the country dissolved in the 1990s, the independence of its constituent nations suddenly made national languages of Slovene, Croatian, Bosnian, Serbian and Montenegrin. When Moldova gained its independence from the Soviet Union, its 1994 constitution cited Moldovan as the national language – despite it being all but identical to Romanian, and known as such prior to independence.* And were you to ask someone from North Macedonia what language they spoke, they would tell you Macedonian. Ask someone from neighbouring Bulgaria what language a Macedonian

---

regional, dialectal and minority languages of Italy over the past century that it now bears much less resemblance to its Florentine roots. The fact that Italian is the official language of Italy at all was enshrined in the country's constitution only in 2017. The decision was a contentious one. At the time that the decision was announced in the Italian parliament, Northern League party member Federico Bricolo objected, explaining that the 'language spoken in my family, in schools, [and] at work' was Venetian, not Italian. 'My language is that of Venice,' he continued, before his microphone was abruptly switched off: he had made his objection in Venetian, breaking a rule that only Italian may be spoken in parliament.

* The precise name of the language of Moldova remains contentious. Although classed as Moldovan in the country's 1994 constitution, the original 1991 declaration of independence maintained that it was Romanian. A decision was finally made by the country's Constitutional Court in 2013, which declared, 'The official language of the Republic of Moldova is Romanian and the phrase "Moldovan language" ... can be equalised semantically with the Romanian language.'

speaks, and they would say Bulgarian, because across the border the two are not considered dissimilar enough to warrant separate names.

Examples such as these show that when our definitions of *language* and *dialect* come up against the real world – with its own fiercely held concepts of statehood and national identity – the two often do not comply. If our maps and politics were drawn differently, it would be easy to imagine a single Scandinavian nation speaking a single Scandinavian language, or an enormous patchwork of linguistically independent Chinese states. Had the likes of Moldova and Macedonia never gained their independence, we wouldn't be left squaring the circle of a language enjoying different names and statuses each side of a national border. But to impose our concepts of *language* and *dialect* unquestionably onto the world would be wrong – misleading at best; at worst it would risk denying a great many languages of their 'languageness' and strip their speakers of a personal and often hard-fought aspect of their identity. The world, quite simply, does not work like that. Or at least, it doesn't any more.

Before we began drawing lines and borders around ourselves, the concept of a national language simply did not exist. The way people spoke would just have changed from place to place, with those living nearby typically speaking more like you than those further away. What we now see as distinct nations and languages were once one long boundaryless blur of similar, yet gradually diverging, ways of speaking.

The shadow of this less restrictive past can still be seen in many places today. Imagine you were to take a boat trip from the Black Sea coast of Turkey, into the Caspian Sea, and down Europe's longest river, the Volga, into the heartland of western Russia. At the start of your journey, you would board a *gemi* – the Turkish word for ship. Sail north down the Don Canal into the Caspian, and you could take a southern detour to Azerbaijan where your ship would now be a *gəmi* (the local letter Ə being pronounced like the 'a' in *cat*). Continue on, and you'd reach Turkmenistan, where your ship would be a *gämi*. Travel north to Kazakhstan, it would be a *keme*. An Uzbek would call it a *kema*. Enter the Volga, and a local Bashkir speaker would call it a *kämä*. Arrive in the city of Kazan, and a Tatar speaker would know it as a *köymä*.

On paper, you would have travelled through several different nations and states, each with its own distinct language. But on the ground (or, rather, on deck) you would have heard little more than a steady shifting of the same word from one destination to the next. Only by the end of your trip would that shift appear more dramatic: *gemi* and *köymä* are indisputably different words, and we would have little problem labelling Turkish and Tatar as different languages as a result. But on a local level, those boundaries would have blurred, and without consulting a map it would have been difficult to tell where one language stopped and another began.

This gradual drifting of endlessly similar forms is called a dialect continuum, examples of which exist all over the world. In southern Europe, a South Slavic continuum connects all the Balkan languages from Slovenia to Bulgaria. West Africa's Manding languages blur into one long continuum from Ghana to the Gambia. In South America, the collapse of the Incan Empire left a fragmented Quechuan continuum strewn across the Andes. And the Ojibwe dialects of North America merge into one another across a long continuum encircling the Great Lakes, from Montana to Michigan.

Within a continuum, one local form simply fades into another. Whatever borders or nations it crosses are of no consequence – as is the arbitrary decision of some of those countries to raise certain dialects to the status of their languages. In fact, labelling anything as a *language* or *dialect* here is of little real use. Adjacent forms will behave like dialects and appear to have much in common (*gemi* vs *gəmi*) but compare those to forms further away and they will show much less similarity, and behave more like distinct languages (*gemi* vs *köymä*). So not only do our strict definitions of *language* and *dialect* risk dismissing people's national identity, in some cases there is no objective difference between them at all.

Consequently, linguists often steer clear of these labels altogether and, when required, talk more neutrally of language *varieties*, or *lects*. The language of an individual person is their *idiolect*. Every family has its own set of linguistic quirks and in-jokes, forming its *familect*. Every household has its *ecolect*. Elsewhere, there are *sociolects*, *ethnolects*, *regiolects* and *genderlects*. And the elevated standard or prestige form of a language – Standard Chinese, Standard Italian, Standard English, and so on – is an *acrolect*. Every one of these can be considered a *dialect* of a single *language* – so, yes, even the Queen's English is just another dialect, linguistically no better than nor superior to any other. The prestige attached to it, therefore, is an entirely social construct.

So we can define human language itself. We can list the features that set our language apart from other forms of communication. And we can define and identify individual languages based on their composite features. But in a world of lines and labels, in which certain forms of a language can be artificially placed on a pedestal and elevated above all others, using a purely linguistic definition of *language* becomes problematic.

If there really were any difference between a language and its dialects, perhaps it is that our 'languages' are essentially the cover stars, the frontispieces, the products in the shop window – if not the name of the shop itself. Behind and inside them, we find a multitude of styles and varieties, from those used more widely, across entire regions and groups of society, down to the unique vernacular of you, your family, and your household. The vagaries of politics and history might lead to one of these varieties becoming the A-lister, taught in schools and textbooks, circulated in literature and journalism, and carefully curated and standardised in dictionaries and style guides. But this elevation is often so haphazard that from a linguistic perspective it is unreliable, if not meaningless. Realistically, all we have are dialects – or, rather, all we have is language.

Q. 3

Where Do Languages Come From?

Now the whole earth had one language and one speech ...
And they said, 'Come, let us build ourselves a city, and a tower
whose top is in the heavens; let us make a name for ourselves,
lest we be scattered abroad over the face of the whole earth.'

But the Lord came down to see the city and the tower which
the sons of men had built. And the Lord said, 'Indeed
the people are one, and they all have one language ...
Come, let Us go down and there confuse their language,
that they may not understand one another's speech.'

Genesis (11:1–9)

E arly one winter morning, two huntsmen went down to a river to catch duck. Each man caught one bird, while the rest of the flock noisily took flight, making a loud whistling sound as they rose into the air. The men set off home and began discussing this peculiar noise as they walked. This, the first explained, was the sound of the birds' wings beating together. No, the second countered – it was the sound of the air passing through their open beaks. And as they continued on their way, their disagreement rumbled on.

Unable to resolve it themselves, they took their quarrel to the local council. But they too failed to reach a consensus and split angrily down the middle, one side adamantly believing one man's account over the other. As the winter months rolled on, so too did this increasingly bitter argument until the entire community was entrenched in two fiercely opposing camps. Eventually, the spring thaw set in, but in the village the situation remained as icy as ever. Enough was enough: unable to reconcile their differences, one side packed up their belongings and left, never to speak to their former friends and neighbours again.

This is a tale told by the native Salishan people of America's Pacific Northwest. As it continues, the departing tribespeople come to encounter new things in their new territory and invent new words for their discoveries. But as ever more disputes occur, the quarrelling groups continue to fragment and the number of these invented words increases, pushing their vocabularies apart. A casual early-morning conversation about ducks is ultimately the Salishan people's explanation for the emergence of all the world's languages.

Other cultures have their own version of these events, of course. We have the Tower of Babel. The Greeks blamed Hermes for dividing our languages. The Aztecs thought languages were bestowed by a dove onto the children of two survivors of a gigantic flood, from whom all humanity is descended. The Ticuna people of the Amazon believe different languages arose from eating forbidden hummingbird eggs. The Naga people of India tell a story of how the king's warriors suddenly began speaking differently while slaying a giant python. And Africa's Wa-Sania people think a punishingly severe famine caused everyone to go so mad they meandered off and never spoke the same way again. Yet of all these tales, the Salishan myth bears an uncanny resemblance to the truth: the birth of a new language is very often sparked by the isolation of an existing one.

With little outside influence to reinforce the norm, the language of an isolated community can easily start to vary and take on features not adopted elsewhere. The more of these novelties that appear, the further the language steps from its roots until eventually it is no longer mutually intelligible with them – just as the language of the Anglo-Saxons diverged from its roots as soon as its speakers found themselves stranded on an island. Areas whose geography is naturally disconnective like this often prove linguistically distinct, as neighbouring communities struggle to maintain close ties across rivers, seas, forests, deserts, canyons and mountains. In the Swiss Alps, it's not uncommon to find adjacent villages speaking entirely different dialects each side of unscalable valley walls. The Goulburn Islands, off the coast of northern Australia, are home to scarcely 450 people but no fewer than nine different languages are scattered across the archipelago. And it is little coincidence that the world's most linguistically diverse nation, Papua New Guinea, is also one of its most mountainous, most densely forested, and least densely populated.*

Yet surely it is preferable to share a language with your neighbours – no matter how distant they may be – than to adopt features

---

* Although precisely what constitutes a separate language is difficult to define, Papua New Guinea is said to be home to around 830 distinct living languages. On average, that equates to one language for every 11,000 people who live there – or every 212 square miles of territory. If the United Kingdom were equally diverse per square mile, it would be home to 440 different languages; the United States would have 17,900; and the world as a whole would speak 270,000.

that render what you're saying incomprehensible to them? Imagine the sense of kinship and the diplomatic advantages that could exist had Proto-Indo-European never broken apart, and all 4 billion people from Reykjavík to Rajasthan were still speaking the same way today. So why do languages change at all?

At least part of the answer is that this change occurs at a near imperceptible pace. Just like the physical world around us, the bedrock of our linguistic world is always shifting, yet the rate of that change is so glacially slow, it's often impossible to notice anything has happened until after it's taken place. Each stage of a language's development is a subtle drip feed of deviations and alterations, introduced gradually across generations, often affecting only a handful of words, sounds or communities at a time. And if you cannot tell something is happening, how can you be expected to stop it?

Even on a personal level, our language can change without us realising it. The so-called chameleon effect is the psychological phenomenon in which a person subconsciously adopts the accent and mannerisms of somebody else as they communicate with them. If you've ever caught yourself doing this (or spotted it in someone else – my half-Scottish dad used to change his accent the moment we crossed the border from England), it can be alarming or even embarrassing, and can sometimes come across as rude or derisive. Yet the chameleon effect is part of what makes us human: we have always naturally mimicked others as a means of forming bonds and fostering new relationships, meeting new people in a physical and phonological middle ground between our two selves. It's partly this phenomenon that is responsible for people 'losing' their accents when they relocate, and perhaps also for new accents and sound features emerging when people from different regions or backgrounds are brought together. As with almost all language change, these developments are often so subtle that they are undetectable, but recent research has been able to show this process in action with remarkable clarity. A 2019 study of scientists in Antarctica showed that some of their vowel sounds changed during their time there, as accents from all over the world mingled in the close quarters of an overwintering station. These changes are so palpable, in fact, that Antarctica is often said to have its own accent – some linguists have even predicted that if humans ever were to colonise Mars, a new Martian accent would no doubt be added into the mix too.

As undetectable as language change may be, however, it is by no means inexplicable. Aside from more personal changes like this, looking at how our languages have developed in the past allows us to pinpoint the kinds of forces and processes that have provoked that change over time. On the one hand, there are external factors, such as conflict and migration, that change languages by shifting and disordering the communities in which they are spoken. Just as in the Salishan tale, relocated people will naturally encounter new things deserving of new words, and as their vocabularies expand to accommodate them, their languages are cast adrift. But the movement of people can reportedly do much more than merely inspire new words.

Research has suggested languages that come to develop in high-altitude locations typically adopt sounds easier to produce in environments where the air is thinner. Languages spoken in forested areas tend to utilise more vowel sounds, as trees naturally interfere with the acoustic transmission of higher-frequency consonants. And an extraordinary study in 2019 even suggested that as our ancestors abandoned their hunter–gatherer past and turned to farming, their jaws realigned to better suit a diet of softer, cultivated foods. This tiny evolutionary development produced an overbite that in time allowed us to touch our lips to our teeth more easily – and in doing so, gave us our 'f' and 'v' sounds for the very first time.

Conversely, language can be affected by internal changes. As the rules of grammar change, the structure of sentences can be uprooted (though more on that later). Words can change too, by coming to mirror or morph into one another over time, via a process called lexical analogy. It was this that changed Old English *weal* into *wealth* (which gained its *–th* on analogy with *health*) and added an L to the French *principe* to make *principle* (on analogy with words like *participle*). Analogical change can affect grammar as well, with irregular words abandoning their abnormalities and falling into line with regular ones, through a process called paradigm levelling. The likes of *dare*, *laugh*, *climb*, *help* and *step* were all once irregular verbs, yet have come to adopt regular past-tense forms (*dared*, *laughed*, *climbed*, *helped*, *stepped*), consigning their original forms (*durst*, *lough*, *clomb*, *halp*, *stop*) to the etymological dustbin.

This zeal for simplification can affect phonology too, as complex sound combinations are manipulated or abandoned in favour of easier equivalents. In epenthesis, an entirely new sound is inserted into a word, often as a means of transitioning more smoothly between incompatible neighbours; it was this that added the B to our words *thimble*, *humble* and *nimble*, so as to bridge the gap between their Ms and Ls more comfortably.* In metathesis, a word's sounds are

---

* Epenthesis is not always driven by ease or simplicity, however. The insertion of a consonant sound specifically is known as excrescence, and 'excrescent P' is a phenomenon in which a word gains a 'p' sound as a result of the emphasis

manoeuvred into a more euphonous order that's easier to pronounce; it was this that changed Old English *brid*, *fersc*, *waps* and *drit* into *bird*, *fresh*, *wasp* and *dirt*. And in a process called phonological deletion, sounds can come to be dropped altogether to create a more streamlined word overall. The male leader of a household, for instance, was once the *hlaford* ('loaf-guardian') in Old English, while his female counterpart was the *hlæfdige* ('loaf-maker'). Several centuries of simplification later, and we have been left with their considerably less cluttered descendants, *lord* and *lady*.

When language change works to diminish complexities, it's easy to see why the results would catch on. But languages sometimes behave more capriciously, and new features can be adopted for purely subjective reasons of fashion and taste. French inherited its 'r' sound from Latin, and its speakers would originally have followed the Romans' lead by pronouncing their Rs as a soft trill, made by lightly vibrating the tip of the tongue just behind the upper teeth – the same rolling 'r' you'll still hear in Italian words like *grazie* ('thank you') and *terra* ('earth'). Towards the end of the seventeenth century, however, a trend emerged in high-society Paris for swapping this teeth-tapping 'r' for a throatier sound, produced around the fleshy uvula at the back of the throat – the same quintessentially French 'r' you'll hear in words like *trois* ('three') and *quatre* ('four'). Quite what prompted the change is unclear, but as this uvular 'r' requires less effort and airflow than the trilled version, it probably proved a more economical

---

with which it is pronounced. It was this that turned *no* and *yes* into *nope* and *yep*, with their final Ps added not to ease their pronunciation, but to mirror the forcefulness of the mouth snapping shut when these words are pronounced more emphatically. In contemporary slang, this process is also in the middle of changing *well* into *welp*.

replacement in fast-paced speech. No matter *why* it caught on, however, what matters is *who* it caught on among.

The upper classes of Paris were the trendsetters of their day. Whatever they did was to be admired and emulated, and so city by city, region by region, use of this fashionable new 'r' sound spread. By the turn of the century it had crossed the border into Germany, Belgium and the Netherlands, and been adopted into the phonologies of German, Flemish and Dutch. By the late 1700s, the 'r' of Danish and Swedish had become uvularised too. Further south, it bled into Spain and Portugal, and from there was taken across the Atlantic to colonies in the Americas. Ultimately, by the mid-1800s, a faddish vocal quirk that had emerged in the salons of upper-class Paris three centuries earlier was now not only an established feature of many major European languages, but had fallen into use 5,000 miles away in Brazilian Portuguese.

Typically, it takes time for developments like these to become permanent. But sometimes circumstances can transpire in which a language not only changes more rapidly, but an entirely new language is produced. A pidgin is contact language that emerges between two or more groups whose own languages are incompatible. The need to communicate forces these input languages to mix, with the result being a linguistic hybrid exhibiting features of both.

Historically, many pidgins arose via international trade, as people from across the globe suddenly found themselves doing business across insurmountable language barriers.* Colonisation and conflict are important instigators too, as superpowers uncompromisingly

---

* The word *pidgin* itself is a replication of the Chinese pronunciation of 'business' heard by European traders in the Far East in the early nineteenth century.

force themselves on regions not sharing their language and culture. As a result, pidgins tend to develop quickly, as the need to seal deals or impose power outweighs any desire or opportunity for one side to learn the other's language. As those of colonisers and conquerors, the languages of Europe have long formed the basis of many pidgins. In North America, the Europeans' arrival created Trader's Jargon, or Pidgin Delaware – a makeshift contact language used between Dutch fur-trappers and Algonquian tribes in the 1620s. West African Pidgin developed as a result of the transatlantic slave trade, built from a combination of several native languages mixed with English and Portuguese. Tây Bôi (literally, 'servant-boy French') was a French-based pidgin that emerged during the colonial era in Vietnam. And an extraordinary English–Dutch–Zulu mixture called Fanagalo arose among mineworkers and labourers in British South Africa; indicative of its use chiefly as a means of giving orders, the name *Fanagalo* comes from a Zulu phrase meaning 'do it like this'.

Not all pidgins have European roots, however, and the widespread misconception they do probably stems from little more than a long-standing European bias in linguistic research. Nefamese is a pidgin spoken in east India and rooted in the local Assamese language. Bimbashi is an Arabic-based pidgin originating in southern Egypt, and now used widely in neighbouring Sudan. And both Nootka and Chinook Jargon were in use among the native peoples of north-west America long before the Europeans arrived; another, Mobilian Jargon, was spoken along the Gulf of Mexico.*

---

* There is considerable debate over whether these pidgins truly were in use before Europeans arrived in North America, and frustratingly evidence seems to support both pre- and post-contact theories. It has been estimated roughly

The speed at which pidgins develop comes at a price. Complexities tend to be discarded in favour of more direct and immediate speech, and so pidgins often exhibit restricted vocabularies, simpler grammatical structures, and are characterised by clipped and curtailed pronunciations. That's not to say they are somehow poor-quality or watered-down languages – far from it. Pidgins demonstrate immense ingenuity and creativity, and are proof of just how vital and robust language can be when it is compelled to change. They are simply driven more by a need to exchange basic information than by conversational niceties. And that directness is no better illustrated than by one of the most unlikely pidgin languages in linguistic history.

In the early seventeenth century, Basque fishermen headed north each summer to hunt whales in the rich waters off Iceland's Westfjords peninsula. Basque and Icelandic could scarcely be more dissimilar, yet the sailors' arrival on the island each year forced the two languages together and a pidgin soon developed. Brilliantly, a handful of phrasebooks of this bizarre Basque–Icelandic mixture survive, in which are recorded such down-to-business phrases as *Jndasunirj* ('Show me'), *Simbatur* ('How much?'), *Cavinit trucka for mi* ('I buy nothing'), and even *For ju mala gissuna* ('You are a bad man'). Proving just how fractious the relationship between

---

15 per cent of Chinook Jargon derives from French, but those words might have been later additions to a language already in use before the first French speakers arrived. Of the three listed here, Nootka appears the most certain to have emerged before the arrival of European settlers: Nootka Sound, an inlet of Vancouver Island, was an important trade post for many Native American peoples, and it's highly likely a pidgin developed among these groups long before the first Europeans landed.

these two groups became, however, one glossary includes the likes of *Jet sat* ('Kiss my ass!'), *Fenicha for ju* ('Fuck you!'), *Caca hiarinsat* ('Eat shit from an asshole!'), and *Sickutta samaria* ('Go fuck a horse!').*

When the Basque whaling industry faltered in the late 1700s, fewer fishermen started journeying to Iceland each year and this extraordinary language simply faded away. This speedy demise is another characteristic feature of pidgins: when the circumstances that give rise to them change, the languages prove surplus to requirements and vanish just as quickly as they emerged. But if a pidgin is allowed

---

* Icelandic is by far one of the most conservative of the Nordic languages, to the extent that native speakers today can even understand some of the ancient Icelandic sagas written eight centuries ago. Basque is classed as a language isolate, and is so unlike anything else in the world today that linguists are not sure to what other language or languages (if any) it is directly related. As a result, the two are about as far removed from one another as it is possible to be in the same part of the world.

Not all the surviving Basque–Icelandic glossaries are quite so profane. Other entries include such run-of-the-mill terms as *elisa* ('church'), *plamuna* ('halibut'), *navaria* ('red wine'), *chatucumia* ('kitten'), and even *kikomiciuka* ('blind-man's-buff'). Nevertheless, relations between the two sides were not easy, and in the winter of 1615 the rumbling hostilities culminated in a brutal confrontation known as *Spánverjavígin*, the 'Slaying of the Spaniards'. Forced to prolong their stay in Iceland after their ships were crushed by ice, many of the Basque fishermen resorted to stealing from local houses and farms to survive. The local council took dramatic action in response, and declared all Basques to be outlaws, and passed a law allowing any Basque in the Westfjords area to be killed with impunity. Over the months that followed, dozens of men were apprehended and summarily murdered, with many suffering the indignity of having their bodies mutilated and unceremoniously dumped into the sea. Incredibly, this centuries-old law was not officially repealed until 2015, when a memorial to the murdered fishermen was unveiled in the village of Hólmavík.

to endure, it can flourish. Its vocabulary can grow, its structure can become more complex and, crucially, children born into the community where it is spoken can come to learn it as their first language. This all has a legitimising effect, so that far from being a merely contact language, the pidgin emerges as a fully fledged language in its own right. This process is called creolisation, and the language that results from it is a creole.

The world's most widely spoken creole is Haitian, used by more than 12 million people across the Caribbean. Another is Tok Pisin, an official language of Papua New Guinea, fashioned from an unlikely mixture of English, German, Malay and several native languages. Bislama is an English-based creole now so firmly established in the Pacific nation of Vanuatu that the national anthem is sung in it. But of all the world's creoles, easily one of the most extraordinary emerged as recently as the 1980s, when an educational programme for deaf children was established in the Central American republic of Nicaragua.

The programme was the first in the country's history, and as such many of its pupils had never learned formal sign language before, nor even met or conversed with other deaf children. Instead, they had each developed their own improvised sign systems at home with their families. Progress was slow, and the pupils struggled to engage with uninspiring classroom lessons teaching Spanish lipreading and fingerspelling. But in the schoolyard, the enthusiastic new deaf community the programme had assembled began sharing one another's homemade signs, and a unique pidgin sign language gradually emerged. New enrollees picked up this schoolyard pidgin more readily than the formal Spanish of their lessons, and as they began contributing to it themselves it graduated into a creole spoken by all the pupils at the school. Today, this extraordinary language – created spontaneously by deaf schoolchildren on their lunch breaks and the school bus – forms the basis of the official Nicaraguan Sign Language system. It remains perhaps the only language in history to have been fully documented from the moment of its birth through to the present day.

The development of pidgins and creoles can give us a rare real-time glimpse into the workings of an emerging language. But they obviously rely on existing languages, from which they can arise. The same goes for the emergence of one language from another, such as English from West Germanic – or, for that matter, West Germanic from Proto-Germanic, and Proto-Germanic from Proto-Indo-European. But what about before then? Where did human language itself originate?

That is a question that has confounded and frustrated inquisitive minds for centuries. It once proved so thorny an issue, in fact, that in 1866 the Société de Linguistique de Paris – one of the earliest academic bodies dedicated to the study of languages – banned its members from discussing it. Two problems lay behind this early antipathy. On the one hand, the Bible had already given us an answer: God bestowed language on Adam in Eden, and that divine language endured until it was scattered by the destruction of the Tower of Babel. Questioning or doubting this scriptural explanation was for a long time controversial (if not tantamount to blasphemy), so that even the earliest editions of the *Encyclopaedia Britannica* describe the origin of language in terms of our descent from Adam.

Much early research likewise concerned itself with simply corroborating the Bible's story by seeking to identify mankind's original language. In 1493, James IV of Scotland allegedly ordered two newborn babies to be sent to the tiny island of Inchkeith, off the coast of Edinburgh, and there be raised in isolation by a deaf-mute foster mother. By being brought up in a language-less vacuum, the king reasoned, whatever language the children came to produce must surely be the God-given language of man. The historian Robert Lindsay recounted the king's experiment in his *Historie and Chronicles of Scotland* (*c.* 1570), and somewhat dubiously suggested that the children were able to speak Hebrew when they were returned to the mainland. In his own *History of Scotland* (1829), however, the author Sir Walter Scott arrived at a different conclusion. 'It is more likely they would scream like their dumb nurse,' he wrote, 'or bleat like the goats and sheep on the island.'*

On the other hand, the origin of language has long suffered from a near fatal lack of evidence. Spoken language is ephemeral, and speech – made literally out of thin air – fades instantaneously, leaving no trace of itself behind. There are no fossilised words to be unearthed here, nor Stone Age conversations encased in amber.

---

* Lindsay's record of it aside, it is debatable whether this experiment really did take place or is nothing more than linguistic folklore. There are certainly other similar tales and experiments on record that might have simply inspired this later tale (or that may be apocryphal themselves, of course). In the thirteenth century, for instance, the Holy Roman Emperor Frederick II supposedly ordered a group of children be raised by mothers who were told never to speak to them. According to one contemporary account, the emperor 'laboured in vain, for the children could not live without clappings of the hands, and gestures, and gladness of countenance, and blandishments'. And 2,000 years earlier, the Egyptian pharaoh Psamtik I is said to have had two infants sent to live with a shepherd in a remote corner of his kingdom, on condition that they never hear him speak. According to Herodotus, after two years the infants suddenly babbled the ancient Phrygian word for bread, *bekòs.*

Language is archaeologically invisible; we simply have no record of it before the development of writing, some 5,000 years ago.

Discussing a subject with no solid proof was therefore seen as futile, and its theories were widely dismissed as conjecture, unworthy of serious debate. As the president of London's Philological Society explained when it joined Paris's moratorium on the subject in 1873, it is simply not worth 'filling waste-paper baskets with reams of paper covered with speculations'. For some, however, it proved too intriguing a subject to ignore.

In the mid-1800s, the German philologist Max Müller, and later the Danish linguist Otto Jespersen, collated the major theories of language origin at the time and added two more of their own. The nicknames they gave them – which were perhaps a little more flippant than their authors would have wished – have remained attached to these ideas ever since.

The bow-wow theory is the notion that all language was originally imitative: our ancestors' first words would have been onomatopoeic attempts to replicate the sounds they heard around them in nature, and thereby became labels with which to refer to them. Variations on this idea have persisted for centuries, reinforced by the fact that onomatopoeia plays a much greater role in our vocabulary than we might credit. Far beyond *snap!*, *crackle!* and *pop!*, the likes of *laugh*, *moan*, *cough*, *sneeze*, *howl*, *brawl*, *raven*, *crow* and even *fanfare* are all thought to be fundamentally imitative words, alongside even less obvious examples such as *pebble* (perhaps invented to mimic the sound of a stone dropped in water) and *shingle* (an echo of waves lapping at a stony shore). But such words are still relatively uncommon overall, and this theory fails to account for things our ancestors would presumably have given early names to, like the sun and the moon, that have no associated sound at all. If language were indeed onomatopoeic by nature, moreover, we might also expect to see greater similarities between our languages today – but while English dogs say *bow-wow*, Turkish dogs say *hev-hev*, Korean dogs say *meong-meong*, and Kazakh dogs (somewhat unfortunately) say *ars-ars*.

A second theory claims language evolved from instinctive vocal responses to stimuli such as pain, fear, rage, happiness, shock and anguish. Müller called this the pooh-pooh theory, but its supporters knew it as the interjectional theory, as it assumes language emerged from a stock vocabulary of *oohs!*, *ahs!*, *ows!*, gasps, laughs and shrieks. Whether these outbursts are varied enough to shape an entire language is arguable – although, unlike onomatopoeias, they do at least tend to travel across borders. An English scream is no different from a Turkish or Kazakh one, and that universality has made this an enduringly popular hypothesis: the Greek philosopher Democritus proposed an early version of the pooh-pooh theory more than 2,500 years ago.

Müller's own suggestion was the ding-dong theory, although that light-hearted name belies just how complex an idea it was.

There is a law which runs through nearly the whole of nature that everything which is struck rings. Each substance has its peculiar ring ... [and] so it was with man ... Man, in his primitive and perfect state, was not only endowed ... with the power of expressing his sensations by interjections ... he possessed likewise the faculty of giving more articulate expression to the rational conceptions of his mind ... [But] the creative faculty which gave to each conception,

as it thrilled for the first time through the brain, a phonetic
expression, became extinct when its object was fulfilled.

Max Müller, *The Theoretical Stage and
the Origin of Language* (1861)

So just as different metals produce different dings and dongs, our
ancestors' words were instinctive and almost metaphysically attuned
reactions to the world as they responded vocally to it for the first time.
Once we had given everything we needed to a name, this preternatural
ability to tune into the things around us faded away. It's an elaborate
concept, which Jespersen more succinctly described as 'a somewhat
mystic harmony between sound and sense'. But even Müller himself
later abandoned this idea in favour of a less enigmatic explanation by
the German philosopher Ludwig Noiré. He believed language began
as little more than grunts and groans, which would naturally have
synchronised when groups of our ancestors worked together on a
physical task. In time these coordinated sounds would have formed
communal chants, and it was on these that the foundations of language would have been laid. Noiré knew this as the sympathy theory;
Müller called it the yo-he-ho theory.

As for Jespersen, his suggestion was the la-la theory, which held
that language initially served an emotional rather than a functional
purpose: our earliest vocalisations were extensions of the sounds we
naturally made during play and courtship. Could these noises have
then shed their emotional connotations to operate freely in a wider
language? Jespersen, at least, believed so.

In the mid-1900s, a resurgence of interest in the origin of language saw several more theories added to this list. In 1930, the
English scientist Sir Richard Paget proposed the ta-ta theory, which

claimed language began as a kind of 'pantomime of the tongue', with the vocal organs mimicking established hand and body gestures. Speech, he believed, arose not through any desire of man for 'expressing his thoughts', but simply 'the difficulty of talking with his hands full'.

More recently a different approach has been adopted, with theorists now focused on not how our first speech might have sounded, but imagining what social contexts and interactions might have inspired it. The from-where-to-what theory suggests language grew out of distress calls between parents and their offspring when they became separated. In more frantic or perilous situations, these calls would naturally be heightened, strengthened or prolonged, establishing different shades of pitch and tone from which a more complex spoken language could have emerged. In 1996, the British anthropologist Robin Dunbar proposed the gossip-and-grooming theory, claiming that as humans came to live in ever larger groups, they would have replaced the communal grooming sessions of their primate ancestors with a less time-consuming 'vocal grooming' – using speech, rather than touch, as a means of consolidating social bonds. And in 2004, the American anthropologist Dean Falk suggested the ingenious putting-the-baby-down theory. Early human mothers, she believed, would have struggled to walk, forage and feed with their babies clinging to their bodies, as in other primates. Having laid them down, the mothers would have then used a comforting language of 'motherese' to entertain and reassure their infant children as they busied themselves elsewhere.

As inventive as these theories are, providing evidence to back them up is still problematic. Without a time machine, it seems, we shall never be able to ascertain whether our first words were spoken by dutiful mothers or gossiping groomers, or what their first words or speech sounds were. So is this entire question doomed to endless conjecture and to remain frustratingly unanswered? From a twenty-first-century perspective, perhaps not.

In recent years, research into the origin of language has become more collaborative, combining linguistic data with that of diverse disciplines including anthropology, archaeology, palaeontology, pathology and medicine. This joint effort – a field known as glossogenetics – is beginning to paint a much clearer picture of our evolutionary ancestors than ever before, and in doing so is coming to firmer and more extraordinary conclusions about their linguistic capabilities.

With some certainty, we can now say the earliest hominins to have had some form of recognisable language were the Early European Modern Humans, or Cro-Magnons – a group of *Homo sapiens* that settled across Europe in the late Stone Age. They used complex tools, produced art, made music, wore clothes and jewellery, carried out long-distance trade, and held elaborate burial rituals for their dead, all of which suggests a level of cultural and cognitive advancement that would make their use of language hard to deny. Examinations of their physical remains, moreover, have shown Cro-Magnons' brains and vocal tracts to be all but identical to modern humans, suggesting they had both the physical and mental capacity to produce complex speech. At a conservative estimate, therefore, the dawn of recognisable language can be dated to around 45,000 years ago.

Our vocal tract itself, however, is much older. Humans have a characteristically low larynx (our voice box) and a spacious pharynx (the descending cavity at the back of the throat), which together with a highly mobile tongue, forms the ideal apparatus for producing the range of sounds required for spoken language. But in evolutionary terms, the lowering of our larynx came at considerable cost: we humans can choke if our larynx becomes blocked, whereas other primates, whose larynxes are higher, such as monkeys, cannot. The risk incurred in developing a lowered larynx must therefore have been outweighed by the advantages it afforded us in being able to produce speech, otherwise we simply wouldn't have maintained it. This is the basis of the laryngeal descent theory, which claims the lowering of our larynx down our ancestors' throats was the true launching point for our ability to speak. Once it was in place, speech would have emerged quickly as our ancestors justifiably seized on the potential of this evolutionary breakthrough.

Quite when this all occurred is difficult to say, not least because the soft tissues of the head and neck do not fossilise as bones do. Analysis of our ancestors' skulls and jaws, however, provides enough anatomical clues to suggest our vocal tract, such as it is, might have emerged with the very first *Homo sapiens*, some 200,000–300,000 years ago. If so, that would potentially push the birth of language back five or six times further than the Cro-Magnons.

This theory is certainly not without controversy, but far from being too generous with the linguistic timeline, some recent studies have suggested it might still be too restrictive, and have pointed to evidence suggesting a lowered larynx is by no means as essential to speech production as it was once believed. If that were the case, then even this earlier cut-off point would be too cautious, and spoken language could have emerged far, far earlier. A less conservative estimate – though perhaps a no less likely one – could therefore place the dawn of recognisable human language at around 100,000 years ago at the very least.

Given an earlier date, it is likely another of our evolutionary cousins shared our ability to talk. Neanderthals first emerged around 300,000 years ago too. Long considered the lowlier cousins of *Homo sapiens*, in 1983 a 60,000-year-old Neanderthal hyoid bone – a small horseshoe-shaped structure that connects to the larynx and supports the tongue – was discovered in Israel and found to be all but identical to a modern human's. This, combined with recent reassessments of Neanderthal intelligence and culture, has led to suggestions that they too might have had vocal skills similar to early *Homo sapiens*.* Evolving new anatomical features is worthless, however, if you're not capable of physically controlling them. It would be like having all the individual parts of a car, but no idea how to assemble them (or how to drive it, even if you did). *Homo ergaster* was a relative of *Homo erectus* that roamed Africa some 1.4–1.7 million years ago. Analysis of its skull has found it had a component in its brain comparable to

---

* This too is not without controversy; those who oppose it are quick to point out the human hyoid is also anatomically identical to that of a pig and should not be taken as a barometer of linguistic competence on its own. More convincingly, however, recent DNA sampling of Neanderthal remains has found a variation of a gene, FOXP2, that we now know to be necessary for the development of language. Combining this cutting-edge genetic research with a growing anthropological understanding of Neanderthal culture makes at least some form of Neanderthal language an increasingly likely proposition. If they truly did have comparable vocal skill to *Homo sapiens*, however, Neanderthal voices would not have been the same. The size and position of their larynx suggests their voices would have been higher, and they would have been able to produce only a relatively limited range of sounds. Some theorists have even suggested that the Neanderthal language, such as it was, was so phonologically limited that it might have impaired their capacity to communicate and pass on learned information and skills, and thereby contributed to their eventual disappearance from the fossil record some 28,000 years ago.

that in modern humans that controls the production and processing of language. Its discovery implied the doors of human language could have been thrown open millions, not merely thousands, of years ago. But subsequent analysis of *Homo ergaster*'s vertebrae has suggested its spinal cord was not robust enough to carry sufficient signalling from the brain to coordinate the chain of bodily organs required to produce speech. In that sense, many of our earliest ancestors might have had some of the physical attributes we associate with language – and were undoubtedly able to vocalise, and perhaps even communicate wordlessly through gesture – but would not have been able to control the production of vocal sound enough to generate anything as complex as speech. So at what point did our primordial calls begin to turn into the diverse library of sounds necessary to talk?

Australopithecus afarensis is another of our ancient ancestors, dating from around 3.5 million years ago. Its remains show evidence of a small cup-shaped projection called a hyoid bulla that would have supported an inflatable air sac at the back of its throat. Most primates retain this feature today: studies of chimpanzees have suggested it might work to amplify their vocalisations, or even prevent them from hyperventilating during prolonged vocal exchanges. But humans have long since lost it and are the only modern primates to have done so. Somewhere in the long evolutionary gap between *Australopithecus* (which had these air sacs) and *Homo heidelbergensis* (the earliest of our known ancestors not to), our hyoid bulla disappeared. But a remarkable experiment at the University of Amsterdam in 2011 sought to determine what our speech would have sounded like had we retained it.

Researchers used plastic tubes to recreate a series of human vocal tracts. Half of these were straightforward cylinders, resembling the tract as it is today, while the other half were fitted with an additional descending chamber, replicating the effect of *Australopithecus'* throat sacs. By passing air through the tubes, different speech sounds could be produced that participants in the experiment were then tasked with identifying. The sounds produced *without* the extra chambers were consistently found to be much clearer than those produced with them. Essentially, the air sacs over-resonated the sounds, muddying their precise articulation and making them difficult to tell apart. Theoretically, *Australopithecus* would have struggled to produce the kind of contrast we can easily hear in words like *pat*, *pet*, *pit* and *pot* – all of which would have sounded to it something like *put*.

Losing our air sacs would therefore have clarified our vocalisations, increased the variety of sounds we could produce clearly, and put us firmly on the path to assembling the kind of varied phonological inventory required for complex speech. Of course, *Homo heidelbergensis* wasn't having the same kind of conversations we have today as he was wandering around the mountains of northern Spain 600,000 years ago. The loss of our hyoid bulla is just one of the many developmental changes that will have been necessary over time for humans to cultivate the physical and mental capacity for speech.

How long all of that took is unclear. Some theorists have suggested it occurred quickly, perhaps sparked by a single genetic mutation that generated a linguistic faculty in our brains and allowed us to take advantage of our bodies' ability to produce complex sounds. Others think the process was piecemeal, spurred on by incremental social and evolutionary changes, and perhaps hastened only when we came to live in larger communities where vocal communication would have served a greater purpose. Some think it might have occurred in only one place or in one population before spreading elsewhere – the so-called monogenetic theory of language. Others believe it might have emerged in several places all but simultaneously – the polygenetic theory. Either way, perhaps our earliest ancestors first evolved a simple protolanguage, comprising only a handful of different sounds or sound combinations, that gradually grew more nuanced with time. Alternatively, those who sign up to the more instantaneous idea of language development would claim it flourished almost immediately, as soon as we were able to produce it.

There is still much to explore then, and much left unanswered – and, regrettably, still much we shall almost assuredly never know. But by combining disciplines, embracing new technologies, and potentially filling ever more gaps in our scant fossil record, the long-opaque picture of our past is slowly becoming clear. A subject once dismissed as undeserving of any kind of serious debate might yet prove one of the most momentous in all linguistic research.

Q. 4

Where Do Words Come From?

Word-making, like other manufactures, should be done
by those who know how to do it. Others should neither
attempt it for themselves, nor assist the deplorable
activities of amateurs by giving currency to fresh
coinages before there has been time to test them.

H. W. Fowler, *A Dictionary of Modern English Usage* (1926)

In the early seventh century, a Spanish writer and cleric known as Isidore of Seville began work on a truly extraordinary project. He called it *Etymologiae* – an enormous twenty-volume encyclopedia intended to summarise the entirety of human knowledge. And in it, as its name might suggest, Isidore set out to explain how anything and everything came to earn its name.

Hail, he claimed, is known as *grando* in Latin because it resembles grain, *granum*. Pigeons, *columba*, are so named because of their colourful necks, *collum*. The Latin for girl, *puella*, comes from the word for purity, *puritas*. Our hands, *manus*, are so called for the service, or *munus*, they provide the body. Horses, *equus*, take their name from the Latin for equal, *aequus*, because they have to be matched by strength and gait when harnessed together. And our spleen derives from *supplementum*, because Isidore believed its only purpose to be 'filling a space opposite the liver' – making it literally an anatomical 'supplement'. Tale after etymological tale, Isidore compiled more than 400 chapters like this, covering terms from every conceivable discipline. It was a remarkable piece of work, with just one drawback. A lot of it was wrong.

In truth, hail has nothing to do with grain. Pigeons have nothing to do with necks. Girls, horses, hands and spleens have nothing to do with purity, equality, services or supplements. Isidore was a product of his time, and working in an age when our understanding of the histories of our words and languages was relatively limited. Many of his etymologies were therefore misguided assumptions, based on only the slightest of similarities between words, aided and abetted by the Greek and Roman encyclopedias on which his own was based. The scale of his work was nevertheless so impressive that *Etymologiae* remained Europe's foremost reference book for centuries to come, and earned its author the nickname 'Schoolmaster of the Middle Ages'. Isidore's lifelong dedication to knowledge was even recognised by the Vatican in the 1990s, when he was nominated for a title that would make his uneasy relationship with accuracy seem all the more appropriate: the patron saint of the internet.

But if Isidore's theories were largely mistaken, where do our words really come from? And for that matter, how do we know?

In simple terms, researching a word's history begins with collecting as much written evidence of it as possible, and tracking that etymological evidence back through the historical record as far as it will go. Any changes in how a word is used or spelled over time act as clues to its original form and meaning, and can thereby reveal its origins by pointing to any older 'parent' word from which it might be descended.

Our word *girl*, for instance, can be traced back more than 600 years, with Geoffrey Chaucer making an early reference to 'the yonge gerles of the diocise' in his *Canterbury Tales*. The way Chaucer used it shows he understood the word to have a different meaning from ours: his *gerles* were just children, as *girl* was originally gender-neutral in English, and used in much the same way as *child* would be today. Our trail of evidence shows it came to be used exclusively of female children only around the 1500s, by which time Chaucer's less specific meaning had died away (probably as a result of English picking up the word *boy* from French). The trail runs cold in Chaucer's time though, so we have no record of *girl* in any earlier English texts. That doesn't mean the word wasn't used in Old English, only that no evidence of it has survived. Venturing back into this uncharted territory will ultimately require some keen etymological detective work.

Our language underwent a series of changes between the Old and Middle English periods that altered its sound, structure and vocabulary, and set it on course to becoming the language we use today. We know enough about those changes now to be able to unpick them, and in that way can reconstruct a hypothetical Anglo-Saxon word, *gyrele*, that could have feasibly developed into something close to Chaucer's *gerle* at a later date.

This is an understandably speculative process – a little like looking at a finished product and trying to imagine what its prototype might have been – but by comparing our invented word with words for which we *do* have earlier evidence, we can nevertheless start to draw some historical parallels. *Gyrele* could be related to *gierela*, an

Old English word for clothing or vestments, and from there we can imagine *girl* might have developed its original gender-neutral meaning in reference to the swaddling-cloths used to dress infants. That's just a theory, of course, and plenty of rival explanations take *girl* in different etymological directions. But in the absence of any hard evidence, hypothetical reconstructions are our best guess.

When historical evidence proves hard to come by, etymology often relies on this kind of linguistic sleuthing, using whatever scant clues we can find to patch together a purely theoretical idea of what could have taken place. But just because our evidence comes to a dead end in English doesn't mean we can't expand our search and look for more clues elsewhere. English has sister and cousin languages, such as German and Norwegian, that share our Germanic ancestry and, through that, a common forefather in Proto-Indo-European. Just as we were able to reconstruct a hypothetical word from Old English, so etymologists can reconstruct even older words from further down our family tree by combining the evidence from English with that from other Germanic languages.

Some German dialects, for example, have a word *göre*, meaning 'child'. In Norwegian, there is *gorre*, or *gurre* (which can also mean 'lamb'). Some Swedish dialects have *gårre*. And in North Frisian, a regional language of north-west Germany (and one of English's closest relatives), the equivalent word is *gor*. Given these languages share the same lineage, it's certainly possible all these words – alongside our *girl*, *gerle* and *gyrele* – derive from a single, now lost, Germanic root. Using what we know of the Germanic languages' history, however, we can reconstruct that root, and through it rebuild an even earlier Proto-Indo-European root from which this entire cluster could be descended. All in all, *girl* could be derived from something along the lines of *gher–*, an ancient etymological tag believed to have been used to form words in Proto-Indo-European bearing some sense of smallness or shortness. Despite our evidence running out around six centuries ago, we can use all the weapons in our etymological armoury to tentatively retrace the history of *girl* back more than 3,000 years.

The further we go down our family tree, of course, the more hypothetical our theories become. We might have relatively little hard evidence of *girl* from the early days of English, but we have no evidence whatsoever of our ancient protolanguages, such as Proto-Germanic and Proto-Indo-European. Our knowledge of those is sheer conjecture, pieced together using the same kind of retrospective deductions that made *gyrele* from *gerle*. So how can we know anything about an ancestral language we can't even prove existed? How do we even know our languages are descended from one another at all?

As far back as the first century BCE, the Greek historian Dionysius noted that the Romans spoke a language 'neither completely barbaric, nor wholly Greek, but mixed from both'. He was certainly onto something by connecting Latin and Greek in this way (whether he realised it or not), and many later writers made similar observations to his for centuries to come. It would take another 1,500 years before anyone began to investigate these similarities in any more detail, however, and start to use them to piece together our language's genealogy.

Marcus van Boxhorn was a professor of history and rhetoric at the University of Leiden, in the Netherlands, in the early seventeenth century. For decades he and his contemporaries had theorised that the languages of Europe and Asia were somehow related, and had even adopted a name, Scythian, for the missing piece of the puzzle: the unknown language that connected them.

The exact nature of that connection was unclear, and scholars were divided on precisely how Europe's existing languages fitted into the Scythian bloodline. In an effort to solve the mystery, Boxhorn adopted a simple yet painstaking approach. Word by word, structure by grammatical structure, he began systematically comparing one language with another, and using any similarities he found to assess how, if at all, they were related. Beginning with Greek and Latin, he expanded his search into Persian, German, Russian, Turkish, Swedish, Czech, Lithuanian and even Welsh. The more parallels he discovered, the more intricate a connection he envisaged – and the more their mysterious link to Scythian revealed itself.

Unlike many of his colleagues, Boxhorn came to see Scythian as a single common ancestor, which had long ago given way to its modern-day offspring. The existing languages of Europe and Asia were therefore not its cousins or siblings but its descendants – brother and sister languages, related by a common Scythian parent. Boxhorn was convinced he had discovered 'something true and important',* but the grand reveal would have to wait. At the age of just forty-one,

---

* Boxhorn was compelled to publish the first of his Scythian theories after an unexpected discovery in the winter of 1647. A violent North Sea storm washed away the sand from a beach at Domburg, near the Dutch border with Belgium, and exposed the ruins of an ancient temple dedicated to a mysterious goddess named Nehalennia. The discovery understandably caused a sensation, and for Boxhorn provided all the proof he needed: the goddess's name, he believed, was unknown to historians and classicists because it was of Scythian origin, and he published an influential treatise outlining how he believed the name *Nehalennia* connected to various words found in modern-day European languages. Although Boxhorn was confident in his theory, the origin of Nehalennia's name – and

he died suddenly in Leiden in 1653, and his revolutionary research spent another century on the academic backburner.

Eventually, it fell to British philologist Sir William Jones to pick up where Boxhorn had left off. While working in India in 1786, he gave a famous speech in which he noted the Latin and Greek of Europe bore 'a stronger affinity ... than could possibly have been produced by accident' with Sanskrit, the oldest of India's languages and one of the oldest recorded languages in the world. These similarities, he believed, proved they must share 'some common source, which perhaps no longer exists', from which they and many of the other Eurasian languages had probably evolved. By this point, Jones was by no means the first person to suggest a connection like this (and it's fair to say some of his other theories from the same speech were a little wide of the mark). But, at the time, his comments on a relationship between Latin, Greek and Sanskrit caused a sensation.

Linguists and historians around the world were soon engaged in figuring out this ancient and mysterious connection, and in doing so they resurrected Boxhorn's meticulous word-by-word research. By the turn of the century, his work had inspired an entirely new field of research – comparative linguistics – and this painstaking work had yielded enough material to draw a fuller picture of our linguistic past than he could have ever imagined. It was now clear that the languages of Europe and Asia were indeed related to one another via a single common ancestor (now known as Proto-Indo-European, not Scythian), but their relationship both to it and to one another was far more complex than anticipated. As the Proto-Indo-Europeans had

---

indeed in which European culture she was venerated – remains largely unsolved to this day.

left their homeland at the end of the Bronze Age, their language had broken apart in not just one but more than a dozen different directions. The Germanic family of languages had emerged in north-west Europe, but elsewhere distinct Italic, Celtic, Balto-Slavic, Hellenic, Anatolian and Indo-Iranian bloodlines had appeared too – alongside many others – from which languages as diverse as Italian, Irish, Polish, Greek, Hittite and Kurdish had developed. Many of these lineages in turn had their own branches and sub-branches, each representing a new stage of evolution scattered across countless generations. Today, Indo-European is known to be the world's largest language family, embracing more than 400 different individual languages, spoken by over 3 billion people across one-quarter of the globe. Retracing the origin of our word *girl* therefore involves piecing together the history of just one of potentially tens of millions of interconnected words.

Not every one of those words needs quite such an in-depth explanation, of course. Take our old friend, the compound noun *doghouse*. Its individual elements, *dog* and *house*, have lengthy and complex histories, but the $x + y$ process that brought them together in English is a simple one, and the word itself is only a few centuries old. New words are being created in this way all the time, without any recourse whatsoever to our languages' prehistoric roots. And compounding is just one of a number of different word-building processes that continue to expand our vocabulary today.

The vast majority of our compound words are so-called endocentric compounds, meaning one of their conjoined $x + y$ words acts as a general headword that is somehow specified or clarified by the other. So a *doghouse* is a house, specifically for a dog. A *blackbird* is a bird, specifically one that's black. In English, these headwords typically fall on the right, so ours is said to be a right-headed language. Other languages are left-headed, like French, which prefers compounds like *stylo-bille* ('pen-ball', for a ballpoint pen) and *oiseau-mouche* ('bird-fly', for a hummingbird). But if you're a native English speaker, you'll be all but hardwired to interpret words such as these from the right. You can test just how innate this right-headedness is, in fact, by switching compound words around and seeing how your brain reappraises them. *Birdblack* doesn't exist as a word in English, but if it did, you'd likely expect it to refer to a substance used to blacken feathers,* while a *housedog* wouldn't be a house for a dog, but be a dog suitable for keeping at home.

All our other types of compound word are far less common. Copulative compounds are pairs of words with an *x and y* relationship. A *dinner-dance* involves both dinner *and* a dance. A *passive-aggressive* person is both passive *and* aggressive. In appositional compounds, the *x* is a *y* and the *y* is an *x*. A *singer-songwriter* is both a singer who writes songs and a songwriter who sings. A *player-manager* is a player who manages and a manager who plays. And in exocentric compounds, the combination *x + y* relates not to a specific *y*, but to an unrelated *z*. *Pickpockets* and *loudmouths* are people, not pockets or mouths.

---

* This relationship is known as *hyponymy*, and endocentric compounds (*x + y*) are classed as *hyponyms* of their heads (*y*). *Streetlights*, *traffic lights*, *penlights*, *nightlights* and *flashlights* are all types of – or hyponyms of – light. The head word itself is known as a *hypernym*. This contrasts with another type of semantic relationship known as meronymy and holonymy. While hyponymy refers to types of things, meronymy refers to parts of things: finger is a meronym of hand, toe is a meronym of foot, and bulb could be classed as a meronym of light. In this kind of relationship, the main noun or head of which the meronyms are part is known as the holonym.

Given all these different forms and structures, the relationship between the components of a compound word is often unpredictable, and even similar pairings don't always follow the same rules. A *mousehole*, for instance, is a hole made *by* a mouse – but an *armhole* is a hole made *for* an arm. And while *steam engines* and *steamboats* are contraptions powered by steam, a *fire engine* isn't powered by fire, and a *gravy boat* certainly isn't powered by gravy.

English also finds room for reduplicative compounds, in which a root is joined to itself, $x + x$ style, to make a matching pair – such as *so-so*, *buddy-buddy*, *twenty-twenty*, *goody-goody*. Exact repetitions like these are rare, however,* and the vast majority of reduplicative words typically exhibit some kind of difference from one half and the other – as in *hocus-pocus*, *hoity-toity* or *namby-pamby*.

Words formed by reduplication are often either onomatopoeic – *choo-choo* or *tick-tock* – or emphatic, and meant to somehow strengthen or reinforce their meaning – *teeny-weeny* or *super-duper*. But humour plays a role here too, and many are just daft extensions or plays on pre-existing words, like *easy-peasy* and *nitty-gritty*.† As

---

* Compound words built from exact repetitions might be rare in English, but the use of repeated words themselves is not. Contrastive focus reduplication is the name of an ingenious language phenomenon in which a word is repeated to in some way reinforce or modify its meaning or implication in a specific context. It is this, for instance, that leads to paper books being called *book-books* to differentiate them from ebooks – and it is this that lies behind otherwise potentially mind-boggling statements such as 'We went out, but not *out* out' and 'I like him, but I don't *like* like him.'

† A slangy phenomenon called *schm– reduplication* is another example of the wittiness of reduplicative words. Although not used to create new standard words, *schm–* reduplication sees words repeated with an initial *schm–* prefix the second time around, creating intentionally dismissive or throwaway phrases

random as many of these *higgledy-piggledy* words might seem, however, there is method to the madness here. Studies have shown infants find it easier to learn words with repeated sounds than those that are mixed, which not only accounts for childish inventions like *choo-choo* and *gee-gee*, but the enduring use of stock phrases such as *bye-bye* and *night-night*. And when a pair of repeated words differs only by its vowel, as in *dilly-dally* or *flip-flop*, the sounds involved always follow a strict sequence, moving from a high vowel (usually 'i' or 'e') to a low vowel (like 'a' or 'o'). This predictable order – known as ablaut reduplication – is what makes pairings like *dally-dilly* and *flop-flip* sound so immediately off-kilter.

When words are merged rather than compounded, the resulting hybrid is called a blend – for example, *smog* (from *smoke* + *fog*) or *ginormous* (from *gigantic* + *enormous*). Blending is a particularly common word-forming process in modern English and has been responsible for such contemporary buzzwords as *flexitarian*, *hangry*, *metrosexual*, *chillax* and *cosplay*. Even more recently, we had an entire pandemicon of coronavirus-related blends, including *covidiot* (someone behaving irresponsibly during lockdown), *scariant* (an alarming virus mutation) and *fauxvid* (symptoms matching Covid-19 that turned out to be nothing).

The slanginess and clunkiness of modern blendventions like these often leads to them being met with a mixture of distaste and dismay (or *dismaste*, as you could call it). But as a word-building process in its own right, blending is by no means new. The long-obsolete word *nimp*, meaning to bite or gnaw, was coined in the fourteenth century from a

---

such as *work-schmerk*, *money-schmoney*. The comedian and activist Fran Drescher founded the charity *Cancer Schmancer* in 2007.

combination of *nim* (to seize) + *nip* (to pinch). *Clasp* is thought to be a medieval combination of *close* + *hasp*. *Dumbfound* (*dumb* + *confound*) dates from 1653. *Flabbergast* (*flabby* + *aghast*) is from 1773. And people have been enjoying *brunch* (*breakfast* + *lunch*) since 1895. In fact, some blends have been with us so long that they scarcely register as combinations any more, like *happenstance* (*happen* + *circumstance*, 1857), *electrocution* (*electric* + *execution*, 1889) and *meld* (*melt* + *weld*, 1936). Those of us who might roll our eyes at clumsy concoctions such as *hacktivism* or *advertorial* will probably have little problem with such subtler combinations as *pixel* (*picture* + *element*) or *cultivar* (*cultivated* + *variety*). Whether we'll be quite so welcoming to twenty-first-century coinages like *Frypo* (a Freudian typo), *bedgasm* (the euphoria of slipping into bed at the end of a long day) and *chairdrobe* (a pile of laundry kept on a bedroom chair) remains to be seen.

The fragments that make up blended words, such as *br–* and *–unch*, are known as splinters. Usually, the splintered head of one word (*breakfast*) is blended with the tail of another (*lunch*), but all manner of different combinations are tolerated. *Sitcom* is head–head (*situation* + *comedy*). *Burbclave*, meaning a gated community, is tail–tail (*suburb* + *enclave*). Sometimes entirely unsplintered words are involved, as in *carjack* (*car* + *hijack*) or *docudrama* (*documentary* + *drama*). Rarely, one splinter is placed directly inside another, creating a so-called intercalative word: *chortle* (*chuckle* + *snort*). Some splinters even break free from their blends to begin operating as prefixes and suffixes in their own right. After the first *walkathon* was held in the 1920s, the ending *–athon* spawned a *runathon* (1932), a *talkathon* (1934), a *readathon* (1936) and a *telethon* (1949). And since 1972's Watergate affair, *–gate* has been used to coin another fifty years of scandals, from *Irangate* (1986) and *Camillagate* (1992) to *Plebgate* (2012) and *Partygate* (2021). Splintered tags such as these – as well as the likes of *Franken–*, *–tastic*, *–licious*, *–aganza*, *–aholic* and *–splaining* – are known as liberated affixes. (Or, appropriately enough, *libfixes*.)

We can of course create new words using standard prefixes and suffixes, like *un–* and *–ness*. This is derivational morphology, and in this book alone you'll find *unprolongable*, *languageness* and *ungenderedness*. Similarly, we can build words by adding Latin and Greek fragments to one another, using a process called neoclassical compounding. It was this that made *photography* from the Greek words for 'light' (*photo–*) and 'writing' (*–graphy*), and named the *television* from the Greek for 'afar' (*tele–*) and the Latin for 'to see' (*visio*). But we can also build new words by removing prefixes and suffixes – or at least, elements that resemble or act like them. So if the device itself is called a *television*, it makes sense to say that to *televise* is to broadcast something to a television. Despite it being the shorter word, the verb *televise* understandably didn't exist in our language until after the television was invented. That makes it a backformation – a word created by cutting down an established word, in a kind of reverse derivation.

It was backformation too that gave us *peddle* from *pedlar*, *burgle* from *burglar*, *buttle* from *butler* and *swindle* from *swindler*. There was no verb *sulk* before the adjective *sulky*, no *raunch* before things were *raunchy*, and no *megaliths* before the *megalithic*. *Gestation*, *automation*, *donation* and *titillation* all existed before their related verbs *gestate*, *automate*, *donate* and *titillate*. Perhaps oddest of all, the verb *escalate* was coined only after the *escalator* had been invented, and English adopted *editor* and *curator* from Latin before chopping off their endings to produce verbs for what they do – *edit* and *curate*.

As a word-forming process in itself, 'chopping bits off' is properly called clipping. *Ad*, *lab*, *bus*, *gym*, *pram*, *exam* and *memo* are all clippings of *advertisement*, *laboratory*, *omnibus*, *gymnasium*, *perambulator*, *examination* and *memorandum*. When the tail of a word is clipped off (as in *rhino* from *rhinoceros*), the process is called apocope. When the head is taken away (as in *phone* from *telephone*), it is called apheresis. When both the head and tail are lost, it is called syncope – a rare form of clipping responsible for only a handful of words including *flu* (cut from the middle of *influenza*), *fridge* (from *refrigerator*) and *shrink*, in the sense of a psychiatrist (from 1950s slang *headshrinker*).

Of course words can be further truncated, so that only their initial letter or sound remains, producing acronyms such as *scuba* ('self-contained underwater breathing apparatus'), and initialisms like *VIP* ('very important person'). The boundaries between these two categories are not always clear, and recent coinages are blurring them more than ever. Do you pronounce *LOL* as an acronym ('loll') or as an initialism ('L-O-L')?* Is it 'A-sap', or 'A-S-A-P'? Some initialisms even go full circle and turn into words coined to replicate strings of initial letters, like *deejay*, *okay* and *enbie*. Inventions such as these are properly known as phonetic respellings but have much more snappily been dubbed 'vocologues'.

A lot of these word-building processes involve simply adapting or reshaping existing words. Clipping and acronymy involve trimming down words we already have, while compounding and blending involve binding them together. But what about words invented

---

* The earliest record of LOL as an acronym is from 1960, when it was used to mean 'little old lady' in a San Francisco newspaper.

without any raw materials whatsoever? Can't we, for want of a better phrase, just make one up?

In 1920, the American mathematician Edward Kasner took a walk in the woods with his nine-year-old nephew, Milton. Kasner had recently been pondering how some quantities that are often labelled as infinite – such as the number of electrons in the universe – are not actually infinite, so long as a digit large enough to quantify them can be named. With that in mind, he asked Milton to come up with 'any amusing name that entered his head' for an appropriately gigantic figure: a 1 followed by 100 zeros.

In standard arithmetic notation, this figure would be ten duotrigintillion, but the name Milton came up with instead was *googol*. Kasner included the word in his bestselling book *Mathematics and the Imagination* in 1940, and from there it quickly fell into standard usage. (Its use became so normalised, in fact, that in 2001 it was the answer to the million-pound question on Major Charles Ingram's infamous edition of *Who Wants to Be a Millionaire?**)

Googol is the quintessential example of a word created out of thin air, but it is by no means alone. Sci-fi author Robert A. Heinlein coined the word *grok* ('to understand intuitively or by empathy', according to the *Oxford English Dictionary*) for his 1961 novel *Stranger in a Strange Land*. In 1964, US physicist Murray Gell-Mann randomly named the *quark* particle (though he was reportedly inspired by a word already concocted by the author James Joyce).

---

* Milton's contribution to our language didn't end there either. When tech entrepreneurs Larry Page and Sergey Brin needed a new name for their search engine BackRub in 1997, they chose one based on the number's name in order to imply the scope of their website, and Google was born.

A *grawlix* is a string of random symbols used to signify swearing in a comic strip, so named in 1980 by American cartoonist Mort Walker, who also named *briffits* (clouds of dust drawn behind a fleeing character), *swalloops* (curves drawn around flailing limbs) and *plewds* (sweat droplets drawn to show stress or exertion). The brand *Kodak* was named by photography pioneer George Eastman in 1888, who wanted a word that was 'short and euphonious, and likely to stick in the public mind'. And, as we're including proper nouns on this list, the tiny town of Ixonia in Wisconsin was named in 1846 by randomly drawing letters out of a bag.

Clearly, words can and indeed are invented entirely at random. Doing so is often remarkably useful too; giving a name to something allows it to be discussed openly and is a simple way of revealing the commonality of feelings and experiences that might otherwise go unspoken. Not every invented word will catch on beyond your own vocabulary, of course, but if it does, posterity awaits. When Beverly Hills High School student Gaby Rasson started using the word *cheugy* among her friends to describe off-trend fashion in 2013, she could scarcely have predicted the word would end up being shared around the world via TikTok and become one of the most talked-about terms of 2021 (and no doubt guaranteeing her a future place in the dictionary).

Go back far enough in time, however, and surely *all* our words were at one point invented out of nothing? According to Max Müller's ding-dong theory, our very first words were our ancestors' instinctual responses to the world around them; they had no etymological basis other than a kind of metaphysical resonance with nature. Müller's theory might be disregarded today, but it still raises one final intriguing question: what were our very first words?

It's fair to say we simply have no way of telling what our very earliest vocalisations were. Depending on what part of our language's evolutionary journey you think qualifies as the first human speech, there's a reasonable argument to be made that it was perhaps some kind of instinctive response, a scream or shout, or an orangutan-style alarm call. But as our communication became more complex and we began to string those basic sounds into longer words, it is impossible to say what our first speech may have been, or indeed why our ancestors chose to label things with certain combinations of sounds over others. As Charles Hockett emphasised in his list of our language's design features, words are fundamentally arbitrary labels – so precisely why our ancestors effectively chose to give the combination 's', 'u' and 'n' to the sun and 'm', 'oo', and 'n' to moon (or whatever their ancient equivalents were) is a mystery lost to evolutionary time. According to one recent study, however, Marcus van Boxhorn's meticulous comparative research can be taken to extreme limits.

Two centuries ago, linguists reconstructed Proto-Indo-European using comparative evidence gleaned from the languages of Europe and Asia. Since then, similar studies have been repeated elsewhere, and entire linguistic dynasties have now been reassembled in every corner of the globe. By applying our comparative word-by-word method to the vocabularies of these ancient protolanguages *themselves*, however, we can very tentatively take our language even further back in time. In essence, we can use the world's protolanguages to reconstruct our proto-protolanguage.

In 2013, researchers at the University of Reading compared words from the Indo-European family of languages to their equivalents in seven other language families: Altaic, the ancestor of modern-day Uzbek and Mongolian; Chukchi-Kamchatkan, a family of Siberian languages; the Dravidian language family of India; the Inuit-Yupik languages of the Arctic; the Kartvelian family, to which Georgian almost uniquely belongs; and the Uralic family, the ancestor of a handful of European outliers, including Hungarian, Finnish and Estonian. Similarities between the root words in these ancient families revealed a core list of around two dozen words the researchers described as 'ultraconserved' – that is, they had remained relatively unchanged in sound and structure over the past 15,000 years:

ashes	*hand*	*old*	*we*
bark	*hear*	*pull*	*what*
black	*I*	*spit*	*who*
fire	*man*	*that*	*worm*
flow	*mother*	*this*	*ye*
give	*not*	*thou*	

There is a handful of words here that we arguably could have expected to find on a list such as this (*man*, *fire*, *mother*), plus a scattering of useful grammatical particles (*this*, *that*, *not*, *I*, *we*). A little less expected are *worm*, *spit*, *ashes* and *flow*. But it's nice to know the medicinal and practical functions of *bark* are nothing new, and there's a reassuring nod to our innate collaborative spirit in the ancientness of the verb *give*.

Admittedly, this study is by no means without controversy; it's certainly possible that it entails too much conjecture and that the correspondences behind it are little more than prehistoric coincidences. But if they're not, then perhaps these words really are capable of giving us a newfound glimpse into the most ancient part of our vocabulary.

What Is the Hardest
Language to Learn?

Learn a new language, get a new soul.
Czech proverb

In the spring of 1816, Lord Byron was facing a crisis. His marriage had collapsed after scarcely a year, and the divorce proceedings now under way had made public a string of infidelities, with both male and female lovers. Mounting debts and a scandalous relationship with his half-sister only worsened his troubles, until he was left with little alternative: just after 9 o'clock in the morning on 25 April, he boarded a packet ship at Dover and abandoned England forever.

By autumn he was in Venice, where it didn't take long for him to fall back into his old ways. An affair with the wife of his landlord was followed by another with a twenty-two-year-old newlywed, who promptly abandoned her marriage to move into Byron's home; when he later ended the relationship, she threw herself into a canal. In an attempt to escape temptation and ignominy once and for all, Byron headed somewhere that offered little chance of either. 'By way of divertissement,' he wrote home to a friend, 'I am studying daily at an Armenian monastery.'

Byron was at San Lazzaro degli Armeni, a friary on Venice's St Lazarus Island. There, under the tutelage of the monks, he had begun learning Armenian. 'I found that my mind wanted something craggy to break upon,' he wrote, 'and this – as the most difficult thing I could discover here for an amusement – I have chosen to torture me into attention.'

Difficult was the word. Armenian is a complex and deeply nuanced language, furnished with a devilish writing system unlike any other on Earth. Purpose-built in the fifth century (to replace an ill-fitting mixture of Greek and Persian in use before then), the Armenian alphabet originally had thirty-six letters; by the time Byron came to learn it, two more had been added (and a thirty-ninth followed in 1924). 'It is, to be sure, a Waterloo of an alphabet,' he wrote. But that was the least of his worries.

Whereas English only inflects nouns for number (*dog* vs. *dogs*), Armenian nouns can be declined in seven different ways to express additional qualities including motion, position and use. A word as simple as 'envelope', *crar*, would require a distinct form depending on whether you're talking about something inside an envelope (*crarum*), being removed from an envelope (*craric'*), or if you're using an envelope to do something (*crarov*). Each then alters again depending on who owns the envelope and how many envelopes there are – so in the sentence 'your papers are inside your envelopes', *crar* would need to be upgraded to its second-person possessive plural locative form, *crarnerumd*.

Complexities like these nevertheless failed to deter Byron, who eventually proved proficient enough to co-author two Armenian textbooks. In 1821, he even aided in the compilation of the first English–Armenian dictionary. It might have been 'the most difficult thing' he could find to distract himself, but mastery of the language had by no means proved impossible.

So if not Armenian, what? Say you wished to follow in Byron's footsteps and test your linguistic mettle. You might not have a string of doomed love affairs to escape from, but which language would pose the greatest challenge to 'break your mind upon'? It's an intriguing question. It's also very difficult to answer.

What makes one language more difficult than another is subjective, and rests on endless variables that change from one learner to the next. Any language more closely related to one you already know, for instance, will naturally pose less of a challenge than one more distant. From an English speaker's perspective, the US Foreign Service Institute categorises seventy of the world's languages into four levels of difficulty, based on the time it takes its diplomatic staff to achieve a 'professional working proficiency'. It's little coincidence that its Category I languages – said to require only twenty-four to thirty weeks' tuition – include many of English's closest relatives, such as Dutch, French and Swedish. The more complex grammar of German lands it in Category II (alongside Swahili), while the increasingly distant Czech, Polish, Finnish and Icelandic find themselves in Category III with Hebrew, Vietnamese, Urdu, Mongolian and Byron's Armenian. The final 'super-hard' languages of Category IV – Arabic, Cantonese, Mandarin, Japanese and Korean – typically require more than 2,000 hours of coaching, often with months of immersive study overseas.

Age is another variable. Children tend to learn languages more readily than adults, as their developing brains are all but hardwired to pick up their mother tongue (and any other language besides) as rapidly as possible. Estimates at the cut-off point of this critical period of learning suggest it lies somewhere between ten and eighteen years of age, after which internal changes to our brains' plasticity and external changes to our lifestyle conspire to make the retention of new linguistic information more difficult. The fact that childhood proficiency is determined as much by biology as eagerness or tuition would seemingly put adult learners at an immediate disadvantage, but happily some studies have suggested quite the opposite: adults may in many ways make *better* learners than children, as they are able to use tried-and-tested memorisation techniques, call on a lifetime of knowledge and experience, and approach the learning process more critically. After all, Byron was in his thirties when he took on Armenian.

And then there's the notion that some people have a natural gift for languages that other people simply don't share. Studies of so-called hyperpolyglots – individuals with mastery of multiple languages* – have suggested there might be some truth to this, as they seem able to store and retrieve linguistic information in their long-term memories much more readily than other people. Yet research has also shown it may not be the lack of a gift that holds many learners back, but rather a lack of confidence. Xenoglossophobia, or

---

* In his 2012 examination of multilingualism *Babel No More*, the linguist Michael Erard set the boundary between a polyglot and a hyperpolyglot at a proficiency of at least six languages. Erard's thinking was based on a survey of naturally multilingual communities, the world's most diverse of which bring together five different languages in a single location. A mastery of six different languages is ultimately a level of multilingualism not seen naturally anywhere in the world, and marks the point at which a person must have learned at least one of those languages intentionally to converse with other communities.

foreign-language anxiety, is a growing field of psychological study that routinely finds factors such as test apprehension, nervousness in a classroom setting and a fear of making mistakes can have hugely detrimental effects on the learning experiences. By adapting teaching methods accordingly, new languages could be opened up to anyone, regardless of any innate skill.

In light of all this, it would be wrong to single out one language as the world's hardest (or indeed, easiest) as the answer would understandably be different for everyone. But all learners, regardless of their starting point, face the same challenges – from learning a new vocabulary to adapting to unfamiliar sounds and sentence structures. So in an effort to come to some kind of conclusion here, we can at least identify the types of difficulties learners encounter and explore how different languages compare around the world. When it comes to learning a new set of words, for example, ironically English presents one of the world's toughest challenges, as its vocabulary is popularly said to be the world's largest. That's a difficult statistic to corroborate (not least because there's no hard and fast way of defining what a word actually is), but with over 200,000 entries in the *Oxford English Dictionary* alone as a starting point, it's fair to say English is on the heftier side. Add to that our sprawling regional variation and a chaotically inconsistent spelling system, and congratulations – if you're reading this, you've already mastered one of the world's toughest languages.

If you're used to the ABCs of English, of course, any language that uses a different writing system will instantly cause a problem. The prospect of learning an entirely new way of reading and writing can seem daunting – but not every writing system poses quite the same challenge.

By definition, all alphabets exhibit a roughly one-to-one correspondence between their letters and the sounds of a language – so A makes an 'ah' sound, B makes a 'b' sound, and so on. Learning a new alphabet ultimately boils down to learning just a new set of these letter–sound correspondences. As unfamiliar as an English speaker might be with the lambdas, epsilons, xis and etas of Greek, once they know they spell *λέξη*, or *léxi*, all that remains is to remember it as the Greek word for – well – 'word'.

A more complex alphabetical set-up is found in a writing system called a syllabary. Here, different characters represent sound pairings or combinations, and so the number and complexity of the letters in a syllabic system tend to be much higher than in an alphabet. Cherokee, for instance, has a robust set of eighty written characters representing all its possible consonant–vowel combinations, such as *ge* (Ꭸ), *ha* (Ꭽ), *qua* (Ꮖ), *dla* (Ꮭ) and *tsu* (Ꮷ). If English were to adopt a similar system, we would need to learn something in the region of 15,000 characters.

More complex again are systems called abjads and abugidas. In an abjad, like Hebrew, only the consonants are written down and readers have to fill in the vowels deductively from the surrounding context. In an abugida, like Thai, each written character typically represents a consonant–vowel pairing, with a basic consonant character modified in some way to indicate the associated vowel. In many abugida systems, these modifications are reduced to dots, dashes, lines and other markers written on or around the consonant in question. Others, like the Inuktitut writing system of Canada, use the direction of the consonant to indicate the vowel, producing mirrored sets of characters like *hai* (ᕴ), *hi* (ᕵ), *hu* (ᕷ), and *ha* (ᕹ).

These systems might seem extraordinary to an English speaker,* spclly gvn tht wtht r vwls, mch f r lngg wld b ll bt nrdbl. But many abjad and abugida languages have evolved in such a way that their consonants simply play a greater role in differentiating words than we're used to in English, and their vowels are reduced to little more than filler material that can be easily deduced from them. Once the rules dictating which vowels appear where are mastered, the rest of the system will simply fall into place. Perhaps the most formidable writing challenge is not then a language that uses a different system of letters, but one that uses no letters at all.

A logography is a writing system in which each individual character, or logogram, represents a distinct word or, in some cases, a morpheme. The most well-known logography in use today is written Chinese, but the hieroglyphic system of Ancient Egypt partly followed a similar arrangement. Such systems are rare, however, not least because logographic writing effectively requires a reader to know as many individual characters as there are words, and no known writing system is entirely logographic. Nevertheless, by sheer volume of material to be learned, Chinese presents an undeniable challenge: estimates at the total number of its written characters, or *hanzi*, range from a conservative 50,000 to well over 100,000.

Just as a proficient English speaker doesn't need to know every word in the dictionary, of course, not every Chinese speaker will know all 100,000 hanzi. In fact, to pass the topmost proficiency test

---

* As alien as this system seems to English speakers, as we shall see our ABCs developed from an abjad, and it was only the quirks of the development of Europe's languages that added vowels to our alphabet. Moreover, English has countless words that would be rendered identical if we were to remove or reduce their vowels (as in *pat, pet, pit, pot, put, peat* and *pout*).

of the Chinese Ministry of Education, a learner need recognise only 3,000 – so learn ten every day, and you'll master enough in a year to pass the Chinese government's own fluency exam.* However, being able to recognise Chinese characters is one thing; being able to pronounce them is another.

Mandarin is a tonal language, so its words and syllables are distinguished not just by their sound, but by how musically pitched or contoured those sounds are in speech. There are four possible tone shapes in Mandarin – high, rising, falling–rising, and falling – plus a fifth neutral tone, equivalent to no noticeable change at all. Depending on which of these is applied to the word *qi*, for instance, will transform it into 'wife', 'strange', 'rise' or 'lifeforce'. *Wu* can mean 'house', 'without', 'five' or 'fog'.

As perplexing as tonal languages can seem to outsiders (and as impenetrable as they can be for people without a musical ear†) they are certainly not uncommon. As many as 70 per cent of the world's languages, spoken by over 1.5 billion people,‡ exhibit some kind of

---

* In writing, many Chinese words are formed from pairings of other characters, producing a relatively large vocabulary from a small number of hanzi; link *fire* and *mountain* together, for instance, and you'll have the word for *volcano*. These 3,000 characters can ultimately be used to form some 11,000 different words.

† Having a natural musicality inbuilt to your language seems to have its advantages, as there is evidence that speakers of tonal languages tend to be more likely to possess perfect pitch – the ability to recognise the musical pitch of an isolated note.

‡ Around the world, tonal languages tend to be clustered in three broad regions: eastern and south-eastern Asia, the western Americas, and sub-Saharan Africa. Given the vague overlaps in climate here, a 2014 study suggested that tonal languages don't tend to occur elsewhere – that is, in more arid or less humid environments – because the colder and drier air inhibits the movement of

tonal contrast – albeit to varying degrees of complexity. Navajo and Xhosa have two tones. Zulu has three. Cantonese has six. The Hmong languages of south-east Asia have up to eight. And in the Wobé language of Côte d'Ivoire, syllables can be pitched at five different levels – very high (1), high (2), mid (3), low (4) and extra-low (5) – with various rising and falling movements between those pitches creating fourteen possible tone shapes. Say the Wobé word *keh* with a solid level 1 tone, and you'll say 'tip'. Pitch the same word at 3 then raise it to 2, and you'll say 'law'. Raise it more dramatically, from 4 to 1, and it will mean 'beak'. Drop it from 2 to 5, and it will mean 'inheritance'. Lower it more subtly, from 4 to 5, and it will mean 'giraffe'. One word, multiple meanings – all differentiated solely by tone.

Tone isn't the only phonological challenge either. While English is an egressive language – meaning our sounds are produced by exhaling – a handful of languages use ingressive sounds, made by sucking air inwards, back into the mouth and lungs. Many of the Scandinavian languages have ingressive sounds, as do some native African and Australian languages. Outside of those, the only time most people will ever hear or use ingressive speech is when they're compelled to continue talking while running out of breath.

The soundscape of Czech includes an extraordinary sound known as the voiced alveolar fricative trill – a simultaneous combination of a trilling 'r' (like the sound made to imitate a cat's purr) plus a harsher 'zh' (like the S in the middle of *vision*). This sound is

---

the vocal folds, reducing the elasticity required to produce tonal differences accurately.

so complex even many native Czech speakers don't master it until late childhood, while those who never do resort to pronouncing the 'r' and 'zh' successively, not simultaneously.

Many southern African languages have click consonants, variously made by tutting, clucking or popping the tongue, lips and mouth. Articulating even one of these sounds accurately is a skill in itself, but Xhosa has eighteen of them: six made with the tongue against the teeth (like a *tut* sound); six made by forcing airflow around the tongue (like the sound used to gee up a horse), and six made by using the tongue to pressurise and then release a pocket of air against the roof of the mouth.

And while English tends to demand every syllable is built around a vowel sound, the Salishan languages of north-west America allow consonants to occupy their own syllables, without any accompanying vowels at all. That rule allows for utterly extraordinary words such as *xłp̓x̌ʷłtłpłłskʷc̓* – 'he had had a bunchberry plant in his possession' in the Nuxalk language of British Columbia.

Even languages whose phonologies are relatively straightforward can still have their difficulties. In 2011, researchers at the University of Lyon analysed the average talking speed of several of the world's major languages, with Mandarin coming in slowest of all (at 5.18 syllables per second), as its tonal syllables required more time to articulate. English was comparatively sluggish too (at 6.19 syllables), while at the faster end of the scale Spanish (7.82) was pipped into second place by the world's fastest language, Japanese (7.84). It has a relatively simple phonology overall, comprising just fifteen different consonant sounds and only five vowels (compared with English's eleven), all of which tend to fall in regular consonant–vowel pairings. Its faster pace, however, means an English learner would have to pick up nearly two extra syllables of spoken information per second.*

There are other complexities in Japanese too, and it certainly has a well-earned reputation as one of the world's most challenging languages. Its writing system effectively bundles three different writing systems into one. *Kanji*, a 50,000-character logography adopted from Chinese, is mixed with two distinct Japanese syllabaries, *hiragana* and *katakana*. Its grammar complicates things further with an extensive set of sentence particles, or *joshi* – short syllables and tags added onto the ends of Japanese words, clauses and sentences to shape their meaning more precisely. Adding *kke* into a Japanese sentence is a way of expressing doubt. Tagging *zo* onto it is a means of showing assertiveness. *Ne* is used to form rhetorical questions or ask for confirmation of a statement. And a robust set of honorific markers, or *keigo*, are used to communicate one of three different levels of Japanese conversational courtesy – *teineigo* (standard politeness), *sonkeigo* (respectfulness) and *kenjougo* (humility).

A great many other languages encode courtesy into everyday speech in this way, of course. French speakers use their plural pronoun *vous* ('you') when talking respectfully to individual people, reserving their actual singular pronoun, *tu*, for close friends, family

---

* The overall effect on a Japanese conversation, however, is limited. This study also sought to quantify how much information each syllable carries, rated on a scale of 0–1 based on the so-called 'information density' of each language. The slowest languages were found to have the most meaningful syllables: English scored an ID of 0.91, slightly behind Mandarin's 0.94, while Japanese and Spanish scored just 0.49 and 0.63 respectively. Despite them having different paces, a story told in English would take roughly the same amount of time to tell in Japanese – it just takes more Japanese syllables to say the same thing.

members and children. The influence of French on English meant for a time we did the same, using the plural pronoun *ye* as a marker of respect, saving singular *thou* for less formal contexts. But this practice disappeared when *you* began assuming both positions in the 1600s – and nor is this the only linguistic complexity for which English simply has no obvious equivalent.

Around a third of the world's languages exhibit an ingenious feature called clusivity, which allows speakers to specify whether or not the person they're talking to is included in the action they're describing. In Chechen (thought to be the only European language to do so) the first-person plural pronoun 'we' is either *waj*, 'we including you', or *txo*, 'we but not you', depending on whether the person being addressed is included. This distinction is impossible in English without broader context, so an English speaker exclaiming, 'We've won the lottery!' could either be bringing their audience good news or be about to make them unendingly envious.

The specificity stakes are raised even higher in Malagasy. Its demonstrative pronouns (equivalent to *this*, *that*, *these* and *those*) can be reshaped to indicate whether *this* or *that* is visible to the speaker, and how far away it is located. That alone would be complex enough, yet Malagasy grammar recognises no fewer than seven different stages of geographical distance, from immediate proximity (*ity*, 'this thing I can see right here'), to nearby (*ito*), not so nearby (*io*), middle distance (*itsy*), far middle distance (*iny*), distant (*iroa*) and most remote of all (*iry*, 'that one I can see way off over there'). If what you're talking about cannot be seen, these change to *izaty* ('the one I can't see but is nearby'), *izato*, *izao*, *izatsy*, *izany*, *izaroa* and the most extreme, *izary* ('that thing out of sight in the far distance').

And then there's Berik, a language spoken in New Guinea. It too recognises distance in its grammar by inflecting its verbs to show how near or how far away the action is taking place. But Berik verbs can also be inflected to show factors including the size and number of objects involved; the gender of the people involved; whether or not the action is taking place in sunlight or by moonlight, and even the height at which it is happening, relative to that of the person speaking. Add to that the usual distinctions of past, present and future, and Berik speakers are capable of expressing mind-boggling levels of exactness with a single conjugated verb. *Kitobafo*, for example, is just one form of the Berik word for 'give' that specifically refers to the act of handing three large-size items to one man under cover of darkness. The verb for 'tie' turns into *faarefant* when talking about someone having tied two large items together in daylight nearby. And the verb for 'place' would become *gwerantetfa* if a man were busy at this very moment placing just one large item at a level above their own height somewhere far away.

And so it goes on, with language after language exhibiting complexity after complexity beyond anything we could ever imagine in English. Thai has a specific form only ever used when speaking to the royal family. In Burushaski, a language of Pakistan, verbs can be inflected to show the intensity of the action – so the verb for closing a door could be inflected to show whether the door is being closed softly, normally or slammed shut. Matsés, an indigenous language of the Amazon, demands its speakers encode into everything they say precisely how they came to know it. A Matsés sentence would change depending on whether the speaker has first-hand experience of what they're talking about ('It is raining – and I know it to be raining because I have been out in the rain'); are only inferring something based on evidence ('It is raining – because I can see other people's clothes are wet'), or are merely speculating ('I bet it is raining!'). And in the Jemez language of New Mexico, nouns are pluralised as part of an extraordinary system called inverted number. Unlike in English, where nouns are typically singular until inflected otherwise, Jemez nouns are either *inherently* singular or *inherently* plural (or even inherently dual, if they tend to occur in pairs). A single inflectional ending, *–sh*, is added onto a word only when the number being talked about is somehow different from this inherent number. So the word for 'person', *pæ*, is normally singular – making its plural form *pæsh*. But the word for 'drum', *pó*, is inherently plural – so its singular form is *pósh*. Put another way, nouns in Jemez are inflected for number only when the number of them you're talking about is somehow grammatically unexpected.

Alongside all the features English doesn't have, there are several features we would find indispensable that other languages do without. The Pirahã language of Brazil, for instance, has no numbers. Its speakers simply make do with a trio of words meaning 'small amount', 'large amount' and 'many'. Guugu Yimithirr, a native Australian language, has no words for left and right. Instead its speakers use the cardinal points of a compass to describe relative locations, as in 'the chair to the west of the table', or 'the tree to the south of the gate'. Incredibly, these directions are reinforced with such regularity in the day-to-day language (*north*, *south*, *east* and *west* account for around 10 per cent of a standard conversation), that by the age of eight a typical Guugu Yimithirr speaker has essentially assembled an inbuilt compass, and will remain permanently aware of their location, relative to north and south, for the rest of their lives.

It's worth mentioning at this point that around two-fifths of the world's languages have no writing system, and so are never written down. True, many of these exist in parallel with sister languages that are written down, like Swiss German (whose enormous array of dialects tends to be replaced in print by the more standardised Swiss High German). But dual statuses do not exist everywhere and hundreds of the world's cultures simply make do without writing. When it comes to taking on a challenging new language, perhaps one you simply cannot read or write would pose the greatest challenge of all.

From the perspective of an English speaker, perhaps this last detail is the most remarkable. It is difficult for us, nourished by centuries of printed learning and literature, to imagine a world in which our language is simply never put down on a page. But the world's unwritten languages are perhaps better thought of as 'non-written' languages: they don't lack a writing system any more than a ship lacks wheels or a car lacks sails, as to their speakers there simply isn't anything missing. It is not that they are somehow deficient or anomalous – or even primitive or undeveloped – but that our notion of what is normal is skewed by the norms of our own language.

When it comes to discussing the difficulty of languages, it is easy to marvel at the eighteen click consonants of Xhosa, or wonder how a Pirahã speaker could ever get by without any concept of counting. But one person's strange is just another person's normal. One person's difficult or extraordinary is another person's easy and everyday. To the speakers of the handful of languages name-checked here, their seemingly bizarre features and complexities will simply be rational, unremarkable elements of how they communicate. From a different perspective, this chapter written in Jemez or Japanese might focus on the fact that English has two completely

different forms of the 'th' sound. As easy as it is for us to tell the word *bath* from the word *bathe*, this is a tricky distinction found in less than 10 per cent of the world's languages.* Even rarer still, English speakers can form simple yes–no questions by simply reshuffling the order of words in a statement, turning *Your pet is a dog* into *Is your pet a dog?* Globally, this seemingly effortless aspect of how we talk to one another is found in barely 1 per cent of the world's languages.†
When it comes to assessing linguistic difficulty, ultimately, not only would our answer change from one learner to the next, but so too would our idea of what is unusual or difficult itself.

---

* The 'th' in *bathe* – as well as in words such as *though* and *this* – is known as the voiced dental fricative, /ð/. The 'th' in *bath* – as well as *thanks* and *thin* – is the unvoiced dental fricative. Voiced sounds involve vibration of the vocal cords, while unvoiced sounds do not. Place a finger and thumb each side of your neck as you say *bath* and *bathe*, and you should be able to feel a little more vibration when saying *bathe* than *bath*. Alternatively, try saying the words *thy* and *thigh*. *Thy* is pronounced with the voiced sound, while *thigh* uses the unvoiced equivalent. Without the difference, the two words would be identical.

† This is the finding of the World Atlas of Language Structures (WALS), which compiles data from almost a thousand of the world's documented languages. Just thirteen of them utilise the same question-forming technique as English.

Q. 6

Why Do Languages
Have Genders?

In German, a young lady has no sex, while a turnip has.
Think what overwrought reverence that shows for the
turnip, and what callous disrespect for the girl . . .

> *Gretchen: Wilhelm, where is the turnip?*
> *Wilhelm: She has gone to the kitchen.*
> *Gretchen: Where is the accomplished*
> *and beautiful English maiden?*
> *Wilhelm: It has gone to the opera.*

Mark Twain, *A Tramp Abroad* (1880)

In French, *beds*, *bathtubs* and *bridges* are masculine, while *boxes*, *bottles* and *bells* are feminine. In Spanish, *ships*, *shoes* and *shoulders* are masculine and *shirts*, *shops* and *shadows* are feminine. From an English speaker's perspective (or for that matter, the perspective of anyone whose language doesn't classify words in this way), a gendered vocabulary can seem an unnecessary complication. From a learner's perspective, meanwhile, having to remember the masculineness or feminineness of a new set of words as well as the words themselves can prove a frustrating stumbling block – especially if that gender seems somehow illogical or counterintuitive. To a French speaker, for instance, *feminism* is masculine, while *masculinity* is feminine.

Correctly matching a word to its gender is nevertheless important. In languages that do operate like this, gender has a knock-on effect in the grammar – a form of agreement called concord – that requires all the other words that interact with a gendered word to be reshaped to match it. So 'a new little black bag' in French would be *un nouveau petit sac noir*, using all the masculine forms of 'a', 'new', 'little' and 'black' to match the masculine noun *sac*. 'A new little black dress', on the other hand, would be *une nouvelle petite robe noire*, comprising all the feminine equivalents to match the feminine noun *robe*.

Then there's the problem of heterogenes – pairs of words that are identical except for their gender. So the French *livre* can mean either a book or a pound, depending on whether it's masculine or feminine. The same goes for *platine* (platinum or a DJ's turntable), as well as *faux* (a falsehood or a scythe), *geste* (a gesture or an epic poem), and even more problematically, *mari* (husband or a slang name for marijuana). Fail to gender any of those correctly, and you'll not only make a grammatical misstep but potentially take your conversation in a seriously questionable direction.

Heterogenic words are rare, however, and overall gender isn't ordinarily quite so troublesome that misgendering a word will cause a total breakdown of communication. Ask someone on the Côte d'Azur *Où est le plage?* rather than *Où est la plage?* and they'll still point you in the direction of the beach, despite you mistakenly using *plage* as a masculine rather than a feminine word.

Nor is gender a universal feature of language, as it has been estimated only two-fifths of all languages at most have gendered vocabularies. Alongside French and Spanish, such global heavy hitters as Arabic, Hindi, Swahili, Russian, German, Portuguese and Italian all gender their words, while the ungendered vocabulary of English stands alongside that of Mandarin, Japanese, Thai, Turkish, Persian, Finnish and Hungarian. Both lists include major languages, spoken by hundreds of millions of people, so whether or not a language utilises gender clearly has little impact on how widely used it can become.

So if not every language uses it – and we can still be understood even when we misuse it – what purpose does a gendered vocabulary actually serve? Where do these apparently arbitrary categorisations come from? And why do some languages utilise them, and others not? To get to the bottom of all that, we first need to know precisely what we're dealing with.

English isn't entirely without gender, of course, as we still have word pairs such as *actor* and *actress*, and we reflect gender in our pronouns (*he*, *him* and *his*, and *she*, *her* and *hers*). In linguistic terms, the effect of an individual's gender on the language used to describe them is known as natural gender – though some languages scarcely go this far. Finnish, for instance, has only one third-person singular personal pronoun, *hän*, used in all male, female, ungendered and gender-nonspecific contexts. The kind of gender that makes *beds* masculine and *beaches* feminine is something different. It is grammatical gender, a feature of language that involves the categorisation of a language's nouns into separate gendered groups. Each of these groups – known as noun classes – is then dealt with differently in the grammar, and so might require a unique set of pronouns or word endings, be introduced with different articles or determiners (equivalent to *the* and *that*), or be described using different forms of adjectives (as with the French *nouveau* vs *nouvelle*).

Labelling these groups as 'genders' and organising their words into classes dubbed 'masculine' and 'feminine' is just one method of this categorisation. Put another way, gender is just a class of class – although some linguists even consider the terms *gender* and *class* more or less interchangeable, regardless of how the categories themselves are named. (Indeed, the word *gender* itself merely means 'type' or 'kind', and is an etymological cousin of *genre* and *genus*.) Other languages use other designations and classify their nouns into groups based on all kinds of criteria. Not being tied to a straightforward masculine/feminine split allows many the freedom to introduce enormous numbers of noun classes, far beyond anything we might think possible.

Languages such as German and Russian add a third neuter gender into the mix. Czech and Slovak do the same, but they further divide their masculine nouns into separate animate and inanimate subclasses for a total of four. A living and breathing bear, *medvěd*, would be a masculine animate noun in Czech, while the forest in which it lives, *les*, would be masculine inanimate. Burushaski, a language of northern Pakistan, also has four genders, though its masculine and feminine groups are joined by a third covering animals and all countable objects, and a fourth comprising abstract concepts, mass nouns and uncountable objects. Apples fall in Burushaski's third gender, while apple trees – seen as homologous masses from which individual apples are obtained – fall in the fourth.

Dyirbal, a native Australian language, likewise has four genders: masculine, feminine, fruits and vegetables, and a final catch-all group for everything else. Dyirbal folklore then expands on these categories in various imaginative ways, so that the borders between them are never quite straightforward. The masculine and feminine classes include animals and birds said to carry the spirits of dead men and women. The moon and sun are wedded in Dyirbal myth, and so fall in the masculine and feminine groups as husband and wife. And because the sun is associated with wildfires and sunburn, her feminine class of words includes terms associated with pain, sickness, danger, wrath, warfare and violence – including scorpions, snakes, biting insects, fire, water and weaponry. Far from being a collection of merely female-associated words, the second gender in Dyirbal is often designated 'women, and dangerous things'.

The Chechen language has six noun classes. Mixtec, a language of southern Mexico, has seven. Yimas, spoken in New Guinea, has ten. Australia's Ngan'gi language has sixteen – as do Swahili and Zulu, though some of Africa's other Bantu languages have more than twenty. The largest of all noun class systems, however, are found in South America. Tuyuca, a native Colombian language, has at least fifty. Miraña, a language of the north-west Amazon, has seventy-two, and classifies its nouns into categories including log-shaped objects, ashy substances, deep containers, rotten things, broken objects, objects with a single hole in them, things that have been deliberately flattened and things with an arrangement of separate fibres pointing in different directions. (That last category means words relating to the splintered stump of a fallen tree and the untidy hair of someone who has just woken up are dealt with the same way in Mirañan grammar.) The largest of all known noun class systems belongs to Miraña's mother language, Bora. Though researchers in Peru are still getting to grips with the full extent of its complexity, it is believed to have 350.

The simple masculine and feminine of French and Spanish don't seem quite so bad now, do they? But, then again, the majority of languages worldwide still have no gender system at all – so what, if anything, do these categories achieve?

In languages like Miraña and Bora, in which nouns are classified into dozens of groups based on functions and attributes, gender might be a way of reinforcing or grammatically signposting the overall theme of a conversation. A chat about something that's broken will naturally come to include many words from the 'broken objects' group, and because those words are all dealt with in the same way in the grammar, the conversation as a whole will become more grammatically harmonised. Once the topic of the conversation shifts, the grammar will shift with it, and a new set of words sharing a new set of attributes and grammatical conventions will take over.

It is possible that multiple noun classes might have a clarificatory benefit too. Conversations don't take place in acoustical vacuums, after all, but in the noisy and clamorous real world. Dogs can bark, winds can blow, and words can be drowned out and distorted amid this background noise. Multiple noun classes might therefore be a means of instilling an extra layer of detail into the spoken language, making conversational threads less likely to be lost or overwhelmed. If a bird were to squawk or thunder were to rumble, a Mirañan speaker might still hear enough to keep track of the conversation, even if they were able to pick out only one of the grammatical tags unique to, say, ashy substances.

The same cannot be said of languages that have only a handful of noun classes, such as French and Spanish. Here, so many words are lumped together under so few categories that they can't possibly all share a common attribute, so the idea that gender somehow helps thematically attune a conversation simply doesn't stand up. Instead, it has been suggested that systems like these might serve a preparatory purpose, and work to accelerate our brain's processing of the language it encounters. Take our examples from earlier, *un nouveau petit sac noir* and *une nouvelle petite robe noire*. As soon as a French speaker's brain hears a masculine *un* rather than a feminine *une*, it knows immediately to expect a masculine noun, and can therefore disregard its databank of feminine words. But an English speaker, whose brain throws all its nouns together in a single ungendered mass, has no equivalent means of narrowing that mental glossary down.

Think of it this way: imagine you had to stop and look up every noun you ever heard in conversation in a dictionary in order to understand it. Naturally, to keep the conversation going, speed would be of the essence – but with no genders or subclasses to go on, an English speaker would have to riffle through one gigantic tome, containing every conceivable noun, and would have to wait until the noun itself was mentioned in order to start their search. A French speaker, however, would have two much shorter volumes – one masculine, one feminine. Hearing *un* rather than *une* would be like a starter's pistol – an immediate clue that the word they need will be in the masculine book, not the feminine book. They could therefore begin their hunt earlier than the English speaker and would have a much smaller and more precise library to search through overall.

It's a vivid theory, certainly, and has been supported by some remarkable findings from real-time language-processing experiments. But, in reality, our language moves on so rapidly – and our brains already operate so astonishingly quickly – that the split-second advantage a gendered vocabulary might give a French speaker over an English speaker must be very small indeed. Instead, a much more obvious advantage of using grammatical gender comes when dealing with ambiguity:

A cat chased a mouse. It ran under the table.

In grammatical terms, the word *it* here is a proform – a word that takes the place of an earlier word or phrase, which is itself called the antecedent. In this instance, *it* is clearly taking the place of the animal that ran under the table, but these sentences are structured in such a way that we have no means of telling precisely what 'it' is. Has a cat gone under the table, or a mouse? We English speakers simply do not – and cannot – know.

In a gendered language like French, however, that ambiguity can be resolved. Because the rules of grammatical concord demand the words interacting with a gendered noun change to match it, the proform has to correspond with the gender of the antecedent. *Cat* is a masculine noun in French, while *mouse* is feminine, so swapping genderless 'it' for a gender-specific proform – either masculine *il*, or feminine *elle* – instantly clarifies what animal it is:

Un chat a chassé une souris. Il a couru sous la table.
(A cat [*m*] chased a mouse [*f*]. It [*m*] ran under the table.)

Un chat a chassé une souris. Elle a couru sous la table.
(A cat [*m*] chased a mouse [*f*]. It [*f*] ran under the table.)

In both sentences there is no confusion, no need to ask for or provide extra details, and while the English speaker is still left in the grammatical dark, the French conversation can happily move on. Unless, of course, both possible antecedents happened to be the same.

As ingenious as this is, a French speaker would have precisely the same problem as an English speaker if both the nouns involved were the same gender. If a dog were to chase a cat, for instance, we'd still have no idea what was under the table because *dog* and *cat* are both masculine. So grammatical gender helps us decode ambiguous antecedents only in a relatively limited set of circumstances – and whatever its benefits to language processing may be, they seem at best marginal and at worst non-existent. All of which raises a good question: why use it at all?

The answer lies in our languages' ancestry. French, Spanish, German, Czech, Russian and many of the other Eurasian languages we've namechecked here all inherited their gender systems from Proto-Indo-European. Passed on from one linguistic generation to the next, these languages have maintained these classifications in much the same way as any family would hold on to its ancestors' heirlooms.

Originally, Proto-Indo-European categorised its nouns into two classes – not masculine and feminine, but animate and inanimate. Aside from obviously separating the living from the non-living and the moving from the non-moving, the ins and outs of that distinction were hazy, and the line between the two categories probably wasn't as clear as their names might suggest. The animate group, for instance, included various abstract and natural phenomena that were somehow considered active or anthropomorphically alive – such as the wind, thunder, lightning and even chance and luck. Proto-Indo-European nouns were therefore classified less on the basis of separating the living from the lifeless, and more on contrasting dynamic, meta-phorically vital things with those that were more passive or inert.

Oddly, some nouns managed to straddle that boundary. Water as a wild elemental force was known by an animate word, *hékweh*. But as a more passive entity – water as merely a substance – it took an inanimate word, *wódr̥*. As Proto-Indo-European began its slow dis-integrating evolution across Europe and Asia, these two terms went their separate ways. The animate root morphed into the Latin *aqua* and Germanic *ahwō*, and through those ended up providing us with words such as *aquarium* and *island*. The inanimate stem, meanwhile, variously developed into the likes of *wet*, *water*, *hydration*, *vitriol*, *whisky*, *vodka* and even *otter*. The same thing happened to fire, whose two roots – animate *h̥gwnís* and inanimate *péhwr̥* – gave us one set of words including *ignition* and *igneous*, and another containing *fire*, *pyre* and *pyrotechnics*.

Quite why the Proto-Indo-European speakers felt the need to classify their words at all is debatable. (After all, many other ancient language families – including Uralic, the family to which Finnish and Hungarian belong – have never utilised any gender system.) But the *water* and *fire* examples show how the animate vs inanimate distinc-tion, still found in a great many of the world's languages today, was probably a practical one.

Not only would an animacy distinction have contrasted active and living things with inert and non-living things, but it would have allowed things that exist in two fundamentally different states to be distinguished by their nature or characteristics. After all, there is a big difference between a wild raging inferno and a simple domestic fire. This distinction would have been useful grammatically too, as animate forces are much more likely to be the causes or instigators of actions than inanimate ones, so dividing words into these two camps could also have been a means of separating the grammatical doers, causers and affecters from the done, the caused and the affected.

In later Proto-Indo-European, however, this distinction fell apart. The animate class split in two, creating a new pair of word classes, masculine and feminine. The inanimate class, meanwhile, became a more generalised neuter gender, home to everything else. (The word *neuter* itself literally means 'not either'.)

What sparked this division is the subject of countless theories and decades of linguistic debate. One explanation is that the change began first with feminine pronouns, the standard ending of which was reinterpreted as a feminine-specific suffix, then applied to other words, and so laid down the foundations of a distinct gender that way. Another theory claims it was abstract words (those referring to invisible concepts) and collective words (mass nouns, like a mountain range or herd of cattle, rather than an individual peak or cow) that emerged as a distinct category first, before overlaps between how collective and feminine words were dealt with in the grammar of Proto-Indo-European led to them all joining forces as a new third gender. Besides what was happening grammatically under the surface of the language, there were probably broader cultural factors at work too. The Proto-Indo-Europeans had a pastoral society, reliant on farming and livestock, and it's fair to say that if you're actively breeding animals, merely knowing that they're 'animate' isn't a particularly useful label. Perhaps a growing need to distinguish male and female creatures simply came to be reflected linguistically and was rolled out through the rest of the vocabulary as a result. Moreover, Proto-Indo-European mythology assigned the likes of the sky and the weather to male gods, and the sun and the Earth to female goddesses.

In much the same way that Dyirbal culture affects how its nouns are categorised, perhaps these godly associations had an influence on the language too, with heavenly words forming the masculine gender, and earthly words the feminine.

No matter how this change took place, however, as the Proto-Indo-Europeans migrated from their homeland towards the end of the Bronze Age, they took their language – and its new three-tier gender system – with them. And as new languages began to emerge from their footprints across Europe and Asia, this multi-layered system endured. In German and Russian, all three genders remain intact. Elsewhere, as in Czech, they underwent further complication, and the animate and inanimate distinction was revived. In French and Spanish, the three-tier system collapsed back into two, with neuter words reassigned to the masculine and feminine groups. And in some places – including Anglo-Saxon England – it disappeared altogether.

Like most of its Indo-European neighbours, English initially retained a system of grammatical gender, and categorised its nouns into masculine, feminine and neuter groups. The rules dictating which words belonged to which gender had by this time become rather murky, but a handful of spelling and sound conventions in Old English made things a little clearer: nouns ending in –*a*, for instance, were almost always masculine, while most overtly male and female words, such as *cyning* ('king') and *cwene* ('queen'), fell in their corresponding genders.*

---

* Those rules weren't implemented across the board, however, and there were still many counterintuitive allocations: *wif* ('wife', 'woman') was neuter in Old English, while *wifhand* ('heiress') was masculine. Perhaps understandably, some

By the early Middle English period, however, English's gender system had begun to disintegrate, and by the fourteenth and fifteenth centuries had almost completely vanished. What happened in the intervening years was a cocktail of internal and external simplifying influences – chief among them the fact that Anglo-Saxon England was invaded not once, but twice.

In the ninth century, Vikings began raiding and ultimately settling across much of northern England, and brought with them their Scandinavian Germanic language, Old Norse. Two centuries later, a second invasion, this time from the south – the Norman Conquest of 1066 – brought a Romance language, Norman French, into the mix. As both began to impose themselves on ancient England, it's likely that English was compelled to change and streamline, and began jettisoning its complexities to make communication between opposing sides more viable. Gradually, this creeping appetite for simplification began to affect how masculine, feminine and neuter words were recognised in the language, and English's inherited system of grammatical gender was slowly abandoned.

Elsewhere, of course, this simply didn't happen. In fact, although gendered vocabularies are in a minority worldwide, a majority of Indo-European languages have held on to theirs. But with new words being created all the time, this is a system that requires near constant upkeep: in May 2020, the Académie française – the official linguistic body in charge of all things French – was compelled to decree *la COVID-19* officially a feminine noun.

Old English writers and scribes ended up making mistakes: some passages in the *Lindisfarne Gospels*, written in the early eighth century, mistakenly treat the word *stan* ('stone') as if it were a neuter word, not a masculine one.

Our human desire for simplification has not gone away, and in an increasingly gender-aware twenty-first century has been joined by a growing interest in neutrality. And with research now increasingly showing that grammatical gender subconsciously perpetuates gender biases and stereotypes,* might other languages follow English's lead and abandon grammatical gender in the future? It would take considerable upheaval to do so, admittedly, but in some cases, it is a process that has already begun.

Danish has long since conflated its masculine and feminine genders, and today has only two genders – common and neuter – where once it had three. A similar change is currently under way in Dutch, with large parts of the Netherlands and the Dutch-speaking world now recognising no grammatical difference between masculine and feminine words; Afrikaans, the Dutch-origin language of southern Africa, has no gender system whatsoever. Like Danish, Swedish too has conflated its masculine and feminine words into a single common gender, but it went a step further in 2015 when a gender-neutral pronoun, *hen*, was added to the official word list of

---

* A 2002 study by Stanford cognitive scientist Professor Lera Boroditsky asked Spanish and German speakers to describe random words from their languages using any three adjectives they wished. Consistently, grammatical gender was found to influence the speakers' descriptions, with the Spanish speakers describing a *bridge* as 'strong', 'big', 'dangerous' and 'sturdy', and the German speakers preferring words such as 'elegant', 'beautiful', 'fragile' and 'pretty'. *Bridge* is a masculine noun in Spanish, but a feminine noun in German.

A 2012 study of more than a hundred different languages and cultures found that those using a gendered language exhibited higher levels of gender inequality socially. Whether our language can indeed frame our opinions and alter how we view things remains a controversial issue linguistically, yet findings of this nature are proving increasingly difficult to ignore.

the hallowed Swedish Academy (Sweden's equivalent of the *Oxford English Dictionary*) alongside its standard gendered pronouns, *han* ('he') or *hon* ('her'). There are even tentative hints of some more conservative gendered languages shifting towards a more inclusive, gender-neutral future. Masculine has always taken precedence over feminine in French grammar, making masculine word forms the norm in mixed or ambiguous contexts. But in contemporary French there is a burgeoning interest in a new neutral alternative, with conversations about the introduction of a gender-neutral pronoun, *iel* (a combination of *il* and *elle*), becoming an increasingly hot topic.

In many places, however, such changes and proposals remain enormously controversial. When *iel* was merely added to the online edition of France's *Le Robert* dictionary in 2021, for instance, education minister Jean-Michel Blanquer tersely tweeted, 'Inclusive writing is not the future of the French language.' Even in English, which operates barely any semblance of a gender system, many people baulk at the use of *they* as a singular pronoun in gender-ambiguous sentences such as 'The student is expected to raise *their* hand if *they* have a question.' Given this usage has been part of our language for over 600 years, any contemporary distaste largely comes down to personal style or preference. Nonetheless, in many languages, appetites for features like these are undeniably growing. Whether they will ever grow strong enough to see all gender swept from our languages is an issue for future generations to decide.

Where Do Our Number Names Come From?

Numbers constitute the only universal language.
Nathanael West, *Miss Lonelyhearts* (1933)

It's fair to say English isn't the most consistent of languages, even at the best of times – but have you ever seen a more disorderly set of words than *one, two, three, four, five, six, seven, eight, nine* and *ten*? These are the building blocks of our counting system, the basis of practically every number that follows them. But while the rest of that system falls into an endlessly neat arithmetic pattern of *twenty-two*s and *thirty-three*s, we first have to work our way through ten utterly mismatched words, as detached from one another as some of their spellings are from their pronunciations.

One sounds like it's missing an initial W. *Two* has a W it doesn't need at all. *Eight* takes five letters to spell something we need three, *ate*, to spell elsewhere. Aside from a little alliteration between *four* and *five* and *six* and *seven*, there's no semblance of a pattern here at all. So why are our basic number names so inconsistent?

At least part of the answer here lies with our numbers' etymological ancestors. This, as best as we can imagine, was how the Proto-Indo-Europeans would have counted to ten:

óynos	*s^wéks*
dwóh	*septm̥*
tréyes	*oktṓ*
k^wetwóres	*h₁néwn̥*
pénk^we	*dék̂m̥*

We're in some decidedly unfamiliar and hypothetical territory here (hence all those dots, dashes and superscripts floating around*), but cut out all that noise and something much more familiar starts to emerge. Our *six* is almost identical to its long-lost relative *s^wéks*. It's easy to imagine how *tréyes* could have morphed into something like *three*. Even the silent W in *two* makes sense when you find out it's descended from something called *dwóh*. Think outside the anglophone box, and even more falls into place. *Pénk^we* and *dék̂m̥* are akin

---

* As no written evidence of Proto-Indo-European survives, linguists have had to recreate it themselves. All the unfamiliar dots and dashes in these early numbers are their attempts to dictate as accurately as possible how each of these would have been pronounced. The accents over the Es and Os are simply stress markers. The circles or 'underrings' below the Ms and Ns show they formed their own syllables, so weren't attached to the consonants before them. (Think about the difference between *calm* and *Callum*, and you'll get a rough idea.) The little 1 in *h₁néwn̥* shows it was pronounced with the first of three different 'h' sounds linguists think Proto-Indo-European had. And those floating Ws show that the consonants before them were pronounced with rounded lips; some English speakers do this today when they exaggerate the pronunciation of words like *red* and *rabbit*, forming an 'ooh' shape with their lips despite there being no phonological reason to do so.

to the Greek words for 'five' and 'ten', *pente* and *deka* – the origins of our *pentagons* and *decagons*. *Kʷetwóres* mirrors the *quatre*, *cuatro* and *quattro* of French, Spanish and Italian. And if you've spotted some overlaps with the calendar here, it's worth remembering September, October, November and December were once the seventh (*septm̥*), eighth (*oḱtṓ*), ninth (*h₁néwn̥*), and tenth (*déḱm̥*) months of the year.

These correspondences are certainly curious, but all they really do is prove that the random names of our first ten numbers today were just as random 6,500 years ago. And that, unfortunately, is where this particular etymological trail vanishes into the mist.

We can certainly trace our numbers back to Proto-Indo-European, but when it comes to figuring out why the Proto-Indo-European numbers *themselves* look the way they do, blanks begin to be drawn. Some indomitable historical linguists have attempted to venture further back and have drawn tentative connections between the likes of *four* and some impossibly ancient word meaning 'pairs', a dual form of that which perhaps gave us our number *eight*. *Five* probably has a connection to a long-lost word meaning 'hand'. *Six* may have meant something along the lines of 'increased' or 'developed', in the sense of your counting extending to your other hand after reaching five. And *nine* was probably the opposite and named as a 'deficient' or 'lacking' number – one short of a perfect ten. Our numbers appear random to us, therefore, because they were assembled randomly in the first place, from whatever vaguely associated words the Proto-Indo-Europeans (or their ancestors) had at their disposal.

As tantalising as etymological theories like these are, with no hard evidence – and our research already straining under six millennia of conjecture – there is little we can say with any real certainty about why the Proto-Indo-Europeans used these ten words. Nonetheless, use them they did, and we've been living with their equally mismatched descendants ever since. The closer we come to the present day, however, the more of these inconsistencies we can explain.

We know the phantom 'w' sound in *one* emerged in the southwest dialects of Middle English, before catching on elsewhere. (Even William Tyndale's Bible spells it *wone* or *wonne*, reflecting the fact that while his book was printed in Antwerp, Tyndale himself hailed from Gloucestershire.) The silent W in *two* hasn't always been silent, and lives on in related words like *twin*, *twain* and *twice*. And the peculiar spelling of *eight* comes from an attempt to replicate its Old English ancestor *acht*, pronounced with the same guttural 'ch' sound as in *loch* and *Bach*. Even the seemingly coincidental alliteration between *four* and *five* probably isn't coincidence at all: etymologists now believe at some point in the Germanic languages' past, *four* embraced the same initial sound as its neighbour to form a matching pair. So as well as *four* and *five* in English, you'll count *vier* and *vijf* in Dutch, *fjórir* and *fimm* in Icelandic, and *fyra* and *fem* in Swedish. (The same probably happened much earlier with *six* and *seven*.)

As soon as we enter double digits though, this inconsistency vanishes. Our counting slips into set after limitless set of neat groups of ten – from our *teens* into the *twenties*, *thirties* and *forties*, on into triple figures and far, far beyond. Just like the digits themselves, our larger number names are assembled in a simple arithmetic format, left to right, largest to smallest unit, and the higher you count the more the straightforwardness of this system compounds itself. 20 + 1 = *twenty-one*. 50 + 6 = *fifty-six*. 100 + 39 = *one hundred and thirty-nine*. Eventually, you find yourself stringing together all the numerical weapons in your armoury to produce mind-boggling figures such as *one octillion one septillion one quadrillion one billion one million two thousand five hundred and sixty-eight.** But long before we get there, there is one final problem. Or rather, two problems.

Eleven and *twelve* just don't fit this flawless system. As the first two numbers in what should be a neat set of ten teens, we might expect them to be named something like 'one-teen' and 'two-teen', matching the template of the other numbers between ten and twenty. Instead, *eleven* and *twelve* appear as mismatched as the numbers below ten, and as different from one another as the remaining teens are alike.

Trace them back through time and you'll find this inconsistency is as old as it is obvious. Even in Old English, *ten* was followed by a pair of unruly outliers called *enleofen* and *twelf*, before falling into line with a more regimented *threotene*, *feowertene* and *fiftene*. Etymologically, these teens came from the Old English word for 'ten', *tene*, which was tagged onto the end of each single-digit base to create a new two-digit equivalent. (The *–ty* ending of our *twenties*, *thirties* and *forties* is another Old English suffix, *–tig*, implying a set or multiple of ten.) But for some reason 'one' and 'two' were left out of this process, meaning *eleven* and *twelve* were given their names in an entirely different way: from an ancient Germanic root, predating the development of English, which effectively meant 'to leave' or 'omit'. So *eleven* is literally the number 'one left' after ten, and *twelve* 'two left' after ten. Via the same root, *eleven* and *twelve* are more closely related to words like *relinquish*, *derelict* and *relic* than they are the numbers around them.

---

* Why single out this number in particular? If you were to write out every single number name in the standard English counting system, you would only ever use twenty-three of the twenty-six letters of the alphabet; no matter how high you counted, you would never need to use J, K or Z (because, no, a *zillion* is not an official number). This figure – 1,001,000,000,001,000, 001,001,002,568 – is therefore the smallest number in the English number system whose name contains all twenty-three of those letters.

So why don't we say 'one-teen' and 'two-teen'? Or, for that matter, why haven't the likes of *thirteen* and *fourteen* been given names meaning 'three-left' and 'four-left'? Oddly, the answer has less to do with etymology, and more to do with our fundamental understanding of how we count.

English has a base-10 number system, so English speakers are all but hardwired to think of our numbers decimally. We learn them in sets of ten. We count them in sets of ten. We like to use and keep to what we consider 'round' numbers, and our entire number system builds up in ever-increasing sets of 10s, 100s and 1,000s, on and on into numerical infinity. There are plenty of good reasons for using a base-10 number system, of course, not least the fact that ten is such an easy number to work with arithmetically. You can count to ten on your fingers, and can calculate endless multiples, factors and divisions of ten with little or no effort. 187 multiplied by 10? 1,870. 187 divided by 10? 18.7. But despite what we see as its simplicity and practicality, a base-10 number system is by no means the only system out there. Around the world, other languages and cultures utilise all manner of different figures as the bases of their counting systems – some of which, to our decimally wired brains, seem utterly astonishing.

Melpa, for instance, is a language spoken in New Guinea. It has a binary counting system, based almost entirely around its words for one, *tenda*, and two, *ragl*. The Melpa word for three, *ragltika*, literally means 'two-one'. Seven is 'two-one past four', *pömp ragltika gudl*. Ten is 'two past eight', *pömp ragl pip*. The now-extinct Ventureño Chumash language of California had a quaternary, or base-4, number system. Its word for five, *yətipake'es*, literally meant 'one comes again (on top of four)'. Six, *yəti'iško*, meant 'two comes again'.

Ndom, another New Guinea language, has a senary counting system, based around the number 6. Its speakers make do with specific names only for the numbers 1, 2, 3, 4, 5, 6, 18 and 36, while everything else is built from a combination of those eight basic figures and their multiples. If you were to count to 100 in Ndom, you'd reach a number called *nif-thef-abo-tondor-abo-mer-abo-thonith* – literally, '72 + 18 + 6 + 4'.

And so it goes on. Basque and Dzongkha, the official language of Bhutan, are vigesimal, or base-20 languages. So too is Tzotzil, the modern descendant of the Mayan language, spoken by half a million people in southern Mexico. Yoruba, one of the official languages of Nigeria, complicates its base-20 number system by mixing both addition and subtraction into its number names. So double-digit numbers ending in 1, 2, 3 or 4 are formed by adding to the previous multiple of 10, while all those ending in 5, 6, 7, 8 or 9 are formed by subtracting from the next multiple of 10 – making 14 *èrinlá* (literally '10 + 4'), but 15 *ẹ́ẹdógún* ('20 − 5'). Not that using subtraction in a counting system is unique to Yoruba, of course – just ask our roman-numeralled monarchs William IV, or the future King Henry IX.

As extraordinary as these counting systems might seem to us, many are still based on finger-counting or dactylonomy, to give it its proper name. Speakers of base-4 languages, for instance, often count the spaces between their fingers rather than the fingers themselves, or else count their four fingers and not their thumbs. In the Kewa language of New Guinea, the word for four, *ki*, literally means 'hand'; five, *kode*, means 'thumb'; and six, *kode laapo*, means 'two thumbs (plus one hand)'. But alongside this dactylonomic system, oddly Kewa has a second counting method set aside for longer or more complex calculations.

Far from using just fingers and thumbs, this secondary Kewan system involves a long chain of anatomical landmarks counted in strict sequence from one side of the body to the other, producing one of the world's most complicated number systems. Beginning with the five fingers of one hand, Kewa speakers count up through a series of points at the palm and wrist then on to the forearm, elbow, upper arm, shoulder, neck, jaw, nose and eyes, before moving down the other side of the body in the same way, to end on the little finger of the opposite hand. Their extraordinary body-part system is ultimately counted in base-47. And nor is it alone.

New Guinea's Konai language has an unusually asymmetrical base-14 system, which runs up just one side of the body and stops at the mouth. Asai has a base-23 number system, though its anatomical chain moves across the chest, rather than the face: its halfway point, 12, is counted at the shallow dint between the collar bones at the base of the neck. Oksapmin has a base-27 system. Bedamuni has a base-33 system. Kutubu has a base-37 system. And among the strangest of all is New Guinea's Yupno language. Its decidedly male-oriented base-33 counting system runs from the fingers of both hands (1–10) to the toes (11–20), ears (21 and 22), eyes (23 and 24), nose (25), nostrils (26 and 27), nipples (28 and 29) and belly button (30), to finish at the counter's testicles (31 and 32) and penis (33). Mercifully, these last two (or, rather, three) anatomical landmarks aren't namechecked directly when counted aloud, but are somewhat euphemistically referred to as 'the bow-strings', and 'the man thing'.

But what do these systems have to do with our *eleven* and *twelve*? Was the counting system of Old English likewise based around some unlikely chain of X-rated body parts? The evidence suggests not. English was and always has been a decimal language, built around

the same sets of ten we still count on our fingers today. But the prolif-
eration of non-decimal number systems around the world has fuelled
an intriguing theory that our language – or at least one of its ancestors – at some point had a duodecimal, or base-12, counting system.

Twelve is a much more challenging number to deal with arithmetically, of course. (187 multiplied by 12? That's going to take a
while . . .) But compared to ten, twelve is a lot more mathematically
productive. Put another way, it might be harder to calculate sets of
twelve in your head, but once you're able to do so, there is an awful
lot more you can do with it.

A set of 10 can be divided only two ways – into 2 sets of 5,
or 5 sets of 2. But a set of 12 can be split four ways – into 2 equal
sets of 6, 3 sets of 4, 4 sets of 3, or 6 sets of 2. Likewise, 20 can be
divided equally only four ways – into 2, 4, 5 or 10 – whereas 24 can
be divided into 2, 3, 4, 6, 8 or 12. Even a nice round figure like 100
has scarcely half the factors (2, 4, 5, 10, 20, 25, 50) of 144 (2, 3, 4,
6, 8, 9, 12, 16, 18, 24, 36, 48, 72). Nor is counting to twelve on your
fingers impossible: take a look at how your knuckles conveniently
divide each of your four fingers into three, and you'll soon see how
easily our numerical ancestors might have used their hands to count
to twelve just as efficiently as we can count to ten. So was our language originally duodecimal, rather than decimal? It's an ingenious
theory, and one that has endured among etymologists for over two
centuries. But, alas, it looks increasingly doubtful.

The more we find out about our language's prehistory, the more a
decimal number system looks to have always been the norm, both in
English and in its Germanic and Proto-Indo-European roots. (After
all, *eleven* and *twelve* might have different names, but both those
names – 'one left' and 'two left' – describe their values in relation to

ten, not twelve.) But that's not to say that the mathematical convenience of twelve passed our ancestors by. We might never have used a wholesale duodecimal counting system, but the fact twelve can be so efficiently divided and enumerated would still have made it and its multiples immensely useful in everyday contexts when it came to dealing with fractions, divisions, allocations, allowances, expenses and measurements. And our linguistic ancestors were so keen to capitalise on that practicality that it seemingly left its mark on our language.

The usefulness of twelve as a divisible number still survives in the 12 inches in a foot, the 12 old pence in a shilling and the 24 carats of pure gold. Quantities of twelve even became so firmly established in everyday life that we invented separate names and nicknames for them, and still speak of *dozens* and *scores* today.* *Eleven* and *twelve* ultimately earned distinct names for themselves – setting them apart from the teens that follow them – because their arithmetical convenience led to them being used much more frequently on their own. Effectively, they would not have been seen as the first two numbers of a new round set of ten, but as the final two figures in a much more mathematically practical set of twelve. We might have always had a decimal system overall, then, but *eleven* and *twelve* don't obey its rules because they simply weren't considered all that much a part of it. And it is only our contemporary decimal-based perspective that makes their names seem so strange.

---

* The name *dozen* itself comes from the French for 'twelve', *douze* – while the use of *gross* to mean 'a dozen dozens', 144, comes from the French for 'fat', *gros*. The names *dozen* and *gross* might have survived to this day, but other quantities have fared less well: little used today are the *long* or *great hundred* (120), the *great dozen* (144), the *long gross* (one gross + one dozen, 156), the *long thousand* (1,200), and the *great gross* (a dozen cubed, 1,728).

Q. 8

Why Is the Alphabet in ABC Order?

Why is the alphabet in that order?
Is it because of that song?
Steven Wright

A little over a thousand years ago, an English Benedictine monk and scholar known as Byrhtferth of Ramsey completed his greatest work. He called it *Enchiridion* – literally, a 'hand-book' to the complex medieval science of *computus*, the reckoning of dates in the ecclesiastical calendar.

At the time, figuring out the precise timing of movable feasts such as Easter was a complicated business, demanding knowledge of solar and lunar cycles, and the ability to predict their changes from one year to the next. Nevertheless, Byrhtferth didn't make a difficult subject any easier for his students. Written in a mix of Latin and English, his handbook is steeped in dense poetic prose, and as one of the most learned men of his day he couldn't help but take the opportunity to indulge in long deviations into pet subjects including grammar, geometry and rhetoric. The novices in his tutelage probably weren't too grateful for all these detours, but we at least can be thankful he included this:

A B C D E F G H I K L M N O P Q R S T V X Y Z & 7 ꝥ Þ Ð Æ

In one of his digressions, Byrhtferth outlined the mystical and numerological interpretation of alphabets, and in doing so wrote out the English alphabet as he knew it. That was in 1011 – making this perhaps the oldest record of our alphabet in its history.

There have clearly been some changes since then, not least given that Byrhtferth's alphabet has twenty-nine letters. His additions are a mixture of the familiar and the forgotten. Z is followed by the ampersand (&), still very much in use today. Built from an overlapping *e* and *t* (the letters in *et*, the Latin for 'and'), in some iterations of the alphabet it would remain in final position until as recently as the 1900s. Next comes *Tironian et* or *ond* (7), another ancient means of abbreviating 'and'. Tiro was a scribe in the service of the Roman statesman Cicero, who devised a vast system of Latin shorthand in the first century BCE, of which this was a relic. And bringing up the rear are four pure Anglo-Saxonisms: the long-lost letters *wynn* (ꝥ), *thorn* (Þ), *eth* (Ð) and *ash* (Æ).

There are omissions from our modern alphabet here too, as Byrhtferth does not include J, U or W. But differences aside, one thing remains strikingly familiar: not one of his letters occupies a position that does not ring true today. A is still followed by B, by C and D, and so on through to Z. Other letters might have come and gone but their overall order appears to be as old as the alphabet itself. But what exactly *is* this order?

Admittedly, there is no single answer here. Our alphabet is more than three times as old as our English language, and over that long history it has been shaped and reshaped by several different cultures and civilisations to better suit their own languages. By retracing those changes, we can account for the appearance and position of around half our letters as they are today. But those developments were not wholesale and perhaps affected only a single letter at a time, so that rather than one tell-all story, we have instead a dozen or so shorter, letter-by-letter explanations. Accounting for the history of the other half of our alphabet, however, is far more problematic. In fact, some of our letters have been in place for so long that the reason behind their order (if there ever were one) is now a complete mystery.

Complicating this story from the outset is the fact this is not even our original alphabet. When the Anglo-Saxons first arrived in Britain, the Germanic language they brought with them was written in a runic script known as Elder Futhark:

ᚠᚢᚦᚨᚱᚲᚷᚹᚺᚾᛁᛃᛈᛇᛉᛊᛏᛒᛖᛗᛚᛜᛟᛞ

The angular shape of these letters is no accident, but hints at how they would once have been written: not smoothly, with ink on paper, but forcefully, carved into wood, bone, metal or rock. Straight lines are easier to make than curves, hence the futhark script acquired a characteristically jagged appearance. (We might prefer pen and pencil today, but our word *write* still comes from a Germanic root meaning to scratch.)

Nor is the name *futhark* a random invention, but the result of the first half-dozen characters here strung together: ᚠ (*f*), ᚢ (*u*), ᚦ (*th*), ᚨ (*a*), ᚱ (*r*), ᚲ (*k*). That's a noticeably different order from our ABCs but knowing what these first few letters are reveals some intriguing similarities. ᚠ looks a little like our F. ᚱ is all but identical to R. With some imagination, ᚲ could be said to tally with K, and further along the line we'd find correspondences like ᚺ for H, ᛏ for T, ᛒ for B and ᛗ for M. These overlaps too are far from coincidence because, despite their dissimilarities, the runic and Latin alphabets share a common ancestor.

Though the origins of runic writing are murky, it's thought Germanic tradesmen operating along the river Rhine picked up these letters from Rhaetia, an ancient region of Alpine Europe, some time in the first century. Our ABCs originated further south, among the Etruscan people of central Italy. Both the Rhaetic and Etruscan alphabets were part of a family of early writing systems called Old Italic, which developed in southern Europe sometime in the first millennium BCE. And Etruscan came to have the upper hand on all of them.

Around 2,500 years ago, the Romans commandeered the Etruscan alphabet and began using it to write Latin. As the influence of Rome spread, so too did its language – and with it came its newly acquired writing system. In many places, entire languages were lost to Latin as the empire expanded, but even where the local languages survived, many abandoned their existing alphabets and switched to the Romans' ABCs. So it was in Germanic Europe, where the likes of English and German survived as distinct languages yet discarded their runic lettering in favour of the Latin script.

That switch didn't happen overnight, of course, and for centuries the two systems coexisted. The runes survived longest of all in Scandinavia, where the twenty-four letters of Elder Futhark were later streamlined into a more practical set of just sixteen, called Younger Futhark. But even this abridged system gradually declined as Latin gradually took hold, before finally being ousted altogether. One of the runes' final strongholds was Iceland, where one futhark character (Þ) remains the thirtieth letter of the alphabet today.

Things were a little different in England. As the dialects of the Angles and Saxons mixed, Old English developed several sounds not found elsewhere in Germanic Europe. As a result, the English futhark system had to be expanded not reduced, and its original twenty-four letters swelled to more than thirty. That began to change when a group of papal missionaries – sent from Rome to Christianise the pagan Anglo-Saxons – landed at Kent in 597 and founded the diocese of Canterbury. Further north, missionaries from Ireland and Scotland began drifting southwards and established themselves on Lindisfarne, off the coast of Northumbria, in 635. From these two bases Christianity spread rapidly, and with it came the Latin alphabet of Christian scripture. Newly founded churches and monasteries became major centres of Anglo-Saxon learning, and their scholars quickly set about adapting the new Latin letters to suit the English language. Within 500 years, our runic letters had all but entirely disappeared.

Old English still had several sounds not covered by this new system, and so these Anglo-Saxon writers had to improvise. Two runic letters, *wynn* (Ƿ ƿ) and *thorn* (Þ þ), were rescued from the scrapheap as Latin had no straightforward way of representing their sounds, 'w' and 'th'. D was struck through with a line to make *eth* (Ð ð), another way of writing 'th', and A and E were fused into a single character or ligature called *ash* (Æ æ), representing a sound midway between the two. Byrhtferth's alphabet had been assembled.

Elsewhere, other characters emerged that didn't make Byrhtferth's final cut. *Ethel* (Œ œ) was another ligature, combining

O and E. *Yogh* (Ȝ ȝ) evolved from lowercase *g*, initially as a means of differentiating the hard 'g' of *gear* from the soft 'g' of *gentle*. But neither these, nor any of Byrhtferth's additions, survived.

After 1066, Norman scribes began sidelining Anglo-Saxon spelling practices in favour of those of their native French. Thorn and eth were ousted in favour of the *th* digraph we use today. Wynn lost out to a practice of using two consecutive letter Us to represent the 'w' sound (hence its name). Ash and ethel were cut down to a single A or E. Yogh survived longer (most notably in Scotland*) as it had arrived somewhat later, but it too eventually fell by the wayside.

French and Latin helped to fill the gaps in Byrhtferth's alphabet too. J was initially introduced as an alternative form of I used for the final character in a Roman numeral (so 'xxiij', not *xxiii*) or the final letter in a Latin *–ii* plural (so 'filij', not *filii*). By the sixteenth century,

---

* In Old English, lowercase *g* was typically pronounced with a softer 'y' sound: *gear* (with a soft G) was the Anglo-Saxon word for 'year', while the word *gear* itself (with a hard G) was borrowed from Old Norse in the 1100s. The potential confusion created by pairs such as these is partly what inspired the introduction of yogh in the early Middle English period, but its use was never fully standardised and it came to represent a number of different sounds over time. The situation was further complicated both by printers (many of whom found themselves without a separate yogh type-piece) and by writers and scribes (who began using a tailed form of the letter Z, ȝ, in their writing too, from which yogh was all but indistinguishable). What had originated as a solution to the confusion of the past had come to prove a source of considerable confusion in the present, and as a result yogh began to fall out of use in the 1500s, replaced in its different roles by *j*, *y* and *gh*, among many others. It survived longest of all in Scotland, but confusion between yogh and tailed Z, ȝ, persisted; it is this that lies behind the differing pronunciations of Scottish names such as *Menzies* and *Dalziel* to this day.

I was being used in so many different ways that understanding it clearly from the text was proving difficult. As a result, J took on all initial 'dzh' sounds, as in *judge* and *jury*, that had previously fallen under the remit of I, leaving I to operate solely as a vowel. Now furnished with a sound all of its own, J was upgraded, and took a place in our alphabet alongside I. It remains our most recent acquisition.

Likewise, U and V came to be listed alongside one another as they too were long considered interchangeable before being given distinct roles as vowel and consonant. Our 'double-U' character W joined them too, and in this way the alphabetical positions of at least some of our more recent innovations can be explained relatively easily: those related to or derived from one another naturally came to occupy neighbouring slots. As for the rest, we need to head even further back in time.

It was around 3,000 years ago that the Etruscans first emerged as a distinct civilisation in central Italy. Around the same time, migrants from Greece began arriving further south in Italy and established a sprawling collection of colonies and trade ports known as Magna Graecia. The Etruscans were the Greeks' Italian neighbours, and trade between the two sides soon thrived. But solid goods weren't the only things to cross the border: with no writing system of their own, the Etruscans soon picked up that of their neighbours, and a distinct Etruscan alphabet appeared around 700 BCE:

ABCDEFIB⊗IKLⱮⱲⱧOⱤMQPSTVX⏀Ƴ8

So, via Latin, this is our alphabetical grandfather – and scanning that line of text certainly throws up enough likenesses to see the family resemblance. But given the Etruscans took their letters from the Greeks, the Greek alphabet must then be our alphabetical great-grandfather:

ΑΒΓΔΕFΖΗΘΙΚΛΜΝΞΟΠΜϘΡΣΤΥΦΧΨΩ

As for the Greeks themselves, they adopted their writing system from the Phoenicians – so our great-great-grandfather is the twenty-two-letter Phoenician alphabet, which emerged in the eastern Mediterranean around 1050 BCE:

𐤊 𐤋 𐤀 𐤄 𐤉 𐤁 𐤄 𐤈 𐤎 𐤓 𐤋 𐤌 𐤍 𐤕 𐤏 𐤐 𐤑 𐤒 𐤓 𐤔 𐤈

We're so far back in history here there's understandably much less of a resemblance than further down our family tree, but even these 3,000-year-old letters show some oddly familiar features. In the centre is a recognisable run of *kap* (𐤊), *lamed* (L), *mem* (𐤌) and *nun* (𐤍), followed by an O-shaped letter *ayin* (Ο), and a P-curved *pe* (𐤐). Before that, there's an H-shaped letter *het* (𐤇). Later, a backwards-facing *res* (𐤓). And if you think the opening five letters here – *alep* (𐤊), *bet* (𐤁), *giml* (𐤂), *dalet* (Δ) and *he* (𐤄) – look somewhat like tilted or mirror-written versions of A, B, C, D and E, you'd be right: Phoenician was written right to left (so strictly speaking the row above is in reverse order). It is popularly claimed that when ink and paper began to replace hammer and chisel, our prevailing right-handedness prompted a change in writing direction, as a rightward-moving hand was less likely to smudge the wet ink of whatever it had just written. Before then, a right-handed mason chiselling letters onto a tablet or wall would have held the hammer in his strongest hand and worked away from him, making leftward-moving text more practical. When the means and direction of our writing changed, some of our written characters simply changed with them.

But not everything here is quite as it seems. That final X-shaped Phoenician letter is *taw*, equivalent to our T. The letter before it might look like a W, but it's *shin*, pronounced 'sh'. And *zayin* (I) might look like an I, but tilt its central line slightly and you'll see how it's actually the ancestor of Z, and so seems wildly out of place in seventh position. As Phoenician became Greek, Greek became Etruscan, and Etruscan became Latin, our series of gradual, letter-by-letter alterations was to begin.

For starters, what we're calling the Phoenician 'alphabet' here was really an abjad – a consonant-only writing system. Even those letters spelled with an initial vowel in English, such as *alep*, were pronounced with breathy *h*-like consonants in front of them in Phoenician, which the Greeks, like us, simply didn't have. Rather than ditch them, the Greeks ingeniously recycled these letters for their vowels. *Alep* (𐤀), *he* (𐤄) and *ayin* (O) became *alpha* (A), *epsilon* (E) and *omicron* (O), while *yodh* (𐤉, pronounced 'y') became *iota* (I, pronounced 'i'). By adding vowels to a vowelless system, the Greeks had turned an abjad into the world's first true alphabet (and in doing so, gave its first two letters, alpha and beta, to the word *alphabet* itself). But they did nothing to change their order, and so the new Greek vowels simply fell into the same random slots vacated by the unused Phoenician consonants. Our vowels have remained haphazardly scattered throughout our alphabet ever since.

Something a little more complicated happened to the sixth Phoenician letter, *waw* (Y). It represented a 'w' sound, which it initially kept as it transformed into an early F-shaped Greek letter called *digamma*. But 'w' wasn't found in all the dialects of Greek, and in those that lacked it, *waw* adopted a simpler 'u' or 'oo' sound, and eventually became the Y-shaped letter *upsilon*. One Phoenician character had therefore produced two Greek letters, F (pronounced 'w') and Y (pronounced 'u'). Yet by the time that distinction was in place, another complication had arisen: the Greeks were now using their alphabet as a counting system too. Alpha was 1. Beta was 2. Gamma was 3. And digamma, fixed in sixth position, was 6. This strict numerical arrangement left no room for the two forms of waw, and upsilon was unceremoniously cast to the end of the line. All the letters that have since evolved from it – U, V, W and Y – still occupy positions at the tail end of the alphabet today. And *waw* wasn't quite done yet.

By chance, many of the Greeks who relocated to Italy came from Euboea, an island region north of Athens where a dialect containing the 'w' sound was used. As a result, the Greek 'w' letter digamma was adopted by the Etruscans, who began using it to represent their own 'w' sound. But the Etruscans had another sound in their language, 'f', for which the Euboeans had no obvious equivalent.* So digamma (F) and eta (H) were combined, and FH became the standard method of writing 'f' in Etruscan texts. When the Romans took over, however, they made some changes. They weren't quite so fussy about their 'w' and 'u' sounds, and so used a single character – a tailless form of upsilon (V) – to represent them both. That left digamma without any sound attached to it at all, so the Romans dropped FH and used digamma alone to represent 'f'. That development became permanent, and so

---

* The Greek letter phi (Φ), which now has this 'f' sound, was originally more of a 'p' sound, and would not become 'f' for another thousand years.

despite being descended from a letter pronounced 'w', F is still pronounced 'f' and still sits in sixth position in our alphabet 2,000 years later.

Developments such as this show how the history of our alphabet relies not just on Greek but on the specific Euboean form of Greek that came to be adopted by the Etruscans. Although the Euboean alphabet was never standardised, we know from surviving texts that it contained several idiosyncrasies that would prove critical in shaping our own alphabet:

A B < ▷ E F I ⊟ ⊗ I Ʞ L Ϻ Ϙ O Γ Ϻ Ϙ P Ϟ T V X Φ Ψ

The final two Greek letters today, psi (Ψ) and omega (Ω), emerged too late to be taken to Italy and so we have no equivalents of them. Euboean Greek also had distinctively shaped versions of gamma (<), delta (▷), lambda (L) and sigma (Ϟ), and retained an old Q-shaped letter called *qoppa* (Ϙ). It didn't use xi (Ξ) in the same form or position as much of the rest of Greece, preferring instead to use chi (X) for the combination 'ks'. All these local quirks would eventually give us our letters C, D, L, S, Q and X.

One final development here resulted in the biggest overhaul of a letter's position in the history of our alphabet. As the Etruscans continued to reshape the Greek system, they scrapped beta (B), delta (Δ) and omicron (O), as their language had no 'b', 'd' or 'o' sounds. It also had no 'g' sound, but rather than omit gamma (Γ) too, the Etruscans repurposed it for 'k'. In Euboean Greek, gamma was written slightly askew (<), and this, combined with the Etruscans' modifications, not only gave us our letter C but handed it gamma's third-place position in the alphabet.

Latin, however, did have 'b', 'd' and 'o' sounds, so after the Romans took over, they restored beta, delta and omicron to their former positions. They also had a 'k' sound, and so found the Etruscans' C-shaped gamma a useful addition – yet they also had a 'g' sound, and with gamma now being used for 'k', no longer had any way of writing it.

Initially, they made do with what they had, and simply used C for both, so that for a time Latin C could be pronounced either 'k' or 'g'. But that multitasking was confusing, and according to linguistic folklore, inspired the Roman writer Ruga to invent a more permanent solution. Perhaps frustrated by having his own name mispronounced, Ruga added an extra clarifying stroke to the Latin letter C whenever it represented a 'g' rather than a 'k' sound and, in doing so, invented our letter G.

When it came to finding G a place in the alphabet, some prime alphabetical real estate had just opened up. At around that time, Latin was in the midst of losing its 'z' sound, leaving the Romans little reason to maintain the Etruscan letter *ze* (daughter of the Greek letter *zeta*, Z). As it disappeared, G took its place as the seventh letter of the alphabet, where it has remained ever since. And that might have been the end of the tale, were it not for one final and rather significant thing: in 146 BCE, Rome conquered Greece.

In the aftermath of the Battle of Corinth, almost the entire Greek peninsula fell under Roman control. As Rome began to impose power, its Latin language naturally picked up a new vocabulary of Greek names and loanwords, many of which contained the Greeks' 'z' sound. The need to represent 'z' in writing re-emerged in Latin as a consequence, and zeta was at long last resurrected. Having now lost its place in the alphabet to G, however, Z was merely tagged onto the end of the line. A combination of the quirks of Euboean handwriting, the limits of Etruscan phonology and the military prowess of Rome had conspired across seven centuries to demote Z some nineteen alphabetical places and it has remained our final letter ever since.*

Not all our letters have endured quite so eventful and unfortunate a history as Z. Take the Phoenician letter *mem* (ᛗ). The Greeks turned that into their letter *mu*, and via Etruscan and Latin, it later became our letter M. But in all that time, M has always represented a 'm' sound; it has always occupied a position in roughly the middle of the alphabet; and it has always had a vaguely undulating, zigzagging shape. The same applies to around half our letters, which have steadfastly remained in vaguely the same shape and position as the Phoenicians had them more than 3,000 years ago. So why were these unchanged letters put in that order in the first place?

Unfortunately, this final part of our question takes us so far back in time that much of its answer is unknown, if not unknowable. But two extraordinary discoveries in the first part of the twentieth century shed at least some light onto the very darkest part of our alphabet's history.

In 1905, the archaeologist Sir Flinders Petrie discovered a set of inscriptions at a remote turquoise mine in Egypt's Sinai Peninsula. The mine had been in use throughout antiquity, but Petrie dated the inscriptions to the Eighteenth Dynasty of Egypt – the era of Tutankhamun – some 3,500 years ago; we know now they're even

---

* The Roman conquest of Greece also led to the Romans adopting the Greek form of upsilon (Y) into Latin too, which was likewise tagged onto the end of the alphabet alongside Z. Bizarrely, this final adaptation means a single Phoenician letter, waw (Y), is today the origin of no fewer than five different letters of our alphabet: F, U, V, W and Y.

older, and date from around 1800 BCE. Petrie noted a handful of Egyptian hieroglyphs scattered among the texts, yet the remainder of the writing was unfamiliar. Unlike true hieroglyphic writing, however, it comprised relatively few different symbols, so he assumed it must be some early alphabetic script – perhaps that of an ancient Semitic language, used by the Canaanite slaves who worked the mines. If that were true, this so-called proto-Sinaitic writing would be related to Phoenician, and therefore to our own ABCs. But with no way of deciphering it, Petrie's theory remained guesswork. At least, for another decade.

In 1916, the Egyptologist Sir Alan Gardiner made an ingenious attempt to translate Petrie's inscriptions. Working on the theory that they were Semitic, Gardiner assigned each letter a Semitic name based on the Egyptian hieroglyph he thought it most resembled. The symbol resembling the Egyptian oxhead ($\forall$), he called *aleph*, 'ox'. The symbol resembling 'house' ($\sqsubset$), he called *beth*. The 'throwstick' ($\backslash$) became *gimel*. Then, based on the theory the writing was alphabetical, he began piecing together what he could of the texts using a technique that underpins many of the world's alphabets called acrophony – taking only the initial sound of each letter's name, 'a' for *aleph*, 'b' for *beth*, 'g' for *gimel*, and so on.

Much of the text remained indecipherable, but Gardiner's painstaking work eventually paid off: one short string of letters, repeated time and again throughout the inscriptions, was found to read *ba'alat*, the Semitic word for 'lady'. Gardiner knew that had been an epithet of the Egyptian goddess Hathor. He also knew one of the artefacts on which it was found was a small sandstone sphinx Petrie had found in a temple dedicated to Hathor herself. And he also knew that above the word *ba'alat* on that sphinx was a true hieroglyphic inscription reading, 'Beloved of Hathor, the Lady of Turquoise'. It was too good a match to be coincidence. The mystery had been solved, and Petrie's theories were validated: the writing was indeed Semitic, and as each symbol corresponded to a single sound, it was an alphabet. What is more, it was now the oldest alphabetical writing in history.

Petrie's proto-Sinaitic inscriptions provided a missing link between the hieroglyphs of Egypt and the alphabetical writing of Phoenicia, from which the Greek, Latin and eventually English alphabets would all later evolve. The Egyptians' oxhead hieroglyph, for instance, had become a more stylised symbol in Sinaitic, drawn as little more than a rounded triangle with two curved lines above it – yet by the time the same shape emerged in Phoenician almost a thousand years later, it had been further reduced to just a trio of overlapping lines (𐤀). When you write a letter A today, you're actually drawing a tiny, millennia-old picture of an ox, with the point at the top forming its snout, and its two downward struts forming all that remains of its horns.

Likewise, the hieroglyphic of a house (𓉐) gradually rotated and folded in on itself, becoming Phoenician *bet* (𐤁), and later our B. The throwstick (𓌙) was turned around in Phoenician (𐤂), became gamma in Greek (Γ), and eventually C in Latin and English. Further on in the alphabet, the left-pointing palm hieroglyph (𓂧) became *kap* (𐤊), and eventually our K. The zigzagging hieroglyphs for water (𓈖) and serpent (𓆓) became *mem* (𐤌) and *nun* (𐤍), and M and N. And the eye (𓁹), mouth (𓂋), and leftwards-facing head (𓁶) became the Phoenicians' *ayin* (𐤏), *pe* (𐤐) and *res* (𐤓), and later our O, P and R.

Precisely who came up with this Egyptian-inspired system is unclear. Some scholars credit it to the Sinai miners themselves, who presumably knew enough Egyptian writing to recreate its symbols, but not enough to use it fully themselves. Others claim the idea was probably already established, and the miners were simply reusing a system they knew from elsewhere. Similar inscriptions later found near Luxor suggest it might have originally been an Egyptian idea, invented as a truncated form of their own hieroglyphic text. No matter its origin, Petrie's inscriptions proved our letters are the modern-day descendants of hieroglyphs. And a decade later, a second chance discovery would give us one final tantalising clue to their order.

In 1928, a farmer ploughing a field on the outskirts of Latakia on the coast of Syria disturbed a large stone slab just below the surface. As he lifted it out of the ground, the earth beneath it collapsed, revealing something truly astonishing: the entrance to a relic-filled tomb from the long-lost city of Ugarit.

Excavations of the area gradually uncovered the ruins of a bustling Mediterranean seaport that for centuries had operated as a major coastal crossroads, before being mysteriously abandoned in 1185 BCE. And among its remains were found a number of clay tablets written in the world's oldest writing system, cuneiform.

Taking its name from the Latin word for 'wedge', *cuneus* (the origin of our word *coin*), cuneiform writing first emerged in Mesopotamia more than 5,000 years ago. From there, it spread rapidly across the Middle East to become the standard writing system of many of the region's ancient languages. Cuneiform characters were made by imprinting or drawing into wet clay with a pointed stylus, producing networks of overlapping lines and triangles that could then be made permanent by drying or baking. The earliest cuneiform texts were pictographic, meaning their written characters were effectively small images of whatever they were meant to describe. But over time these icons became more abstract and gradually evolved into logo-syllables – individual characters that could either represent entire words, or act as smaller syllabic components of longer ones. Hundreds of these logo-syllables have now been found and catalogued, many of which date from the dawn of written language. Those found at Ugarit, however, were different.

Much like Sir Flinders Petrie's Sinaitic inscriptions, Ugaritic cuneiform comprised a limited number of distinct characters. That suggested it was an alphabet, not a logo-syllabic system, and on that basis the lettering was quickly deciphered. Then, in 1948, another set of clay tablets found at Ugarit not only confirmed the writing was alphabetic, but listed all thirty of its letters in strict alphabetical order:

$'a$	b	g	$\underline{h}$	d	h	w	z	$\dot{h}$	$\d{t}$

y	k	$\check{s}$	l	m	$\underline{d}$	n	$\d{z}$	s_1	$'$

p	$\d{s}$	q	r	$\underline{t}$	$\dot{g}$	t	$'i$	$'u$	s_2

Discard a few of those unfamiliar and duplicate characters and replace g, w and z with c, f and g, and the bones of our ABC order will reveal themselves. So here was an entirely different set of letters, in a 3,500-year-old writing system – several centuries older than Phoenician – sharing our alphabetical order. And that's not all these Ugaritic tablets could tell us.

This stock order was found written out like this on dozens of tablets. For many archaeologists, that suggested these tablets were educational: the cuneiform alphabet of Ugarit was being actively taught and passed on to the city's schoolchildren and scribes, who would have written it out repeatedly in their lessons. A standardised order would have made the learning process understandably easier, and so it's conceivable our ABC sequence – or, as it is known in the context of Ugaritic, the *abgad* order – stems from some ancient mnemonic once used as a cuneiform teaching aid. Perhaps these letters were arranged to match the words of a story, or the lyrics of a simple rhyme or poem. Some intrepid historical linguists have even gone so far as to try to recreate a potential *abgad* mnemonic, and have proposed Semitic words for 'father' (*'ab*) and 'grandfather' (*gad*) as a putative starting point. After Ugarit fell in the 1100s BCE and its cuneiform lettering dwindled out of use, the order of its alphabet had presumably become established enough locally for the Phoenicians to arrange their own Egyptian-inspired characters in the same *abgad* order, and eventually pass it on to most of the alphabets of Europe.

It's a tantalising theory. But just because the earliest evidence of our alphabetical order has been unearthed at Ugarit doesn't necessarily mean it was invented there. The city appears to have been a cosmopolitan one, so it's entirely feasible this order was developed outside its walls and introduced to Ugarit from elsewhere. In fact, other theories have claimed our ABCs were arranged by the Babylonians, who perhaps used this order as a means of classifying or cataloguing their constellations or calendar. Another claims it derives from a method of teaching or arranging Egyptian hieroglyphics. (Intriguingly, the hieroglyphic equivalents of the neighbouring Ugaritic letters *y* and *k* were 'hand' and 'palm', while ʿ and *p* were 'eye' and 'mouth'.) Or maybe there was some kind of alphanumerical sequence at work here, like the 'alpha = 1' system later used in Greek. And then again, perhaps we're looking for order out of chaos, and there is simply no real reason for this order at all.

Undoubtedly, more evidence will be unearthed in the future that will be able to shed more light on this long and intricate story, but the theory that the bones of our alphabet were arranged as a teaching aid is nevertheless a compelling one. Until a tablet bearing some kind of explanatory Ugaritic mnemonic is discovered, however – or indeed anything else that proves or disproves another of these theories – this most ancient of mysteries will have to remain at least partly unsolved.

Q. 9

Why Do We Have Vowels and Consonants?

In the name of every consonant there is a vowel, for the consonants can neither be names nor pronounced without a vowel.

Anonymous Icelandic scholar (c. 1100s)

What is the commonest vowel in the English language? If you said E, you'd be wrong. Well, no – let's be fair. You'd be half wrong.

It's certainly true that in written language, E is not only our most frequently used vowel, but our most frequently used letter overall. In a standard English text, you can expect an E to appear roughly once every twelve letters or so (compared with around 1 in 500 for a Q or a J). But letters are just the written representations of sounds, and as spoken language predates written language, the only reason we have vowels and consonants in our alphabet is because we already had them in our speech. If we strip our language back to its spoken basics, then, what is our commonest vowel sound? And for that matter, what even are vowels and consonants at all? To answer that, we first need to understand a little bit more about how speech actually works.

We'll come on to the production of spoken language in more detail later, but for now all that matters is that vocal sound is the result of three physical processes: respiration, phonation and articulation.

Like putting fuel in a car, respiration provides the raw energy that powers our spoken language. Speech is made from airflow; to produce it we first need to draw air into the lungs, and then expel it upwards and outwards, under pressure, through our vocal tract – the throat, the mouth and the nose. The air we use in this way is known as pulmonic egressive air – pulmonic because it is inhaled into and expelled from the lungs, and egressive because it exits or egresses from the body. That certainly isn't true of all speech sounds, and we've already touched on some languages that contain ingressive sounds (made by inhaling air) and click sounds (made by forming pockets of pressurised air inside the mouth and throat, rather than the chest). If you were to do an impression of Donald Duck, moreover, you would use a pocket of so-called buccal air, stored against the inside of your cheek. But the vast majority of speech, in the vast majority of languages, is formed of the air in our lungs. And in order to provide enough of that air to produce speech, our natural pattern of breathing has to change.

At rest, an average person will inhale and exhale roughly ten to twelve times every minute. The split between the two halves of that respiratory exchange will be roughly the same, so that under normal circumstances we tend to spend as long breathing in as we do breathing out. When we talk, however, that ratio alters to give us enough fuel to produce sound. There are obvious variables to this process, like the loudness of what we're saying, and our emotional state (as crying or laughing can understandably disrupt things). But in ordinary conversation, we typically spend only around one-tenth of our time inhaling, and the remaining nine-tenths exhaling. That enormous shift towards a predominantly outward airflow is what allows us to string together long and complex utterances using a single controlled expulsion of air. To compensate, the length of our inhalations has to be cut down – sometimes to a mere quarter of a second or thereabouts – so that we can refill our lungs and refuel our speech as quickly and as uninterruptedly as possible.

The outward path this pulmonic air takes out of the body isn't itself uninterrupted. As it is pushed from the lungs and sent up through the windpipe, it arrives at its first obstacle, the larynx. Place your fingers lightly against the front of your throat and you'll be able to feel the tough outer part of the larynx just below the skin. It might feel like bone, but it's actually a vaguely cylindrical mass of cartilage and muscle, inside which, protected at its centre, are our vocal cords.

Despite their name, the vocal cords aren't string-like 'cords', but a pair of broad movable membranes – hence their more appropriate name, the vocal folds. When we breathe, these folds are relaxed and open, widening the space between them (known as the glottis) to allow as much air as possible in and out of the lungs. With no interference from the vocal folds, this inhaled and exhaled air remains just that – air. Even if you were to try to breathe out as noisily or as harshly as possible, as if trying to fog up a window or the lens of a pair of spectacles, the sound you would make would still scarcely be louder than a whisper and wouldn't resemble any of the sounds in ordinary speech. Make a long 'aah' sound, however, as if a doctor were examining your throat, and the result will be very different.

When we make a deliberate 'aah', our vocal folds are tensed and shaped into action by the nerves and muscles of the larynx, and thereby restrict the air being pushed out of the lungs. As they move to narrow the gap between them, the pressure of the air beneath them increases – rather like an eager crowd of people all trying to get through the same closed door. Eventually, this so-called subglottal pressure proves too great, and the vocal folds are forced apart to produce a sudden burst of air that can then continue up and out of the mouth.

With its movement no longer impeded, this puff of air acceler-ates through the gap – rather like an eager crowd of people now finding themselves all able to get through an open door. That alters the balance of air pressure in the throat, and naturally creates a sucking effect behind it that draws the vocal folds closed again so the same pressure-building process can restart. This extraor-dinary opening and self-closing mechanism is due in part to the natural elasticity of the vocal folds themselves, and in part to the Bernoulli effect, one of the fundamental principles of fluid dynamics. Ultimately, the same process that lifts aeroplanes into the sky and makes you feel as if you're being pulled towards a fast-moving truck as it speeds past you at a roadside is happening on a minute scale inside your throat, yanking your vocal folds back together every time you talk.*

---

* It was once thought that the opening and closing of our vocal folds during the production of speech was a deliberate movement, precisely controlled by the nerves of the larynx – an idea called the neurochronaxic theory. In fact, we know now that our nerves are simply not capable of operating fast enough to produce the kind of oscillation needed to produce sound. The movement of our vocal folds must instead be involuntary, and driven by a combination of their

As complex as this opening-and-closing process might seem, it occurs dozens of times a second during speech to produce a rapidly oscillating sound wave that we then hear as a voice. And the higher the frequency of that oscillation, the higher that voice's pitch. In normal conversation, male voices tend to have a baseline frequency of around 100 Hz (that is, 100 opening-and-closings of the vocal folds per second), while female voices tend be around an octave higher, somewhere in the region of 200 Hz. These frequencies change from person to person and situation to situation, of course, and human speech in general can range from around 80 Hz at its lowest to 250 Hz at its highest. A newborn baby will cry at around 400 Hz. Soprano opera singers can produce notes in excess of 1,000 Hz. And the lowest vocal sound ever produced by a human being was recorded at just 0.189 Hz, far below the hearing threshold of our ears. (To put that into perspective, you would need a piano with an additional eight octaves of keys to play notes within the same frequency.)

You will be able to feel this opening-and-closing movement if you place your fingers against the front of your throat and make a 'zzz' sound. Each individual pulse of that vibrating or buzzing sensation beneath the skin is just one oscillation of the vocal folds.* Not

---

natural elasticity and the action of the pressurised air released between them – the so-called myoelastic theory. You can create a similar effect by trying to open and close your lips as many times as possible by deliberately moving your jaw. Now try simply blowing air through your lips, as if producing a raspberry or an exasperated 'pfft!'. By relying on the movement of air alone to push your lips apart, you will be able to produce many more openings and closings than you could ever manage by attempting to control that movement yourself.

* This effect can be even more obvious if you use your fingers to plug your ears. Place a finger over each earhole and make a 'zzz' sound, and you should hear a

all the sounds we produce in speech involve the vocal folds in this way, however. Keep your fingers against your throat and make a 'sss' sound, and you'll feel no vibration at all. The way these two sounds are produced – 'sss' and 'zzz' – is physically the same, with the edges of the tongue raised up to touch the roof of the mouth, and air still moving gradually upwards from the lungs. The only difference is that 'zzz' involves vibration of the vocal folds, while 'sss' does not.

In linguistic terms, this vibration (or lack of it) is known as phonation, and is the second part of our production of speech. A sound that uses the vocal folds, like 'z', is said to be a voiced sound, while its opposite, 's', is an unvoiced or voiceless sound. Languages typically contain many pairs of sounds that are identical except for their voicedness. A 'b' sound is the voiced equivalent of a voiceless 'p' sound – you should feel the same vibration in your throat when you say 'b' as when you say 'p', despite the two being produced identically. The same applies to pairings such as 'v' and 'f', 'd' and 't', and 'g' and 'k'.

As it moves onwards and upwards from the larynx, the air being forced from the lungs continues up through the resonating pharynx and enters into the top part of the vocal tract – the mouth, the nose and the back of the throat. Here, it undergoes the last of our speech-producing processes, articulation. This is effectively our body's last chance to manipulate its outflow of pulmonic air, so that if a sound is left untouched by the vocal folds, it is here that its shape is created.

Inside this part of the vocal tract is an assembly of movable and immovable organs that can mould or 'articulate' the air within to form more precise sounds. The immovable organs, known as

---

loud buzzing sound resonating throughout your head. Make a 'sss' sound, however, and there'll be no vibration at all.

passive articulators, include the teeth, the hard palate on the roof of the mouth and the tough bony slope of gum just behind the upper teeth, called the alveolar ridge. We use our teeth to produce sounds like 'v'. We raise our tongue to the hard palate to produce sounds such as 'y'. And we tap the tongue against the alveolar ridge to make sounds like 't'. The movable organs, or active articulators, include the tongue, the lips and the soft palate or velum – the wide band of spongy tissue at the back of the roof of the mouth. We use the tongue to make sounds such as 'l' and 'r'. We use our lips to make sounds like 'f' and 'b'. And we can use the soft palate to direct airflow up into the cavities of the nose, to produce nasal sounds such as 'm', 'n' and 'ng'. All of these sounds, however, have one thing in common: they all involve the airflow through the vocal tract being stopped, narrowed or obstructed in some way. And for that reason, they are all consonants.

By definition, a consonant is any sound that involves blocking or disrupting the otherwise unbroken flow of air through the vocal tract. Some consonants, such as 'b', impede this airflow entirely, so as to build up a momentary pocket of pressure and produce a short burst of sound; it is for good reason that sounds made this way are called stops, or plosives. Other sounds, such as 'l', involve simply man-oeuvring something in front of the flow of air, allowing it to pass through or around an obstacle; because the airflow passes around the sides of the tongue to make a 'l' sound, it is classed as a lateral sound. All of our consonants can be categorised into a dozen or so groups in this way, depending on the manner and place in the vocal tract in which the airflow is disrupted. Fricative sounds, such as 'f' or 'z', involve narrowing the airflow to produce a turbulent friction. Trills, such as a rolled 'r' sound, involve disrupting the airflow with a rapid flapping of the tongue or uvula. And so-called approximant sounds, such as an unrolled 'r' sound, involve bringing the mouth's articulators close enough together to restrict the flow of air, but not enough to produce any kind of barrier or turbulence. Some sounds, however, do nothing at all to block this flow of air – and we know those as our vowels.

If you produce the five basic vowel sounds one after the other (not their letter names, but their sounds, 'ah', 'ee', 'i', 'oh', 'oo'), you'll notice that your mouth simply reshapes to form them, but no part of it meets any other. Our tongue can lift or drop to change their height, and we can round or widen our lips, but the main channel of airflow through the mouth itself remains unrestricted. Vowels, therefore, are sounds made from open airflow through the vocal tract, while consonants are made by impinging or blocking that airflow somehow. But why does our language need both?

When a doctor asks you to make an 'aah' sound, you could (theoretically, at least) keep that sound going for as long as you wanted; the only limitation would be the amount of breath in your lungs. Try to prolong a 'b' sound, however, and you'll have trouble. Because consonants involve occluding the flow of air through the vocal tract in some way, all we can really do with a 'b' is hold on to that blockage a little longer, and thereby increase the pressure behind it. That won't prolong it, but merely delay it, and make it seem more forceful when the pressure behind it is finally released. The only way we can prolong a 'b' sound, in fact, is by attaching a vowel to it: you can make a word like *bee*, *boo* or *bay* go on as long as you like, but in all cases the 'b' sound itself would remain limited.

We could, of course, imagine a speech system comprised of nothing but consonant sounds, and invent coarse, rattling words built from maddening strings of blocked sounds such as *b-k-r-z* or *t-p-d-v*. Conversely, we could construct a speech system from nothing but free-flowing vowel sounds, full of smooth, open, vocalic words such as *oo-ah-ee-oh*. But neither system would be particularly workable, nor particularly efficient. A constant string of consonants would be physically demanding and involve a never-ending realignment of the articulators of the mouth and throat. A constant string of vowel sounds, on the other hand, would quickly exhaust the air in our lungs, and with no articulators to break those sounds apart, one would simply slide into another, making them difficult to tell apart. A combination of consonants and vowels, therefore, gives us the best of both worlds, while simultaneously creating a varied library of sounds from which to build an equally vast library of spoken words. But in the case of English, at least, perhaps that collection of sounds is a little too vast.

From the action of our vocal folds to the movement of our articulators, like our lips and teeth, there are so many variables involved in the production of speech sounds that no language could ever possibly use them all. As we've already mentioned, even the world's most robust sound systems, like those of southern Africa, contain at most around a hundred different phonemes – but the total number of *possible* human speech sounds is far higher. English might not have as many as Botswanan Taa, but with roughly forty-five different phonemes it is still among the world's most well-furnished languages. Arabic and French, for instance, only have around thirty-five, while Japanese and Korean have fewer than thirty. This relatively large collection of English speech sounds ultimately leaves our twenty-six-character alphabet with something of a shortfall, and so forces many of our letters to multitask and take on multiple sounds in order to overcome the deficit. And nowhere is that more true than among our vowels.

Around twenty of the forty-five sounds in the English language are vowel sounds. Some, such as the 'a' in *cat* or the 'o' in *dog*, are classed as short vowels. Others, such as the 'ee' in *bead* or the 'ooh' in *mood*, are long vowels. And some are diphthongs – conjoined sounds that slide from one vowel to another, such as the 'ah-ee' sound you'll hear in words like *high* or *buy*. But with only five basic characters to represent all these different vowels, our A, E, I, O and U have to work overtime. E, for instance, doesn't take its usual 'ee' sound every time we see it. In *pretty*, it has the same short 'i' sound we might better associated with I. In *debut*, it has an 'ay' sound. In *bet* it has a short 'eh' sound. In *water*, *butter*, *after* and even *the*, it has a short, vague 'uh' sound – and, oddly, it is this that is the commonest vowel in our language.

Known as schwa – and represented by an upturned *e*, /ə/, in phonetic transcription – this vague 'uh' sound has been estimated to account for somewhere in the region of 10 per cent of all the sounds we produce in spoken English. The reason for that frequency is partly to do with how it is produced, and partly to do with where it tends to occur. Schwa is the sound we make when all the potential articulators of our vocal tract are relaxed. In technical terms, it is classed as an unrounded mid-central vowel: it is effectively made right in the middle of our vocal space, with nothing working to lift or lower its place of articulation upwards or downwards, push it forwards or backwards in the mouth, or alter its sound by rounding or widening our lips. Schwa is simply the lowest-effort sound our vocal tract can produce.

Because of that vagueness, schwa only ever occurs in unstressed syllables. When we say *water*, for instance, we don't work to pronounce that final –*er* as an obvious 'er' sound, as in *confer* or *prefer*. The primary stress in *water* falls on the first syllable, which reduces its second unstressed syllable to just 'uh'. Throughout our language this happens time and time again with unstressed sounds, which, no matter how they're spelled, are reduced to little more than an 'uh' in speech.

Despite its commonness, in standard written English, schwa doesn't have its own letter or symbol. In fact, such are the shortfalls of our spelling system that not only is this the E in *water*, but it's the A in *about*, the I in *rapid*, the O in *error*, the U in *column* and even the Y in *syringe*. True, when read as individual words, you might be tempted to pronounce them more precisely – making a clear 'a' sound in *about*, or a bright 'i' sound in *rapid* – but in the relaxed, fast-flowing speech of everyday communication, we don't tend to speak quite so precisely. As a result these words, along with a great many more like them, will typically be reduced to little more than 'uhbout' or 'rapuhd'.

It is not lazy, or in some way 'bad English', to produce a schwa where a word's spelling might appear to demand something else. This reduction happens naturally and unconsciously, and is simply an aspect of how our spoken language ordinarily operates. And it is the ease at which this occurs that makes schwa – our vaguest, gruntingest 'uh' of a vowel – the most common vowel sound in our entire language.

Q. 10

Why Do We Capitalise *I*?

*The proudest word in English, to judge
by its way of carrying itself, is I.*

Julius Charles and Augustus William Hare,
Guesses at Truth by Two Brothers (1827)

In 1683, an English printer and mapmaker named Joseph Moxon
published the second of two instructional guidebooks he called his
Mechanic Exercises or 'The Doctrine of Handiworks'. Each volume
contained several detailed how-tos covering an array of practical and
technical disciplines, with the first expounding as diverse a set of skills
as bricklaying, blacksmithing, joinery and even the construction of
sundials. In the second, Moxon was on more familiar ground: this
was an instruction manual for fellow printers.

Moxon explained how to handle paper, how to mix and prepare
ink, when best to use italic lettering, how to proof and correct manuscripts, how to forge new type-pieces for lost or unfamiliar characters,
and even how best to arrange the equipment in a printer's workshop.
Any prospective master printer, he advised, should furnish themselves
with two sets of letters – one in standard roman type, the other in

italic. Each set should then be split between two wooden trays or cases, with the first containing capitals, numerals, accented letters and mathematical operators, and the second containing standard-size letters as well as punctuation marks, dashes, shapes and various other miscellaneous symbols. It was good practice, he advised, to position the first case above the second, further from the printer's reach, as the standard-sized letters of the second box would naturally be needed more frequently than the capitalised letters of the first. This pair of cases ultimately came to be 'described with the most common way of laying them' in a printer's workshop: the 'upper case' contained capital letters, and the 'lower case' contained smaller letters.

It sounds like an etymological story too neat to be true, but it is nevertheless genuine: we call our capital and non-capital letters 'uppercase' and 'lowercase' because of the two tiers of wooden trays into which their corresponding type was sorted in the printworks of Moxon's day – and his *Mechanic Exercises* gives us the earliest recorded evidence of that practice. But knowing how these two forms of each letter earned their names is one thing. Knowing why we have them at all is another.

An alphabet that uses a mix of upper- and lowercase letters like ours is called a bicameral writing system. Not all alphabets are the same, of course, and those that don't divide their letters this way, such as Arabic or Georgian, are known as unicameral systems. As with a lot of what we're discovering here, however, the distinction we make in English today isn't one we made in the past. Our ABCs may be bicameral now, but originally they were unicameral.

All the alphabets from which ours is descended, including those of Greece and Rome, initially consisted of uppercase letters only.

This so-called majuscule text was typically written between two well-defined horizontal lines – without punctuation or spacing – so that it filled out row after solid row of text, with each letter standing roughly the same width as the others and the full height of the line. As the needs and tools of writers changed, however, smaller and more rounded versions of these majuscule letters began to develop.

Early writing had been produced on stone or relatively rough surfaces, like papyrus, that made larger letters built from multiple straight strokes more practical than smaller and more complex ones. But as paper-making techniques improved and writing switched to smoother parchments and vellums, the speed at which letters could be written increased, and writing itself became a more workable and commonplace process. Letters could now take on simpler, looser forms that required fewer individual strokes and could be written much more swiftly than larger majuscule figures. Cursive writing emerged too, as the smoother surfaces allowed fluid handwritten letters to be joined with a single flowing line of ink. As a result, these smaller characters acquired additional tails, bars and other connectors that allowed them to be linked together. In fact, many of the features that still set our lowercase letters apart from their uppercase equivalents today – such as the long ascending stems of *b* and *d*, as opposed to our solid capitals *B* and *D* – first emerged some 2,000 years ago as a means of connecting the majuscule letters of Roman cursive text.

These developments gradually led to an entirely new style of handwriting known as uncial (literally 'inch-high'), the earliest examples of which appeared in the first and second centuries. Despite sharing many of the features we would recognise in our lowercase letters today, uncial was still a unicameral system and its letters were effectively little more than optional variants of their majuscule forms. Documents could therefore be written in either style, with the decision to use one over the other made on purely stylistic or practical grounds.

As it could be written more quickly and compactly than standard majuscule, uncial proved popular and several regional forms of it developed as its use spread across Europe. A Byzantine style developed in mainland Greece. A Roman North African style developed in Algeria. A later Merovingian style emerged in France. And a distinct Insular style emerged in the monasteries of medieval Ireland. It was this that was introduced to Anglo-Saxon England along with Christianity in the sixth and seventh centuries, and before long an entire family of Insular styles was in use across the British Isles; the name *insular* itself derives from the Latin word for 'island'.

As uncial writing continued to evolve, more letters began to adopt what we would now recognise as their lowercase features. The two upper bars of *E* came together to create a closed semicircle, more like that of the modern-day *e*. *H* lost its second upper stroke, becoming more like *h*. *L* lost much of its lower stroke, becoming more like *l*. Other letters started to shift in size relative to those around them, and a more variable style of lettering known as half-uncial emerged that began to ascend and descend outside the strict confines of the line for the first time. *G* sank down to become more like *g*. *K* gradually elongated to make *k*. *R* shrank to *r*. *F* became longer and narrower, and gained a descending tail, *f*. So too did *P*, to become *p*, and the additional stroke of *Q* fell beneath the line to make *q*. Other letters – such as *c*, *o*, *u* and *x* – simply formed more compact versions of their larger selves. Yet still the larger and smaller forms of our letters were not combined, and effectively operated side by side as two optional systems of writing. It would take several more centuries – and the influence of one of the medieval world's most important figures – for the two to merge into a pair of interconnected cases.

The Frankish king Charlemagne was reportedly so fascinated by the written word that he would keep blank writing tablets under his pillows to practise handwriting in bed. Despite all these late-night efforts, he never became fully literate himself, but his appreciation for written learning remained a lifelong obsession. Throughout his reign, Charlemagne instigated a series of early cultural and educational reforms that hauled Europe out of the Dark Ages and established a new period of enlightenment known as the Carolingian Renaissance. And as part of these endeavours, he surrounded himself with many of the greatest minds of the day – among them, an English scholar and cleric named Alcuin of York.

Described as 'the most learned man anywhere to be found' by one of Charlemagne's courtiers, in 781 Alcuin accepted an invitation to travel to Europe to work and teach at the king's court in Aachen. A decade later, partly in recognition of Alcuin's service (and partly so that he remained close enough to still be at his beck and call) Charlemagne conferred on him the abbacy of a grand monastery at Tours, in western France, where he remained until his death in 804. And in both locations, Alcuin was closely involved in Charlemagne's cultural enlightenment and oversaw one of the key aspects of his educational drive: producing new copies of many early manuscripts and documents that were now disintegrating after centuries of use.

The production of written literature flourished during Charlemagne's reign, but the invention of the printing press was another six centuries away. Any reproduced document was therefore still being written out by hand. To keep up with the demanding work-load, Alcuin and Charlemagne's scribes adopted a new writing style that accelerated their handiwork while prioritising the legibility of the text, ensuring all the precious texts on which they were work-ing remained as legible and as accessible as possible. Elements of their ancient majuscule writing were combined with those of both the Insular writing Alcuin knew from home, and the half-uncial style now popular across Europe. The result was a clear, speedily written and aesthetically pleasing new style that became known as Carolingian minuscule.

Although Alcuin is sometimes credited with inventing this style single-handedly (he supposedly complained of the 'rustic-ity' of the writers on his arrival at Tours), aspects of it were almost certainly already in use before he arrived in France, and his input may have been limited only to furthering its use or standardising its appearance. No matter the extent of his involvement, however, the books and texts produced in France during his time there established a great many of the written conventions we still use today. Letter shapes became more consistent, spacing and punc-tuation became more organised, and older complexities – like conjoined ligatures and scribal shorthand – were largely discarded. And what we would now recognise as upper- and lowercase let-ters began to be used consistently and systematically within the same documents.

One of the Carolingian system's greatest innovations was the set-ting aside of larger, squarer capital letters for titles, headings, opening lines, and the first characters of new chapters, sentences, and lines of text. That left the smaller, neater, faster-written minuscule letters for use everywhere else. What had once been a purely stylistic distinction was now a much more formalised one, and after Charlemagne rose to become Holy Roman Emperor in 800 – uniting much of western Europe for the first time since the fall of Rome – this new bicameral writing system came to be introduced far and wide.

Under Charlemagne's influence, Carolingian minuscule remained the standard writing style of much of Europe for the next 200 years, before tastes changed once more and the squarer, heavier Blackletter styles of the Middle Ages became more popular (more on which a little later). But even as these newer styles emerged, many of the standards of the Carolingian system remained in place, and majuscule and minuscule letters continued to be used alongside one another. The printing press circulated these standards even further in the 1400s and 1500s, and would eventually give these dual-tier lettering styles their names: Moxon's upper- and lowercase letters.

Although a mix of capital and non-capital letters eventually became the norm everywhere, for centuries the precise rules dictating when and where these two cases should be used remained flexible. Capitalisation was for a long time seen as little more than a means of adding emphasis to a word or section of text, regardless of whether it was a title or a heading, the first word of a new page or sentence, or simply a particularly important WORD somewhere in the Middle of an Otherwise perfectly Ordinary SENTENCE. Later grammarians weren't quite so keen on this freeform system, however, and in the eighteenth and nineteenth centuries they began advocating much more stringent rules-based approaches to capital letters in their manuals and textbooks. As these instructions became standard practice, they started to be passed on in school lessons and grammatical primers, and gradually established themselves as the rules we follow today. Although, even now, not everyone sees eye to eye. Or rather, *I* to *i*.

The use of upper and lowercase letters themselves is now established across all the languages using the Latin alphabet, but the conventions behind them are not. In English, for instance, our rules dictate capital letters be set aside for the beginnings of sentences, and to highlight all proper nouns such as names, titles, places and the days and months of the year. But in languages like French, days and months are not capitalised, while most other proper nouns are, and in German it has become standard practice to capitalise *all* nouns, regardless of their relative importance – giving us uppercase spellings such as *Katze* ('cat') and *Hund* ('dog'). As a result, many of our languages are united by a common writing style and alphabet, but not by common rules underpinning how that style be used. And anomalous among all these rules is a convention now set so deeply into the grammar of English that you might never even have thought to question it: why do English speakers capitalise our first-person singular subject pronoun, *I*?

Objectively, it seems like an unusual rule to adopt. After all, we don't do it to our other first-person pronouns, like *me*, *mine*, and *myself*. We don't do it to our other single-letter word, *a*. Nor was the etymological ancestor of our *I*, the Old English pronoun *ic*, capitalised. And nor is this a convention found in other languages; the likes of the French first-person pronoun *je*, the Spanish *yo*, and German *ich* all remain steadfastly lowercase. So why do we, and seemingly we alone, do it?

Speaking of German, it does have a rule that capitalises the formal or polite forms of its second-person pronoun, *Sie* ('you'), along with its declined forms, like *Ihr* and *Euer* ('your'). This is part of a broader language phenomenon we've already touched upon here called the T–V distinction, in which pronouns are altered to show formality and respect.* So is this what's happening in English? Do we really think so highly of ourselves that we've grown accustomed to capitalising the pronoun that refers to us? Some etymologists have certainly suggested so, and have theorised that there is some kind of latently egocentric, psychological reason behind uppercase *I*. But if that were the case, it seems odd that no other language has followed suit. And surely we would expect a rule like that to filter down to the likes of *me* and *myself* too? When pronouns relating to God are capitalised in the Bible, for instance, the convention is rightly rolled out across the board, giving us an appropriately godly *He*, *Him*, and *Himself*.

Perhaps instead there is something much more pragmatic going on. An alternative theory claims that because *I* falls so frequently in sentence-first position, it is only natural that its capitalisation would come to be implemented throughout the language. That's certainly a more plausible idea: *I* is a subject pronoun, while *me* is an object pronoun ordinarily never found at the beginning of a sentence. As a result, *I eat pizza* is perfectly grammatical, but constructions such as *Me eat pizza* or *The pizza is for I* are not. If this theory were true, however, it seems odd that such a rule has not affected any of our other subject pronouns, like *you*, *she* or *they*.

---

* The T–V distinction takes its name from a feature of Latin in which the second-person pronoun *tu* ('you') was swapped for its plural form, *vos*, as a sign of respect when the person being addressed was esteemed. Using a plural pronoun to address a single person like this in formal or polite conversation remains a feature of a great many languages (not just those that have since evolved from Latin, such as French), and various incarnations of the T–V distinction are found in languages all over the globe.

Instead, the most likely explanation here is a surprisingly straightforward one, instigated by the fact that around the time capital *I* first began to appear in English writing – in the Middle English period (so Chaucer's *Canterbury Tales* provides much of our early evidence of it) – there was a series of broad phonological changes taking place in our language. At that time, many of the dialects of English were busy reducing and simplifying Old English *ic* (which was pronounced a little like *itch* but without the T) down to a single short 'i' sound, rendering its final C no longer necessary. In written English, however, a single lowercase letter *i* can look a little lost on its own – and in a densely handwritten document, it's easy to imagine how a solitary stroke could easily have been misread, overlooked, or even dismissed as a smudge, a dash or a flourish of the pen. As a result, early Middle English scribes are simply thought to have begun writing the letter *I* a little larger, so that it would sit more proudly in a cramped line of text. As the wider distinction between upper and lowercase letters took hold in our language, this slightly larger *I* was upgraded to a capital, and the rule enforcing capitalised *I* as the standard form of our first-person pronoun became established. There is nothing inherently egotistical or self-aggrandising about it, nor is there any shortfall in our rules or our grammar that has failed to be rolled out onto similar words and pronouns. Our capital *I* is simply the natural consequence of our language's eternal drive towards simpler forms, alongside the invention of upper- and lowercase letters themselves.

Q. 11

Why Does i Have a Dot?

A kiss, when all is said, what is it? . . .
A rosy dot placed on the i in 'loving'.

Edmond Rostand,
Cyrano de Bergerac (1897)

Let's pick up our history of European writing where we left off. By the mid-ninth century, Charlemagne's Carolingian style had introduced a distinction between upper- and lowercase letters. But by the dawn of the new millennium, tastes were beginning to change. Charlemagne's educational reforms were now paying dividends, and an appetite was growing for a newer style that now prioritised content over clarity. In short, there was a new kid on the writers' block: Blackletter.

Blackletter is the thick, often quite linear, style of calligraphic writing whose offspring we still see today everywhere from passports and banknotes to newspaper mastheads and Taylor Swift albums, lending them all an air of gravitas or antiquity. Often wrongly labelled 'Gothic' or even 'Old English' lettering, Blackletter probably emerged first in France sometime around the mid-1100s, before catching on across the rest of Europe in the thirteen and fourteenth centuries. From region to region, several different styles of Blackletter developed throughout the Middle Ages, a handful of which even endured through to modern times; in Germany, a Blackletter style named Fraktur remained the norm in published literature until as recently as the 1940s.

𝔄. 𝔅 ℭ 𝔇 𝔈 𝔉 𝔊 𝔥 𝔦 𝔍 𝔎 𝔏 𝔐 𝔑 𝔒 𝔭 𝔔 𝔕 𝔖 𝔗 𝔘 𝔙 𝔚 𝔛 𝔜 𝔷
𝔞 𝔟 𝔠 𝔡 𝔢 𝔣 𝔤 𝔥 𝔦 𝔧 𝔨 𝔩 𝔪 𝔫 𝔬 𝔭 𝔮 𝔯 𝔰 𝔱 𝔲 𝔳 𝔴 𝔵 𝔶 𝔷

At least part of Blackletter's success lay in its economy. Despite its dissimilarity from the broad, clear characters of Carolingian, Blackletter was its descendant, and evolved naturally from it as books began to be produced more widely and profusely than ever before. A narrower, more compact style of writing allowed more words to be packed onto each line, and therefore more information to be packed into each text. Books written this way ultimately required less time, less paper and thereby less expense to produce. But like a lot of cost-cutting ventures, there was a downside.

Compressing letters to save time and space this way meant compromising on their legibility. As the Blackletter script developed, the open, fluid shapes of the Carolingian style – in particular its lowercase letters – became more constrained, and handwritten texts took on a tighter, denser appearance as a result. Letters were no longer constructed from steady curves and clear strokes and loops, but a regimented network of interconnecting downward and diagonal blocks. Texts were still readable, but by prioritising the informational weight of a document over its clarity, deciphering written literature undoubtedly became more of a challenge – which neatly leads us to the question at the start of this chapter.

Each of the short individual quill-strokes made by a writer's pen is known as a minim (ı). A lowercase letter *l* or *i* – which was written at the time without its accompanying dot – would constitute nothing more than a single minim (ı). An *n* or *u* would be built from two minims (ıı). And an *m* or *w* would be written as three minims (ııı). Letters were still being written at different heights and in different cases (thanks to the new standards Carolingian minuscule had established), so these dense forests of minims weren't always as impenetrable as they might appear. But if a string of minim-heavy letters were nevertheless to fall next to one another, the result could be something of a blur. Take the word *minim* itself, which would have been built from an unavoidable combination of ten individual downstrokes:

ıııııııııı

Telling an *m* from a *ni* or an *iu* in writing like this was clearly now much more difficult, and in few places would this have been more evident than in words using the Latin plural ending –*ii* (found in words such as *genii* or *radii* today). Written in dotless medieval Blackletter, that –*ii* tag could easily have been misread as a lowercase *n*, *u* or *v*, instantly transforming *genii* into *genu* . . .

genıı

genıı

. . . which has the somewhat undesirable effect of being the Latin word for a knee, not a group of geniuses. The context of a sentence would have helped to clear a lot of this ambiguity up, of course, but reading was no longer as immediately user-friendly as it once was.

The problem was aptly summed up in the thirteenth century by one anonymous French writer, who turned to a page in his notebook and doodled this curious Latin sentence:

mimi numinum niuium minimi munium nimium
uini muniminum imminui uiui minimum uolunt

If we were to write this out today, it would read *mimi numinum niuium minimi munium nimium uini muniminum imminui uiui minimum uolunt* – or, in other words, 'The very short mimes of the gods of snow do not at all wish that, during their lifetime, the very great burden of distributing the wine of the walls be lightened.' Quite what that's meant to mean is debatable – as, for that matter, is this line's provenance. It's often said to have been invented as little more than a joke, highlighting medieval writers' frustrations at the illegibility of this new style. Alternatively, a popular (though very likely apocryphal) anecdote claims something like this sentence was used as a genuine message of protest concocted by a troupe of disgruntled actors. More plausibly, however, many historians claim this is a kind of riddle, or a test of a student's reading or writing capabilities – or perhaps nothing more than a light-hearted penmanship exercise used to practise their calligraphic strokes. Regardless of its origins, this bizarre string of words illustrates just how much the writing of the Middle Ages had moved on from Charlemagne's day and embraced a newer, denser norm.

Just as Blackletter text began to take hold, however, a simple solution presented itself. Writers began adding a small dot or flick of the quill above lowercase *i* to show, without doubt, that it was to be read as a separate character. *Genu* now became much more obviously *genii*, and the problem created by *minim* itself was all but instantly eased:

minim

The dot above the *i* – or the tittle, to give it its proper name – wasn't invented purely for Blackletter, of course, as adornments like this had been in use in various Carolingian and uncial styles, as well as even earlier European writing systems stretching back into antiquity. But it was in the minim-heavy texts of Blackletter that this literal stroke of genius showed its worth. Like all the best solutions, it soon became a permanent fixture.

In English, however, it's fair to say that the tittle remains something of an anomaly. As a rule, we don't tend to add much in the way of clarificatory adornments to our letters, relying instead on context and instinct. Other languages, meanwhile, attach an often enormously well-furnished system of dots and dashes to their letters, known as diacritics, to help reflect the nuances of their pronunciation.

French has one of the most robust diacritic systems of all European languages, and scatters acute accents (*café*), grave accents (*père*), cedillas (*façade*), circumflexes (*château*), and diaereses (*naïve*) throughout its vocabulary. Spanish and Portuguese use a tilde to indicate a nasal quality in words such as *señor* and *São Paulo*. A hook-shaped marker called an ogonek does the same in Polish, as in *dziękuję* ('thank you'). German has its double-dot umlaut (*fünf*). In Swedish, a tiny circle called an overring is added to the A in words such as *ålder* ('age') and *åtta* ('eight'). Czech uses a V-shaped háček to turn C, S and Z into 'tsh' (*č*), 'sh' (*š*) and 'zh' (*ž*). And all of this is before we've even set foot outside Europe.

It might appear to be just another mark written above just another letter, but the tittle above *i* (and later its cousin *j* too) doesn't really belong on this list. Graves, tildes, cedillas and the like are all used to indicate alterations of pronunciation, but the dot above our *i* and *j* was a scribal invention, used to clarify written texts not spoken language. The pronunciation of *i* is unaffected by the dot we write above it; tellingly, uppercase *I* and *J* don't use one at all. So where do all these other tags and tails come from?

Admittedly, outlining the origins of every diacritic marker used by the world's languages would provide enough material for another book, let alone a few pages in this one. Suffice to say many have relatively straightforward histories and have simply always been a feature of their respective languages. When the Hangul alphabet was devised to write Korean in the mid-1400s, for example, two simple dotted markers, (·) and (:), were included to flag the difference in print between the high and rising pitches of Korean vowels (although both were quietly discarded in the early 1900s). Other diacritics are more complex, however, and were later developments added to their respective languages' written inventories long after the languages themselves had developed a written form.

The ringed-A of Swedish, *å*, for instance, arrived as recently as the sixteenth century. It evolved from a tiny letter O written above an A where once a double-A spelling had been preferred. The Spanish tilde, *ñ*, began life as a medieval scribal abbreviation that saved space on a page by condensing words such as 'domini' (as in *Anno Domini*) down to '*dñi*'. Later, it came to be used more specifically as a means of reducing double-N spellings to a single letter; the word *señor* was originally *sennor* in Old Spanish. And the German umlaut, *ü*, likewise didn't emerge until well into the Blackletter period, and has been a permanent fixture of German writing only since the late Middle Ages. Before then, all manner of conventions were used to mark the same kind of vowel quality an umlaut indicates in German today – including adding a tiny lowercase *e* beneath the vowel in question, or even adding a whole extra E into the word itself (the same rule that turns the names *Schönberg* and *Göthe* into *Schoenberg* and *Goethe*). With space at a premium in Blackletter writing, the simple double-dot (¨) eventually won out.

Conversely, many of the diacritic markers of French have the odd distinction of being far older than the language itself. The Greek grammarian and librarian Aristophanes of Byzantium is credited with devising a trio of written markers – (´), (`) and (^) – as a means of flagging the high, low and falling pitches of syllables in Ancient Greek in the third century BCE. It wasn't until the 1500s that these dashes were adopted by French writers as a means of differentiating identical words – as in *la* (feminine 'the') and *là* ('over there') – or to flag distinct vowel sounds – separating the 'ay'-like E of *clé* ('key') and *né* ('born') from the 'eh'-like E of *mère* ('mother') and *père* ('father').

Last of all to arrive in French was the circumflex, *î*, which the renowned sixteenth-century translator and printer Étienne Dolet suggested (among many other proposals) as a means of highlighting the omission of a letter that had fallen out of use as Old French had developed into Middle French. Not all Dolet's suggestions caught on (probably a consequence of him later falling foul of the French Inquisition and eventually being burned to death on top of a pile of his own books), but his use of the circumflex to show omission was one of those that did. When the Académie française published the third edition of its landmark French dictionary in 1740, the circumflex was hauled out of obscurity and scattered across the French lexicon, this time to show where silent Ss were currently disappearing from the language. *Conqueste* became *conquête*, *ancestre* became *ancêtre*, *tempeste* became *tempête*, and *vestements* became *vêtements*; so intertwined are the histories of French and English that restoring an S to a French word spelled with a circumflex will often instantly reveal its English equivalent.

It was around the 1500s too that the cedilla, ç, made its way into French as a means of differentiating the hard ('k') and soft ('s') pronunciations of the letter C. Originally, however, it was a Spanish invention. Inspired by the final letter of Spain's ancient Visigothic alphabet, *zet* (ç), the cedilla was used in medieval Spanish to represent a sound known as the voiceless alveolar sibilant affricate – something a little similar to the soft 'ts' sound at the end of *bets*. Once introduced to the written language, it quickly simplified to ç before jumping across the border into France, where it eventually became the letter we find in *façade* and *soupçon* today.

We could go on and explore the origins of the Czech háček (originally a dot later expanded into a V shape, probably for clarity), the Polish ogonek (literally a 'little tail', perhaps inspired by a Cyrillic letter known as little *yus*, Ѧ), or even the dense and complex systems of diacritics used to clarify abjad languages including Arabic and Hebrew. But to do so avoids the other obvious question here:

why have none of these symbols been adopted into English? In fact, English appears so utterly determined not to use diacritic markers that even when we borrow a word from another language that uses them – *café, niçoise, jalapeño, cortège, ångström* – we often strip them of their unruliness and make do with the likes of *cafe, nicoise, jalapeno, cortege* and *angstrom*.

English's long-standing drive towards simplicity is at least partly responsible for our dislike of all these accessories. After all, if we're going to jettison our entire system of grammatical gender along the way, why should we bother implementing anything as trivial as an extra dot above the I in *naïve*? Another reason is that, after an early period of flux, our spellings became standardised relatively early in our language's development with the introduction of the mechanical printing press in the fifteenth century. That has left us with a wildly outdated spelling system that we have scarcely updated since the Middle Ages. And if we're not going to drop our silent letters or fix the unruly pronunciation of a string of letters such as *–ough*, what chance do we have of successfully and systematically rolling out accent markers too?

There's a point of perspective to be made here too. To us English speakers – with our plain, largely unadorned ABCs – it's easy to look at a Spanish *ñ* or a Swedish *å* and simply see a familiar letter with something unfamiliar added to it. But in the Spanish alphabet, Ñ occupies its own slot between N and O, and is considered a distinct letter. In the Swedish alphabet, Å is listed after Z in twenty-seventh place (and is followed by a further two more letters, Ä and Ö). Likewise, Polish separates A from Ą, C from Ć, and Z from both Ź and Ż. And the 42-letter Czech alphabet even manages to find separate slots for the likes of Č, Ů and Ý. Many diacritics therefore serve such an important purpose in their respective languages that they are not seen as optional extras or trivial adornments, but an inherent part of a single, immutable letter warranting its own distinct place in the alphabet. Which, in retrospect, sounds an awful lot like our *i*.

Q. 12

Why Is Q
Always Followed by U?

*Delete the letter Q from the alphabet. It's a
useless heritage from the Etruscans.*

Mildred Vandenburgh,
The Spelling Progress Bulletin (1969)

When it came to ranking the relative difficulties of different languages in Q. 5, we found that arguably an English speaker wasn't the best person to ask. The English language is hardly a bastion of common sense, after all; it's riddled with inconsistencies and complexities that make it notoriously difficult to master. True, it does have its fair share of simplicities: our vocabulary is ungendered, and we have no real sense of grammatical case (as we'll see in Q. 15), both of which can make the fundamentals of English comparatively easy to pick up. But we have a hefty supply of stumbling blocks too, including perplexing idioms, enormous regional variation, and dozens of phrasal and prepositional verbs – the kinds of constructions that mean we agree *with* but care *for* people, and do three very different things when we throw *on* something, throw *out* something, and throw *up* something. Chief among all our challenges, however, is our spelling system.

English spelling – or orthography, to give it its proper name – is notoriously chaotic. Our written language is littered with homophones and homonyms, double and silent letters, and complex and unpredictable letter strings such as *ough*, which can famously be pronounced at least nine different ways in *bought, cough, enough, hiccough, lough, plough, thorough, though* and *through*. Conversely, depending on your accent, a sound as straightforward as 'ee' has more than a dozen different spellings in written English – as in *be, bee, beach, ski, algae, key, keyed, quay, yield, seize, beguine, amoeba, guyot, chamois, bologna* and *dengue*. Elsewhere, *laughter* rhymes with *after*, but not with *slaughter* or *daughter*. *Comb* rhymes with *home*, but not with *tomb* (and neither pronounces its Bs). And *cow* rhymes with *bow* – but only when *bow* is pronounced like *sow*, and not like *sow* rhyming with *sew*, which rhymes with *bow*.

All in all, our spelling system is clearly something of a minefield. But why is it so infinitely disorderly?

It's worth remembering that the English alphabet, such as it is, isn't really our own. The system we use today is a redeployed version of the alphabet fine-tuned by the Romans to suit Latin more than 2,000 years ago. However, English is not a Latinate language but a Germanic one, and that clash of bloodlines is at least partly responsible for some of our most fundamental orthographic problems. When our runic letters were ousted by our ABCs in the sixth century, there was an immediate discrepancy between the sounds of Old English and the Latin letters now at our disposal. As a result, some had to take on multiple roles, and we're still dealing with the repercussions of that shortfall today.

Elsewhere, a number of our Germanic cousins, including German and Swedish, appear to fare much more successfully with the Latin alphabet than we do, and have far more consistent spelling systems as a consequence. Blaming all our orthographic problems on the deficiencies of Latin is therefore a little short-sighted. To explain the remainder of our more troublesome spellings we need to turn not to the history of the English language, but to the history of England itself.

After 1066, as Norman scribes began to operate in a newly conquered England, a French-inspired *je ne sais quoi* was scattered throughout our orthography. As a result, Anglo-Saxon spelling practices were sidelined, and with no real means of reasserting their own preferences, there was little English speakers could do about the encroaching Norman influence. By the time their language finally began to reassert itself in the fourteenth and fifteenth centuries (Henry IV was the first king for 333 years to have spoken English as his first language) French influence on our language was well and truly in place.

This too immediately complicated matters. Whereas the spelling system of Old English had largely mirrored English pronunciation literally to the letter, the Norman writers had imposed even more Latin-inspired spelling conventions onto a language that effectively didn't suit them. Where once English had merely had *hus*, now there was *house*. Where once there had been *circe*, now there was *church*. And where there had been *niht*, now there was *night*. None of this had been standardised yet, however, and spelling choices remained largely the decision of individual writers. Consequently, by the medieval period, there was so much variation in our language that a single Middle English word could be found in multiple guises not just in the same document but in the same sentence. Even a word as mundane as *which* is found as *hwic, hwilc, hwilch, hwuch, huyche, quilc, quhilk, whiche, whilk, whillc, whyche, wilc, wilche, woche* and *wuch* in Middle English writing. Fortunately, this mind-boggling variation could not last forever, and the first steps towards a more standardised spelling system were just around the corner. Unfortunately, the timing could scarcely have been worse.

With the arrival of the printing press in England in the 1400s, the spelling system of Middle English finally had a chance to calm down. Documents were now capable of being mass produced – identically, time and again – and as the printed spellings were circulated repeatedly, handwritten scribal variation began to lose its stranglehold on our orthography. But the earliest gatekeepers of English printing proved in some ways just as idiosyncratic as the writers of the past, and they too exerted considerable influence on our spelling system – often at the expense of more straightforward options.

William Caxton, who brought the first press to England in 1476, had learned his trade in Bruges, and brought with him a staff of Belgian typesetters to help run his printworks in the City of Westminster. As they worked to produce new editions of the likes of Chaucer's *Canterbury Tales* and Aesop's *Fables*, continental influence began to creep back into English spelling – this time from Flemish and Dutch. It was this that famously led to an H being added to words such as *ghost* and *ghastly*: English and Flemish are linguistic cousins from the same West Germanic family of languages, and as Caxton's Flemish-speaking printing team naturally noticed similarities between the two vocabularies, they joined the dots between them with additions like this.

That's not to say all of Caxton's spelling choices were quite so eccentric. He recognised the confusion caused by the erraticism of Middle English in a translation of Virgil's *Aeneid* he printed in 1490.

Writing in the prologue, Caxton recounted a tale he had heard about a merchant ship sailing down the Thames that was forced to anchor in Kent when the wind suddenly dropped. The crew took the opportunity to head into the nearest village for provisions, where one of the men asked a local woman if he could buy some 'egges'. Despite them both being English, the woman somewhat puzzlingly answered that she could not speak French – which, in Caxton's words, angered the merchant, 'for he also coude speke no frenshe'. When another of the crew stepped in and asked if they could buy 'eyren', rather than eggs, 'the good wyf sayd that she understood hym wel'.

In Caxton's time, both *egg* (derived from Old Norse) and *ey* (the Anglo-Saxon word) were in use for precisely the same thing in different parts of England. 'What sholde a man in thyse dayes now wryte,' Caxton bemoaned, 'egges or eyren?' In an attempt to resolve this inconsistency, he implemented as standardised a spelling system as he could in the books he produced, ensuring the editions produced by his printworks at least matched one another as routinely as possible, even if the rest of the language did not. As other printers did the same, an increasingly fixed orthographic system gradually began to emerge in England and our spelling system finally settled down. It's just a shame it happened about 400 years too early. Around the time that our written language was becoming standardised by printed literature, our spoken language was in a deep and confusing state of flux.

The Great Vowel Shift was a curious series of phonological changes that was rolled out across English from the early fourteenth to the late seventeenth centuries. Quite why these changes took place is unclear (and their full impact and nature is far beyond the scope of this chapter). But, in essence, the vowel sounds of English shifted and drifted, with some simple sounds morphing into paired sounds, or diphthongs, and others changing in the way they were shaped or formed in the mouth. Among the earliest to change were our 'ee' and 'oo' sounds, which underwent a process known as vowel breaking, or diphthongisation, to become 'ai' and 'ow'. Later, some of our other vowels began to change too, shifting in how they were articulated via another process called vowel raising. 'Ay' shifted upwards in the mouth to become more like 'ee'. 'Oh' became more like 'oo'. And 'ah' became more like 'ay'.

These changes didn't happen concurrently, nor everywhere at the same time. And nor did they shift from one sound directly to the other, but instead went through a subtle series of incremental stages, all played out across more than 300 years of linguistic evolution. But with our spelling system still effectively frozen in Caxton's day, by the time these changes were complete – and English had settled into its so-called Early Modern form – many of our words no longer resembled their pronunciations. What had once been a straightforward association between orthography and phonology had been irreparably severed. And worse was yet to come.

By the 1700s, the Renaissance was well under way across Europe, and scholars and scientists began adopting countless classically inspired words into their vocabularies to describe the newly enlightened world in which they were now working. In English, this ushered in a third wave of continental influence, as more Latin and Greek terms and spelling conventions were adopted into the scientific and socio-political writing of the day. This new terminology sparked a fashion for imposing classical spelling rules onto existing English words, often in an attempt to lend an air of sophistication to straightforward Anglo-Saxonisms, or else to highlight etymological connections to much-venerated Latin and Greek. Unnecessary Bs were added to *debt* and *doubt* to show their descent from Latin *debitum* and *dubitare*. A C was added to *indict* to highlight its root in the Latin *dictare*. And a P was inserted into receipt to connect it with its ancestor, the Latin verb *recipere*. (Before then, these had simply been spelled *dette*, *dout*, *indite* and *receit*.*) As if these changes were not flawed enough, some of them proved entirely misguided. The name of the *ptarmigan* bird, for instance, gained a silent P in the seventeenth century as the writers of the day erroneously presumed it must have Greek roots, and derive from the Greek word for 'wing', *pteron* (the origin of *helicopter* and *pterodactyl*). In truth, *ptarmigan* comes from Gaelic, *tarmachan*, and has no connection to Greek whatsoever.

Taking all this upheaval into account, it's perhaps unsurprising that there have been several attempts to try to reform English orthography or introduce an updated (or, in some cases, entirely new) spelling system. Such luminaries as Benjamin Franklin, George Bernard Shaw and Isaac Pitman, the inventor of Pitman shorthand, all made suggestions along those lines in the eighteenth and nineteenth centuries, some of which were more radical than others. Franklin's suggestion, outlined in 1768, was that the letters C, J, Q, W, X and Y be dropped from the alphabet entirely, and replaced with six new characters of his own invention. A century later, in 1873, Pitman suggested much the same thing: he advocated ditching C, Q and X and adding no fewer than fifteen new letters in their place. And Shaw's idea was even more far-reaching. After his death in 1950, he left funding for the creation and introduction

---

* For a time, the P in *receipt* was added to its etymological cousins *conceit* and *deceit*. But in typically inconsistent fashion, it endured in only one of the three, leaving us with a mismatched set of spellings today.

of an entirely new alphabet, based on three demanding provisos: it must have at least forty letters; it must exhibit as close to a one-to-one, letter-to-sound correspondence as possible, and it must be entirely distinct from the existing Latin alphabet. Legal wrangling over the precise details of his request delayed the production of this so-called Shavian alphabet, but a winning design was finally chosen in the early 1960s; to mark the occasion, an edition of Shaw's play *Androcles and the Lion* was published entirely in Shavian in 1962. Unfortunately (though perhaps not unpredictably) the system failed to catch on.

Although an appetite for spelling reform remains thanks to dedicated organisations such as the English Spelling Society, few wholesale orthographic reforms have ever been accepted in our language. Arguably the most successful reformer was Noah Webster, who used the publication of his 1828 *American Dictionary of the English Language* to introduce many of the variant spellings – like *center, color* and *dialog* – that still divide British and American English today. Yet even he failed to see all his suggestions come to fruition, as American English speakers steadfastly refused to accept the spellings he advocated for words like *tung, dawter, masheen, wimmin, grotesk, porpess* and *beleev*. Despite all our problematic orthography, resistance to change runs deep.

That being said, it's not true that English is entirely averse to spelling reform. We saw in Q.1 how words like *website* and *email* have changed in recent years, and it's becoming equally rare to see hyphens inside words such as *cooperate* and *coordinate*. Some contemporary dictionaries even list the likes of *caligraphy, liquify, nickle, miniscule* and *dextrous* as acceptable alternatives to their more traditional spellings, *calligraphy, liquefy, nickel, minuscule* and *dexterous*.

It's also the case that while English spelling might be inconsistent, it is by no means random. True, some of our spelling rules certainly aren't among the most reliable of instructions given the number of words that break them (most famously 'I before E except after C'), but others are far more successful. That which demands Q always be followed by a U, for instance, works almost unfalteringly. But none of our other letters have such a singular strict law reinforcing their use – so where has this rule come from?

Much like the origin of our most inconsistent spellings, the roots of our *qu* convention lie at the very outset of our language. In the Old English period, when spelling much more reliably reflected pronunciation than it does today, words like *queen*, *quick*, *quake* and *quell* were spelled with a simple *cw*– pairing, giving us *cwen*, *cwic*, *cwac* and *cwell*. Originally, the letter Q wasn't used in English at all, but after the Norman Conquest a French convention of using *qu* to represent the 'kw' sound was rolled out, ousting the older *cw* spelling and turning it into yet another casualty of the Norman scribes' distaste for Anglo-Saxon orthography.*

French had adopted this *qu* convention from Latin, which had in turn picked up its letter Q from the Etruscan alphabet. The Etruscans, who had inherited their lettering system from the Euboean Greeks, ended up with three different letter forms used to represent the 'k' sound: a slanted C-like form of the letter gamma (<), the K-shaped Greek kappa (K), and a final Q-shaped letter qoppa (Ϙ). That

---

* Just as the pronunciation of English later changed, so too did the pronunciation of French, which later reduced its 'kw' sound down to a simple 'k'. For that reason, words that were adopted into English *after* that change took place – including *etiquette*, *mystique*, *bouquet*, *antique* and *unique* – are likewise pronounced with a 'k' sound in English, despite being spelled with a *qu*.

allowed them to introduce a three-way distinction in their writing: C-shaped gamma was used when the following vowel was either an 'e' or 'i'; K-shaped kappa was used when the vowel afterwards was an 'a'; and qoppa was set aside for use before an 'u' sound. This three-tier arrangement was adopted into the very earliest Latin texts too, but the system gradually simplified and C came to be used in most iterations of the 'k' sound in Latin. The use of Q to represent 'k' when it formed part of a 'kw' sound, however, was maintained, and was eventually passed on to French and then English.

So the association between Q and U was introduced from French, which took it from Latin, which in turn adopted it from a convention used by the Etruscans around 3,000 years ago. It is ultimately one of our oldest traceable spelling conventions – but even this rule is not entirely watertight. Today, English contains several words that break it. Clipped forms, like *tranq* (for 'tranquilliser') and *freq* (for 'frequency') have abandoned their Us because they would be all but redundant in their contexts. The jumbled arrangement of lettered keys of a keyboard has given us the U-less word *qwerty*. And such is the sponge-like nature of English to absorb words from other languages that our dictionaries now list such bizarre-looking words as *umiaq* (an Inuit canoe), *qiviut* (the wool of the muskox), *qindar* (the currency of Albania), *qanat* (an underground water conduit in Middle Eastern countries) and – ironically enough – the name of the letter *qoppa* itself. Admittedly, however, the vast majority of these rule-breaking words are borrowings from other languages, which don't follow the orthographic rules of English simply because they're not subject to them. If we leave exceptions such as these to one side, then this most ancient of spelling rules remains one of our most reliable.

Q. 13

Why Do We Have
Double Letters?

He put so many unnecessary letters into short words,
that they sometimes quite lost their English appearance.

Charles Dickens, *Bleak House* (1852)

As English speakers, we tend to accept double letters as just another quirk of our sprawling, chaotic language. There were two pairs of them in that last sentence and you probably didn't give them a second thought. It's certainly true that double letters don't tend to cause us too many problems, and their presence in many words is often perfectly logical, if not unavoidable. Compound words often contain double letters simply from being built from two shorter words that share a common boundary, as in *bathhouse* or *coattails*. The same applies to words formed using prefixes and suffixes, which can produce accidental pairings like those in *unnoticed* and *shelfful*. We often use doubles to flag the difference between long and short vowels in English, creating neat duos such as *met* and *meet*, and *rot* and *root*. And then there's the so-called Three-Letter Rule – a curiosity of our spelling system that demands all our content words – nouns and verbs – have at least three letters, while our function words – pronouns and prepositions – need not. That rule not only explains why so many of our function words appear so puny (*a, I, he, it, of*), but why so many of our shortest words seem so unnecessarily bulked out (*egg, bee, ill, ebb, inn*).*

Examples such as these are easy to account for, and their spellings unlikely to be fumbled. Drop an H from *bathhouse*, for instance, and you'll end up with a house full of chiropterans, not bathtubs. But in words whose structures aren't quite so transparent, double letters can prove more troublesome, if not a little counterintuitive. As we've established, letters are the written representations of sounds – so if P makes a 'p' sound, why have two of them in *apple*? And if two Os make an 'ooh' sound, why doesn't *good* rhyme with *mood*? Couldn't we just spell it *gud* and be done with it? Add to that all our seemingly idiosyncratic double-letter spellings – *accommodate, questionnaire, embarrassed* – and wouldn't everything just be a lot easier without them?

It's tempting to think so, and indeed many of the reformers mentioned in Q.12 advocated ridding our language of them as a means of simplifying this most impractical of quirks. Just because a word

---

* Despite the Three-Letter Rule being a popular teaching aid among English learners, it's really more of a quirky observation than a solid, verifiable rule. In fact, English has plenty of two-letter nouns and verbs (*be, go, ox*) and just as many noticeably lengthy function words (*because, therefore, themselves*). Nonetheless the rule does have some sound thinking behind it: frequently used words do tend to be kept short in most languages, while many content words have been artificially bulked over time so that they hold their own a little more when dropped into a sentence.

has an odd or difficult spelling, however, doesn't mean that spelling can't be justified.

At the centre of *accommodate*, for instance, is the Latin word *modus*, meaning a measure or proportion. To that was added the prefix *com*–, used here to intensify the meaning of the root word. Added to that in turn was the prefix *ac*–, a form of the Latin *ad*, meaning 'to' or 'towards', used to build words bearing some sense of doing something purposefully or entirely. Altogether, that produced the Latin verb *accommodare*, which was adopted into English as *accommodate* in the sixteenth century. And just as *bath* + *house* makes *bathhouse*, *ac* + *com* + *modus* gives us a word containing two Cs and two Ms.

The sandwiching of one morphological element to another in this way can produce double letters in English even if the actual *x* + *y* process itself occurred centuries before. *Innocent* contains two Ns because it comes from *in*– + *nocere* (Latin for 'to harm'), but *inoculate* contains only one, because it is built from *in*– + *oculus* ('eye'). *Accident* comes from *ac*– + *cadere* ('to fall') but *recommend* comes from *re*– + *commendare* ('to entrust'). Understanding the arrangement of word-building elements can prove the key to unlocking many of our otherwise infuriatingly irrational spellings.

Justifying double letters like this is one thing, but whether or not we should still tolerate them in our language today is another. Yes, *accommodate* contains two pairs of double letters because its Latin morphology just so happened to place them there – but do we really need to maintain those letters in English, all these centuries later? What would happen if we just abandoned double letters altogether? If we just folowed the ideas of the speling reformers, and simply stoped using leter pairs? There are over 80,000 words in this book, containing more than 4,000 pairs of double letters. Think how much time, space, paper and ink could be saved if we simply excised them from our spelling system altogether.

It's a compelling idea, certainly, but a flawed one. Double letters might seem an unnecessary nuisance, but beneath the surface of our language they're often playing a much more meaningful role than we might ever have realised, and without them our comprehension of written English would be hugely impaired.

Take a pair of words such as *later* and *latter*. They share the same etymology, and both essentially refer to one thing being subsequent to another. But they are very different words: only *later* can be used to mean 'more late', while *latter* is typically used to specify the second or ultimate of a set of choices. Confusing the two can consequently prove ungrammatical – or, worse still, alter what you intend to mean entirely:

We can take the 4 p.m. train or the 3 p.m. bus, but we'd prefer the later.
We can take the 4 p.m. train or the 3 p.m. bus, but we'd prefer the latter.

Despite these differences, the entwined etymologies of *later* and *latter* have left them almost identical in our language today, with their only obvious difference being the pronunciation of their vowels: *latter* takes a short 'a', while *later* has a longer 'ay'. In writing, however, it's not the A that bears this distinction out, but the T.

What's going on here – and in countless more English words – is illustrative of a well-established spelling convention that uses doubled consonants to flag an immediately preceding short vowel. *Later* vs *latter*. *Ruder* vs *rudder*. *Coma* vs *comma*. *Super* vs *supper*. *Diner* vs *dinner*. Time and again, double letters follow short vowels in English, and every time this convention comes into play, it ensures we recognise and pronounce our words correctly, and avoid muddling up words that could otherwise be identical.

The link between double consonants in writing and short vowel sounds in speech is so potent that it even underpins some of our most fundamental spelling rules. The so-called 1-1-1 rule dictates that words comprising one syllable, containing one short vowel, in front of one final consonant, must double that consonant when a suffix is added to them. So *slim*, with its short 'i' and its single final M, forms double-M derivatives including *slimming* and *slimmer* to highlight that its vowel sound remains unchanged. Likewise *fit*, *shop*, *hem*, *jog* and *grin* form the derivatives *fitting*, *shopper*, *hemming*, *jogger* and *grinned*. If this rule didn't come into play, these short vowels could all easily be misinterpreted as long (and you might inadvertently end up joining a dubious-sounding organisation called Sliming World).

A similar rule doubles the final consonant of two-syllable verbs containing a short vowel. So *admit*, *regret*, *deter* and *forget* form *admitting*, *regretted*, *deterrence* and *forgetting*. It's this rule too that accounts for the double letters in troublesome words such as *beginning*, *occurring* and *preferred*.

Admittedly, this being English we're dealing with, these 'short vowel = double consonant' rules don't operate everywhere. Only vowel-initial suffixes, such as *–ing* and *–ed*, trigger this doubling process, and words that already end in two consonants, like *walk* or *jump*, are exempt too. But the number of instances in which these rules do apply is vast, and accounts for a great many of the double letters you'll encounter in our language. It's why things that are fun are *funny*. It's why female gods are *goddesses*. It's why nuns live in *nunneries*, and pigs live in *piggeries*. It's why we play *cribbage*, say good *riddance*, and have *scrummages*, *stoppages* and *slippages*. It's why we *madden*, *sadden* and *gladden* when we become mad, sad and glad. And it even explains why *Star Trek* fans are *Trekkies* and *Trekkers*. In fact, the association between double letters and short vowels is so deeply ingrained in our mental rulebooks that we even apply it to words we've only just encountered. You won't know what the word *zwotting* means, because I've just made it up – but I bet you rhymed it with *rotting*, not *voting*, because those two consecutive Ts tell your brain to interpret the O in front of them as a short vowel, not a long one.

Whether we knew it was there or not, the association between double consonants and short vowels in English is clearly a well-established one. So where did it come from? Oddly, the answer lies in a feature that fell out of use in our language nearly a thousand years ago.

In the Old English period, our language marked not only a distinction between long and short vowel sounds, but long and short consonants too. Such sounds were called geminates, and the long-forgotten process that created them was gemination.

Strictly speaking, these geminate consonants weren't lengthened in the same way that we can lengthen a vowel sound such as 'oh' or an 'ah' in English today (not least because it's all but impossible to prolong an unprolongable sound, such as 't' or 'p'.) Instead, these consonants were essentially duplicated, with the resulting pair of consonants pronounced individually. (The word *gemination* itself literally means a 'pairing', and comes from the same etymological root as the zodiacal twins, *Gemini*).

As English abandoned gemination long ago, this can be a difficult concept to comprehend, but the same effect is unintentionally produced today when two identical consonants happen to fall together at the boundary of neighbouring words. Compare the single 'd' sound in the words *redder* or *ladder*, for example, with the pair of 'd' sounds that meet in *red door* or *lead door*. Or think about how you pronounce the word *layman* as opposed to the near-identical *lame man*. Notice a slightly lengthened, almost stutter-like hold in those second examples? That's gemination.

It's a subtle difference, certainly, but in many of the languages that still employ it, gemination can prove the only distinguishing factor between two otherwise identical words. The Italian word for 'ball', for instance, is *palla*, with a geminated 'l' sound split across its two syllables, 'PAL-*la*'. But *pala*, pronounced with an ungeminated 'l', 'PA-*la*', is the Italian word for a shovel. Not articulating the difference between the two could easily cause confusion, especially if you happen to work for an Italian gardener.

Like a lot of the European languages that still feature gemination today, Italian is a descendant of Latin, and it has been the convention in Latinate languages to represent geminated consonants with double letters for over 2,000 years; the technique is popularly said to have been introduced by the Roman poet Quintus Ennius in the second century BCE. Before then, Latin geminates tended to be written either as a single letter (regardless of any potential confusion or ambiguity) or else were signposted with a tiny sickle-shaped symbol called a *sicilicus*, ('), drawn above the consonant in question. Neither method proved particularly reliable, as effectively ignoring the gemination by using a single letter could lead to identical words being misinterpreted, while a tiny sicilicus could easily be omitted or go unnoticed in cramped or untidy text. Ennius's letter-doubling technique solved both these problems by flagging geminated consonants much more visibly. The solution caught on quickly – even in languages not directly descended from Latin.

As a Germanic language, English might have been expected to have remained unaffected by Ennius's innovations. But when the Germanic family switched from their runic alphabet to the Roman ABCs, many Latin spelling conventions came with them. Geminate sounds in the Germanic languages consequently began to be represented with double letters, and when English split from its Germanic ancestors this linguistic heirloom was passed on from ancestor to offspring. Old English *æppel* ('apple'), *sunne* ('sun') and *readda* ('robin') all came to be spelled with double letters, as they maintained the geminated 'p', 'n' and 'd' sounds of their Germanic forebear. Meanwhile, the broader phonological rules of the West Germanic languages permitted these geminate consonants to fall only after short vowels,* and so this rule – coupled with the ancient spelling

---

* A full explanation of why West Germanic geminate consonants only ever appeared after short vowels – or, for that matter, why gemination even occurred at all in the Germanic language family – could fill another book, let alone a footnote. But here, at least, is a summary. When Europe's Proto-Germanic branch of Proto-Indo-European first began to split into its constituent North, East and West Germanic branches sometime around 500, in the West Germanic branch in particular – the branch from which English would later emerge – words that in Proto-Germanic had contained (a) a short vowel followed by (b) a single consonant, in turn followed by (c) a 'y' sound began to be pronounced with that single central consonant, (b), doubled or geminated. There are two theories as to why this happened (driven by rivalling explanations of how the syllables in Proto-Germanic words were arranged), but what matters here is the outcome: as the West Germanic languages developed, these newly formed geminate sounds only ever appeared where there had once been a preceding short vowel, (a). The Proto-Germanic word *bidjana*, for example, became *biddijan* in West Germanic, with a new central pair of 'd' sounds following a short 'i'. As West Germanic morphed into Old English in Anglo-Saxon England, *biddijan* became *biddan*, and initially maintained its geminate 'd'. After gemination was lost from English, *biddan* further simplified to *bid* – the word that remains in

rules of Ennius's Latin poetry – created an association between short vowels and double-letter spellings that lives on in English today and, moreover, in your English-speaking brain without you even knowing about it.

English no longer tolerates geminated consonants today, of course. As our language continued to develop, the precise articulation of these consonant pairs began to slacken, and the two neighbouring 'p' sounds in *æppel*, along with many more pairings like them, coalesced. Gemination essentially proved too onerous to maintain and fell by the linguistic wayside as our language continued on its unending march towards simplification – but, by then, permanent damage had been done. The boom in written and later printed literature in the late Middle English period circulated and standardised many of the older double-letter spellings in our written language so that they survived in text long after the phonological process that had originally motivated them had been abandoned. *Apple* ultimately kept its double P.

Around the same time our language was abandoning its Old English geminates, however, its vocabulary was expanding. The Norman Conquest had essentially doubled the English vocabulary overnight and opened the floodgates to greater French and Latin influence than ever before. New words, spellings and sounds – many never heard or used in English before – soon fell into use, and in response to all this upheaval even some of our older and more established words began to change. That presented the writers (and, later, printers) of medieval England with an old problem, as the alphabet

---

use in our language today. The spectre of our geminated past still lingers on, however, in irregular double-letter derivatives including *unbidden* and *forbidden*.

at their disposal was again no longer exhaustive enough to represent the full range of sounds now being used.

One solution could have been to adopt or invent new letters or symbols to get around this shortfall, or even fall back on our Germanic past and resurrect some of our runic characters, as we had done earlier with eth and wynn. But under the influence of Norman scribes reluctant to use any obvious Anglo-Saxonisms, the writers of the day turned to simpler solutions and tried-and-tested conventions to make up the deficit. And doubling a consonant to signpost a short vowel was just one of the rules they recycled.

So not only was this convention employed long after gemination had been discarded, but it was actively redeployed onto new words, including many that had never been geminated in the first place. Old English *butere*, for instance, became *butter*. It had not undergone gemination in Old English, but later writers nevertheless doubled its T to signal that its preceding 'uh' vowel was short. Likewise, *cetil* became *kettle*. *Sumor* became *summer*. *Ganot* became *gannet*. *Otor* became *otter*. *Popig* became *poppy*, and *pipor* became *pepper*. Far from ridding our language of double letters, the spelling rules of the time proliferated them and established many new pairings where historically there had been none. And once those spellings were in place – along with the long-established conventions that underpinned them – our long-standing unwillingness to update our spelling system has maintained them ever since.

Q. 14

Does Anything Rhyme
with Orange?

The second James a daughter had,
Too fine to lick a porringer;
He sought her out a noble lad,
And gave the Prince of Orange her.

Anonymous, c. 1800s

Somewhere in this book, there is a pangram. That is to say, one of the sentences here contains all twenty-six letters of the alphabet, like *The quick brown fox jumped over the lazy dog*. And no, it's not that one – that's just an example. In fact, I'm not going to tell you where it is. I'm not even going to tell you whether you've already read it or not. But it's in here somewhere, as a little bonus. Just for fun.

And that's the point here – fun. Wordplay and word games show how language has now far outstepped its origins as a tool of communication, and strayed into the realms of creativity, curiosity and entertainment. Not that this is anything new, of course. For as long as we have written evidence of language, we have evidence of writers playing with language. The Sumerians saw meaning in inventing punning nicknames for the gods of Mesopotamia some 5,000 years ago or so.* Greek poets used to secrete their names into their works as acrostics so that the first letters of successive lines spelled them out as a kind of copyright trap for would-be plagiarists. The Romans were so astounded by the cleverness of the Sator Square – a five-by-five Latin word square, SATOR AREPO TENET OPERA ROTAS – that it became the meme of its day and has been found scrawled on the ruins of their empire everywhere from Syria to Cirencester. And puns, homophones and soundalike words were even used as a means of interpreting dreams in antiquity. Dreaming of a raven (*arbu*) in Babylonia was said to foretell an increase in income (*irbu*). Dreaming of a pea (*pisos*) in Ancient Greece signified confidence (*pistis*). And dreaming of a harp (*bjnt*) was considered unlucky to the Egyptians, because it sounded so much like 'evil' (*bjn*) – while dreaming of baring your backside (*pḥwj*) was just as ill-fated because the same word could signify a person heading towards the 'rear end' of their life.

In English, the Elizabethan poet John Taylor is credited with writing one of the earliest palindromic sentences in 1613, capitalising on the ampersand's erstwhile place in our alphabet to pen *Lewd did I live & evil I did dwel*. (A modern equivalent, which still works

---

* There is even a theory that the story of Eve being created from Adam's rib in the Garden of Eden is based on a Sumerian pun, which influenced the creation myth of ancient Mesopotamia. In Sumerian, the words 'life' and 'rib' were homonyms, *ti*. The reason the first woman was created from the first man's rib is because 'rib' happened to be lexically identical to life itself. The pun was lost when the story was passed on and recorded in the Hebrew of the Old Testament, and the punning cleverness of a millennia-old bit of wordplay has since disappeared.

forwards and backwards, is 'Evil I did dwell, lewd did I live'.) In the correspondence-driven newspapers of the eighteenth and nineteenth centuries, a trend emerged for challenging fellow readers to word-hunting conundrums, such as naming the three English words ending –*amt* and –*cion*, the adjectives ending in –*dous*, or the words containing –*nkst*– and –*shion*–. A version still popular today is to name the three words ending in –*gry*. (Answers to all those can be found on page 275.) Some of the earliest collections of tongue-twisters appeared in the 1800s too, with Peter Piper taking centre stage in an alphabetical anthology of nonsense verse in 1813, alongside a host of less-well-remembered characters, like Andrew Airpump, Francis Fribble, and Quixote Quicksight. And nineteenth-century England also saw the publication of surely one of the oddest collections of poetic wordplay: an anonymous set of verses entitled *Uncle, Can You Find a Rhyme for Orange?*

Published in 1869, each of the book's four-line poems was an attempt to engineer a rhyming partner for our language's most notoriously unrhymable word, *orange*. It opens with this introductory verse, setting the tone for what lies ahead:

> *Fair reader, here do I of thoughts*
> *A new and old depot range*
> *Side by side, truth, fable, fun,*
> *Come, pri'thee, taste my Orange.*

The remaining poems follow a similar template, with ever more devious contrivances set up to rhyme with *orange*, which remains the last word of each verse. Among the candidates on offer are 'low cringe', 'sore twinge', 'Stow Grange', 'trapdoor hind and fore hinge', 'on the banks of the Po range', and 'Mont Blanc, beyond the snow range'. Others are even more outlandish:

> *Without you, what is wealth? or life?*
> *A blank – oh! aid me, or ang-*
> *ina pectoris will end*
> *My taste for rhyming orange.*

As contrived as they may be, the book nevertheless contains over a hundred poems like this, each seemingly achieving the poetically impossible: rhyming something with *orange*.

If you were to look *orange* up in a rhyming dictionary, of course, it's unlikely *angina pectoris* would be among the suggested possibilities. For that matter, if I were to tell you the answer to the question in the title of this chapter was *trapdoor fore-hinge*, you'd be forgiven for hurling this book in the bin. The reason why *Uncle, Can You Find a Rhyme for Orange?* succeeds in finding so many *orange* rhymes is that there are so many different methods of forming rhymes in the first place – yet not all of them work as precisely as others, and not all would be considered a true rhyme.

The *angina* example, for instance, is a so-called split rhyme – a poetic device in which a word or set of words is splintered across successive lines of verse (a technique called enjambment) so that only a fragment of it is drawn into the rhyme itself. The *fore-hinge* example is a mosaic rhyme, in which separate words are coupled together to construct a match. The likes of *twinge* and *cringe* – words that are vaguely similar enough to work as a rhyme within the confines of a poem but are not exactly identical to the one we want – are variously known as imperfect rhymes, slant rhymes or pararhymes. And poets and writers often exploit eye rhymes, which look as if they should match on the written page but aren't quite so closely allied when read aloud, such as *grange* and *orange*. None of these would typically find its way onto the pages of a standard rhyming dictionary, and nor would any make a suitable answer to the question we're posing here. So what exactly do we mean when we say that two words rhyme?

To avoid filling their pages with endless half rhymes and mosaic rhymes and *low cringes* and *Po ranges*, rhyming dictionaries typically limit themselves to standard dictionary words and pronunciations, and list only so-called perfect or full rhymes – that is, seamless sound-by-sound matches. And when we think of words that rhyme, it's usually this kind of perfect match that we have in mind.

The standard used by most British English dictionaries is Received Pronunciation, or RP – the basic yardstick of spoken Standard British English. Naturally, the same isn't true elsewhere, and disparities between different global standards can often prove significant. American English dictionaries, for instance, typically use a General American or GA standard, and based on that will tell you *iron*, pronounced with a heavy 'r' sound, has no rhymes except derivatives like *gridiron* and *flatiron*. In RP, however, *iron* doesn't have the same hard 'r' as in an American accent, so a British rhyming dictionary will quite happily match it with the likes of *cyan*, *Mayan*, *lion*, *Ryan* and *Paraguayan*. American poets could certainly engineer a rhyme for *iron*, along the same lines as *fore hinge* or *sore twinge*, but so convoluted an invention would not be valid here, nor make it into a dictionary. Here, only perfect rhymes matter.

For two words to form a perfect rhyme, by definition their final stressed syllables need to contain the same vowel sound, and all the other sounds *after* it – right up to the end of the word – need to be identical too.* Even the slightest deviation from that template will ruin the rhyme and leave the two simply not close enough to count as a perfect match. So *jeepers* rhymes with *creepers* because they both share the same stressed vowel (that central 'ee'), plus everything that comes after it (the subsequent *–pers*). They don't rhyme with *dippers* or *drapers* because, despite their identical second syllables, the vowels in their first syllables are different. They might work as pararhymes and make a perfectly serviceable match in a poem, but for the purposes of rhyming one word with another they're just not close enough. So, with that definition in mind, is there a perfect rhyme for *orange*?

Working back from the end of the word, the final stressed vowel in *orange* is its initial 'oh' sound. To find a perfect rhyme for it we therefore need a word that shares that 'oh', plus everything else that follows it – namely, the awkward-sounding 'runj' of *–range*. A great many words that are often touted as rhymes for *orange* simply don't work based on that outline. *Lozenge* is scuppered by the switch from 'r' to 'z'. *Syringe* has an 'i' where *orange* has an 'oh' and an 'uh'. *Binge* is missing that stressed 'oh' and the 'r'. And *door hinge* is a near miss too, ruined by its 'h' and 'i'. (Perhaps in time a closed compound, *doorhinge*, might come to be reduced to something like 'dorringe' in spoken English, but we'd all have to start talking an awful lot more about door hinges before we see that kind of change take place.) Ultimately, in a standard

---

* Strictly speaking, for a truly perfect rhyme, the sounds immediately in front of the stressed vowel – the 'r' and 't' of *rhyme* and *time* – need to be different too. If they were to match, as in *rhyme* and *rime*, or *time* and *thyme*, we wouldn't have a perfect rhyme, but a so-called tautological rhyme, which some writers claim isn't a rhyme at all. The same goes for words whose rhymes are entirely subsumed by other words – we could not, for instance, claim *rhythm* rhymes with *algorithm*, because regardless of the extra material in *algorithm*, the part that actually rhymes is still the same.

English dictionary, at least, it's true that the combination of sounds that make up the word *orange* is simply so unusual that nothing else matches it and the word has no perfect rhymes. Cast our net a little further, however, and there is a handful of more obscure matches.

The Blorenge is the name of a hill near Abergavenny in southeast Wales. Henry Honychurch Gorringe was the American naval officer who oversaw the transportation of Cleopatra's Needle from Egypt to New York in 1880. And *sporange* – an obsolete form of *sporangium*, a spore-producing structure in ferns, mosses, and fungi – is sometimes proposed as a rhyme for *orange*, although on the rare occasions it needs to be read aloud, it tends to be stressed on its second syllable ('*spuh*-RANJ'), not its first (making it a better match for *flange* than *orange*).

Whether obscure proper nouns and obsolete botanical terminology count as feasible matches is up to you. You probably wouldn't find *Blorenge* or *Gorringe* listed in a standard dictionary (and even if they were, it would be a challenge to fit a Welsh mountain or a nineteenth-century naval officer into a poem about oranges).* But these words nevertheless exist in our language and match the tail end

---

* Naturally, that didn't stop the author of *Uncle, Can You Find a Rhyme for Orange?*:

> *Not so – we'll roam thro' Cambria's vales,*
>   *And Snowdon's heights we'll o'er range;*
> *And when we reach its summit, say*
>   *Delicious is this orange.*
>
> *Then round by Cader's glorious steeps,*
>   *And beautiful Mount Blorenge,*
> *And here and there we'll sweetly quaff*
>   *Our Claret cup, with orange.*

of *orange* perfectly. It might involve widening our goalposts but there are in fact a handful of perfect rhymes for *orange*. And nor is it alone.

So long as you're happy to raid the more obscure corners of our language, a great many words that are often said to be unrhymable (or 'refractory', as they are more properly known) actually do have rhymes. *Wasp* rhymes with *cosp*, the metal hasp that locks a gate. *Filth* rhymes with *spilth*, the quantity of a substance that has been spilled. *Bulb* rhymes with *culb*, a seventeenth-century word for a sharp, cutting reply. *Silver* rhymes with *chilver*, a thousand-year-old word for a ewe-lamb. *Purple* rhymes with *hirple* (to walk awkwardly), *curple* (a Scots word for the encircling leather strap or crupper around a horse's saddle) and *turple* (a Yorkshire dialect word meaning to perish). *Beige* rhymes with *greige*, the colour of undyed fabric. And *circus* rhymes with *murcous*, a seventeenth-century medical adjective (should you ever require it) describing a person's hand that is missing a thumb.

Despite even our sizeable vocabulary, however, a lot of our words still don't have workable rhymes – among them *ninth*, *spoilt*, *scarce*, *pierced*, *oblige*, *carpet*, *penguin*, *month*, *dynamo*, *liquid* and *breadth*. So just how rare are unrhymable words?

The answer to that again rests on our definition of a rhyme. Because perfect rhymes require their final stressed vowel plus everything after it to correspond, the further back from the end of a word that vowel is located, logically the more complex its rhyming tail becomes, and the more the chances of finding a perfect match for it diminish. While a handful of monosyllabic words, like *month* and *scarce*, simply contain too troublesome a combination of sounds for anything to match them, in some longer polysyllabic words, the stress is positioned so far back that its rhyming tail unavoidably extends to an unmatchable extent. So whereas in *orange* the stress falls on the penultimate or second-last syllable (O-*range*), in *dynamo* it falls on the antepenultimate, or second from last syllable (DY-*na-mo*), making its rhyming ending, –*ynamo*, much more complicated. The same goes for other antepenult words including *seminar*, *ambulance*, *recipe*, *interface*, *fantasy*, *corridor* and *velocity*, none of which have perfect rhymes in English. But then, you could always concoct something if need be:

> *Having once gained the summit, and managed to cross it, he*
> *Rolls down the side with uncommon velocity.*

Thomas Ingoldsby,
The Ingoldsby Legends (1837)

Not all words with early stress like this are unrhymable. *Minister* rhymes with *sinister*. *Jealousy* rhymes with *prelacy*. *Bicycle* rhymes with *tricycle*. And even a word as complicated as *constabulary* – which has preantepenultimate, or third-from-last stress – rhymes with *vocabulary*. The only problem here is that if you were to use any of these words in a poem, these would be the only perfect rhymes on offer: all of these are so-called closed pairings – that is, words that, thanks to the limits of our language and the complexity of their structures, rhyme with only one another and absolutely nothing else.

Following the rules of perfect rhymes then, perhaps unrhymable words are not as rare as we might think. If we're willing to expand our search for rhymes into far more obscure fare, a great many trickily structured and seemingly unmatchable words can in fact be paired up. How useful those pairings are in practical and poetic terms, however, perhaps rests on little more than the inventiveness and sheer determination of our poets.

Q. 15

Why Do Our Words Go in the Order They Do?

Good prose is the selection of the best words;
poetry is the best words in the best order; and
journalese is any old words in any old order.

Anonymous letter to *The Times* (1987)

I magine we had a rule in English that required the subject of a sentence (that is, the main person or thing in control of the action) always had to be flagged by adding *–sub* onto the end of it. *The dog-sub chased the cat. The prince-sub killed the dragon.* Now imagine we had another rule requiring the object of a sentence (the person or thing at the receiving end of the action) had to be flagged with *–ob.* *The dog-sub chased the cat-ob. The prince-sub killed the dragon-ob.* It would soon prove a tiresome way of going about things, admittedly, but in simple terms this is the principle behind grammatical case.

Case is a feature of language that deals with how the different parts of a sentence function in relation to one another. Sentences are surprisingly complex things, after all. We might think of them as little more than strings of words but knowing what the words in a sentence mean isn't enough on its own to understand what's going on. Knowing that *dog*, *cat* and *chase* mean 'canine animal', 'feline animal' and 'pursue at speed' is one thing, but in a meaningful sentence we also need to know who or what has chased what or whom. Every sentence we produce is therefore a balancing act between the meanings of its words and the relationships between them – or, in more technical terms, between its semantics and its syntax. Fail to align those two correctly, and you simply won't communicate the right idea. If a canine animal had pursued a feline animal at speed, we could say *The dog chased the cat*, but not *The cat chased the dog*; even though the semantic information ('canine animal', 'feline animal', 'pursue at speed') is the same, the syntactic relationship (how the dog relates to the cat) is different.

Case helps us signpost relationships like these more clearly – put another way, it is case that tells us who or what has done what to whom. Each role in a sentence, such as subject or object, has its corresponding case. The subject is in the nominative case. The object is in the accusative case. And just like our *prince-sub* and *dragon-ob* example, many languages flag these roles overtly, using inflections or affixes, so that the words taking on each role in a sentence can be spotted easily. In German, for instance, the prince would be *der Prinz* if he were the subject of a sentence – but if the story had a less happy ending and he were the object, he would be *den Prinzen*:

Der Prinz tötete den Drachen	The prince killed the dragon
Der Drache tötete den Prinzen	The dragon killed the prince

Of the languages that flag case in this way, many have a much more complex system than just *subs* and *obs*. German has four cases in total: the nominative and accusative are joined by a third genitive case, to show possession, and a fourth dative case to show the indirect object of a sentence (the person or thing less actively involved in the action). So if *The prince gave the princess a kiss* after slaying the dragon, the thing being given (*the kiss*) would be in the accusative case, while the person less directly involved (*the princess*) would be in the dative.

Latin complicated things further with a fifth ablative case (used for whatever part of a sentence shows with, from, while or by which something happened), plus a sixth vocative case (used when someone is named or called on directly*). Older forms of Latin had a seventh locative case, used for places and locations. Sanskrit has eight cases. Basque has fourteen. Hungarian has eighteen. Tsez, a language of the Caucasus Mountains, is said to have over sixty. These numbers climb so high because many languages use case to flag roles in their sentences far beyond just the subject and the object. Czech has an instrumental case, used to show how or with what a verb is performed – so the Czech word for 'pen', *pero*, would become *perem* if you were to write *with* a pen. Basque has a terminative case, used to show progression up to or just as far as something – the Basque word for river, *ibai*, would turn into *ibairaino* if you were to talk about walking *up to* a riverbank. And Finnish goes several steps further with a half-dozen locational cases called the inessive, illative, elative, adessive, allative and, as with Latin, the ablative. A word like *kaappi*, 'cupboard', can therefore be inflected

---

* If the movie *Dude, Where's My Car?* were made in Ancient Rome, then 'dude' would have been declined in the vocative case. English does not utilise the vocative case at all, but the influence of Latin can be seen in a handful of stock phrases and titles, like *O ye of little faith* – a biblical quote in which *ye* was used to translate the Latin vocative. Bach's famous chorale *Jesu, Joy of Man's Desiring* is so named because *Jesu* is the vocative declension of the name Jesus.

to show whether what you're talking about is inside a cupboard (*kaapissa*), being put into a cupboard (*kaappiin*), being taken out of a cupboard (*kaapista*), is on top of a cupboard (*kaapilla*), being put onto a cupboard (*kaapille*), or being removed from the top of a cupboard (*kaapilta*). It was a similar set-up that made the grammar of Armenian such a formidable challenge for Lord Byron.

Given how complex it can clearly be, perhaps we're lucky that English scarcely recognises case at all. The only words we alter in response to it are our pronouns – so if *I* were to say something, that would be different from something being said to *me*, or my words being *mine*. *I*, *me* and *mine* all refer to the same person, but the pronoun used to refer to me changes depending on my role in the sentence. Apart from our pronouns, the rest of our language remains largely unchanged in different cases, so that if *the dog* and *the cat* were to swap roles, the words themselves would look the same. *The cat chased the dog*. Were we to do the same with a sentence built from pronouns, however, the words would have to be replaced. *She chased him* would become *He chased her*, not *Him chased she*. In fact, failing to match a pronoun to the appropriate case is what lies behind common grammatical slip-ups such as *You and me are going* and *He told you and I*.

We might not have much of an overt case system in English today, but historically that wasn't— well, the case. Old English had five cases, and altered its nouns, adjectives and articles in response to them as well as its pronouns. Even a word as simple as 'the', *se*, had no fewer than eleven different iterations across Old English's three genders (masculine, feminine, neuter) and five cases (nominative, accusative, genitive, dative, instrumental).

The nominative, accusative and genitive of Old English live on as the subjective, objective and possessive cases of Modern English (albeit in the pronouns-only way we now recognise them*). The dative and the instrumental have long since fallen by the grammatical wayside; in fact, the instrumental case was already on its way out when the English language first emerged 1,500 years ago and was seldom used even in the earliest Anglo-Saxon texts. So what happened? Why did we abandon so much of our case system? Why do so many other languages have such a complex array of grammatical cases? And what does all this have to do with how the words in our sentences are ordered? For that, we need to return to our dogs and cats and princes and dragons.

As daft as *The dog-sub chased the cat-ob* sounded, it proved a point: if we really were to flag the different parts of a sentence overtly in this way, theoretically we could put them in any order we wanted. Even if we were to say something as topsy-turvy as *Chased the dog-sub the cat-ob*, we would still know it was the dog that had chased the cat, because the dog is still marked as the subject. Likewise, were we to say *The dragon-ob killed the prince-sub*, or *Killed the prince-sub the dragon-ob*, we'd still know the prince was safe and the dragon slain, despite the individual parts of the sentence being mixed up.

Some languages allow the components of their sentences to be moved around like this. In Russian, the ordinary order of a sentence is the same as in English, subject–verb–object (SVO), but the rules of

---

* The genitive case of Old English was typically marked by attaching *–es* onto the end of the noun in question – so the Old English word for 'prince', *æþeling*, would become *æþelinges*, essentially meaning 'belonging to', or 'of the prince'. As our language evolved, this *–es* ending was gradually reduced to just *'s* – the same tag we now use to mark the possessive form of a noun, e.g. *the prince's horse*. The historical origins of our apostrophe-S are why it is still sometimes referred to as the 'Saxon genitive' in English today.

Russian grammar are so fluid that all six permutations of that order are permitted. svo may be the norm, but sov, vso, vos, osv, and ovs are all perfectly acceptable, with each simply emphasising a different part of the sentence.

In English, we can achieve a similar effect to this only rhetorically, by messing around with the expected order of things to 'topicalise' what we want to say. *This one, I like. That one, I don't. Pizza, I ate.* But this emphatic order-jumbling (a rhetorical technique called anastrophe) is by no means standard practice – indeed its effectiveness relies on the fact it deliberately breaks our rules. In Russian, however, any change to the usual svo order of things is entirely within the grammatical by-laws.

But how can a Russian speaker know what's going on if a sentence can apparently be put together in any random order? The case system picks up the slack. Russian has six grammatical cases, so even if the usual sentence order (svo) were completely reversed (ovs), each individual element would still be sufficiently signposted to make it clear who or what has done what to whom. In English, where only the scantest case system remains, we simply cannot do this. If *The dog chased the cat* (svo) were inverted to *The cat chased the dog* (ovs), we wouldn't have somehow emphasised it was a cat the dog chased rather than a squirrel or the postman; we would have wholly and irretrievably changed the meaning of the sentence.

The difference is that English is an analytic language, while Russian is a synthetic language. In an analytic language, the words in a sentence are just that – words. They each have a meaning, but they carry relatively little syntactic information about how that meaning is meant to operate in relation to the words around it. When it comes to figuring out who or what has done what to whom, the words in a sentence simply aren't enough on their own. Instead, they rely on being placed in a strict and predictable order, and only by being analysed in that order, first to last, can the meaning of the whole be deciphered. *The dog chased the cat.* If that order were jumbled or disrupted, the words alone wouldn't be able to communicate the same idea, and the sentence would either change (*The cat chased the dog*) or fall apart entirely and make no sense (*Chased the cat the dog*).

In a synthetic language, words have this functional information encoded directly into them. *The dog-sub chased the cat-ob.* Because these additions alter the words themselves, the information they carry survives no matter the order in which they are placed. Synthetic languages can therefore afford to be much less reliant on word order, as the function of each part of a sentence is made clear regardless. Despite their differences, *The cat-ob chased the dog-sub* and *Chased the cat-ob the dog-sub* mean the same thing.

No language is entirely synthetic or analytic, and these terms are really better thought of as part of a continuum. Russian might be more synthetic than English, but it is much less synthetic than Inuktitut. It is a so-called polysynthetic language, meaning so much information can be encoded into a single word that one Inuktitut word alone often carries a full sentence-worth of information. 'He wants to try to pretend to eat it', for instance, would be *nirinngua-gasuarunajuq.** Similarly, English might be more analytic than Russian, but it is much less analytic than Vietnamese. It is an isolating

---

* Synthetic languages can be further divided into *agglutinative* and *fusional* languages. In a fusional language, such as Spanish, a single inflection often carries a great deal of grammatical information bundled into one. When the verb *hablar*, 'to speak', is rendered as *hablé*, that final *–é* ending alone tells you it is the first person, singular, simple past (preterite) tense, 'I spoke'. In an agglutinative

language, without any inflections whatsoever. Instead, separate stand-alone words and particles have to be added to a Vietnamese sentence to shape its meaning – so *Tôi uống cà phê* ('I drink coffee') becomes *Tôi đã uống cà phê* ('I drank coffee'), and then *Tôi đã uống hai ly cà phê* ('I drank two coffees'). As the sentence becomes more complex, entirely new independent elements have to be added to it, while the four original words remain unchanged.

That languages exist on a scale like this rather than in discrete categories gives them room to manoeuvre. As a language evolves it can slide along the continuum, becoming more or less analytic or synthetic. With its quintet of grammatical cases, Old English was more synthetic than Modern English, and so could take a more flexible approach to word order, as Russian does. The usual order of an Old English sentence was still subject–verb–object, but other combinations were by all means tolerated: it wasn't uncommon to find verbs shunted to the end of clauses and sentences in Old English, and objects hauled closer to their subjects. This flexibility endured for centuries, and English settled into its fixed svo order only around 500 years ago. By the time Shakespeare was writing lines like 'That handkerchief did an Egyptian to my mother give' in the early 1600s, the disrupted word order he was using would have already sounded archaic to his audience, telling us it was being exploited for rhetorical and poetic effect, not because of the grammar of the time. Writers have continued to play around with the usual order of things for rhetorical effect ever since, from John F. Kennedy's 'Though embattled we are', to Yoda's 'The greatest teacher failure is.' But evidence of our

---

language, such as Turkish, each different shade of meaning like this would typically require its own individual addition to the sentence.

language's more flexible past still endures in a handful of stock phrases that have remained frozen in their old-fashioned order while the rest of the language has become more analytic around them. Thanks to the sixteenth-century *Book of Common Prayer*, for instance, a bride and a groom will still say *I thee wed*.

The reason for our language's shift from a synthetic to an analytic basis is the same as it was for its shift from a gendered to an ungendered vocabulary: Anglo-Saxon England was invaded. Twice.

Neither the Norse-speaking Vikings of the ninth century nor the French-speaking Normans of the eleventh century shared a common language with the English-speaking Anglo-Saxons. English, Norse and French were therefore compelled to mix over centuries, and a simpler, leaner, less intricate English emerged as a result. As older complexities were discarded to make way for this more streamlined English 2.0, one of the many casualties was our old and rather convoluted system of case.

Unable now to rely on a shifting set of inflections to show the function of each part of a sentence, the standard subject–verb–object order of English gradually became immovable. The flexibility of the past was gone. English had been knocked along the continuum by five centuries of buffeting from outside influences, unshackling it from its densely inflected, case-driven past – yet shackling it to a newly undeviating SVO order. Aside from the age-old vows of newlyweds and a few stock phrases and proverbs, this order has remained in place ever since.

But why *this* order in particular? That is to say, we know now why English has a strict word order, but why subject–verb–object? Why not subject–object–verb, or any of the other possible combinations here? SVO languages such as ours are in a global minority, as some 40 per cent of the world's languages actually prefer SOV. So why isn't English one of them? Well, according to one theory at least, it once was.

Journey far enough back in time, and English would have used an SOV order. So too would Norse and French. And Russian. And German, for that matter. In fact, regardless of what theory or timeline of language origin you ascribe to, the very earliest human language from which all modern language is descended is now widely presumed to have used a subject–object–verb order. Every other combination in use today, including that of English, is simply a later divergence from that. But how can we know something with such certainty about language from 100,000 years ago? Remarkably, evidence is increasingly suggesting that subject–object–verb is not just the standard word order of the majority of the world's languages, but the default language-processing order of the human brain.

In 2005, a unique sign language used by a small deaf community among the al-Sayyid Bedouin people of Israel was studied in detail for the first time. The language had emerged spontaneously – created by its users, without any outside influence, in the middle of the Negev Desert – over the previous seventy years. Unlike the principal languages of the region, like Arabic (VSO) and Hebrew (SVO), al-Sayyid had adopted an SOV word order. Its users couldn't possibly have picked up this sequence from anywhere else, given the circumstances, so its researchers believed they must simply have found this order the most natural and expedient way to communicate with one another. Other studies of similar emergent languages have suggested the same thing: when our language is left to its own devices, SOV proves the automatic default.

This conclusion has since been backed up by experimentation. In a groundbreaking study at the University of Chicago in 2008, volunteers were tasked with communicating simple sentences using only their hands. Regardless of the natural word order of their mother tongue, all the participants ended up gesturing in an SOV order. Even English speakers, when prompted, will tend to mime *You a letter write* or *I the door opened* rather than *You write a letter* or *I opened the door*. Based on evidence like this, we can presume our earliest ancestors' language used an SOV order too, as this appears to be the natural and inbuilt order of human communication.

Quite why SOV is so naturally preferable is unclear, but it could simply be that the subject and object of sentence (known as the agent and the patient in this context) are often much more tangible than the action that links them together. Moreover, verbs rely on agents and patients to carry them out and cannot easily be envisaged on their own. Without a dog, there would be no cat-chasing – yet without the cat too, there is only the vague concept of *chasing*, which can scarcely be conceived of at all without a chaser and chasee. An SOV order would prioritise a sentence's most substantial information, establishing its agents and patients first before revealing the less tangible action that links them together. *This thing, to that thing, did this thing.* But if SOV really is as logical as this theory would suggest, why has English – along with nearly two-thirds of the world's languages – abandoned it?

A problem arises in SOV sentences when the agents and patients involved are potentially reversible. A cat could just as easily chase a dog. The dragon could quite easily have killed the prince. Placing a reversible agent and patient alongside one another could create confusion, especially as languages advance and sentences become more complex, adopting more detailed descriptions and verbs requiring multiple agents or patients. For example, the sentence *The handsome prince gave the beautiful princess the golden key to the old king's grand castle* proves much more befuddling when all its tangible elements are introduced at once: *The handsome prince the beautiful princess the golden key to the old king's grand castle gave.* Using the verb to divide agent and patient – turning SOV into SVO – might have emerged simply as a means of keeping these potentially confusable elements apart.

The implication that an SVO order helps clarify complex sentences shouldn't be taken to mean that languages still using SOV are in any way less complex, less advanced, or less logical. After all, some of the world's most intricate and poetic languages – Turkish, Japanese and even Lord Byron's Armenian – use an SOV order. The reason why so many of them maintain it merely brings us back to where we began.

Over 80 per cent of the languages that use an SOV word order also have a system of grammatical case. Among SVO languages, that figure drops to below 30 per cent. The one, it seems, feeds into the other. In languages that mark the roles of the words in their sentences overtly using case markers, an SOV order poses little interpretative difficulty. But when a language abandons its case system, for whatever reason, SOV has the potential to be confusing and so another sequence steps in as a clarificatory replacement. Backing up this theory, many languages have been found to have moved from SOV to SVO over time, yet very few have ever been found to have moved the other way. And many creole languages – having thrown their case systems and other complexities overboard – have been found to adopt an SVO order, even if the languages from which they emerge use SOV.

Much of this remains theoretical, however, and research into our languages' histories and our brains' approach to word order is still ongoing. If one thing is clear though, very little about our language is ever truly fixed or static – not even the apparently inflexible order in which our words themselves are placed.

Q. 16

How Do We Read?

What is reading but silent conversation?
Walter Savage Landor,
Imaginary Conversations (1824)

Have you ever glanced at a ticking clock, and thought for a moment that its second hand wasn't moving? That it seemed to somehow stay in place a little longer than it should, before ticking on as normal, as if nothing had happened? You'd by no means be alone if so, because this bizarre sensation is the result of a phenomenon called chronostasis – or, appropriately enough, the stopped-clock illusion.

What causes this to happen is that despite what appears to be an uninterrupted stream of information passing our eyes, our eyes themselves don't take in the world in one long, smooth, running image. Instead, what we see is the result of a stuttering chain of short-lived glances, called fixations, punctuated by a series of enormously rapid eye movements, called saccades, as our eyes leap from one interesting thing to the next. This constant fixating and saccading leaves our brain with a fairly disorderly input of visual information, more like a series of individual snapshots or scenes rather than one long blockbuster movie. As a result, it not only has to interpret and make sense of what we're seeing but quality-control our perception of it too. And it's how our brain does that that creates the illusion of the stopped clock.

As our eyes move from one fixed point to another, each saccadic movement in between lasts just a fraction of a second. But that immense speed means our eyes move far too quickly during a saccade for any kind of clear image to be perceived. If we really were to 'see' what our eyes were taking in as they moved like this, it would to us appear as little more than a dizzying and disorientating blur. Not having a constant stream of clear vision would understandably be of little use to us, and so to maintain a consistent level of perception, our brain simply cuts these momentary blurs out. The gap that leaves in our perception is then filled in retrospectively with an image of the new fixation.

So as we look around, our eyes fixate on something, then move via a split-second saccade onto something else, and then fixate on that. But what we perceive as that process unfolds is the first fixation all but instantaneously followed by the second – an image of which is then artificially prolonged by the brain to mask the blurry gap in between. You can test this out yourself by darting your eyes from one side to the other. Do you *see* the rushing blur between the two glances? Or just two separate images, one after the other? In order to create the impression that we're watching that long blockbuster movie, our brain effectively leaves all the visual content from our saccades on the cutting-room floor.

Normally, this editing process happens so quickly that the brain's subterfuge goes unnoticed, and we remain blissfully unaware that our smooth and uninterrupted view of the world is really more of a hastily assembled clipshow. But when we move our eyes to fixate on something that is *itself* moving in strict time – like the ticking second hand of a clock – the deception reveals itself. Because our brain uses an image of the new fixation (the clock) to cover up the blurry saccade before it (what our eyes see as they *move* to the clock), it makes the first split second of the fixation appear unnaturally long, creating the illusion that time has briefly stopped.

It's not just our sense of vision that operates this way. The so-called dead phone illusion proves that aural information is manipulated by our brains too, giving us the impression that a ringing telephone is not quite ringing as regularly as it really is. But it's in our visual perception that this effect proves particularly noticeable – and the fact that our vision is broken up into fixations and saccades at all proves even more significant when it comes to how we read.

As you scan a line of text like this one, it's again easy to presume your eyes are moving smoothly and uninterruptedly across it, taking it all in as if it were a long tickertape of information. We can certainly force. Ourselves. To. Read. Much. More. Deliberately. Like. This. Yet doing so feels uneven and unnatural, and nothing at all like the smooth, free-flowing feeling of ordinary reading. Just as our visual perception is built from a stuttering series of fixations and saccades, however, so too is our reading. In fact, if you were to watch someone's eyes as they read something – or if you were to video yourself reading and watch the footage back – you would soon see this process is not remotely smooth at all.

As easy and effortless as reading the words on this page will undoubtedly feel (as long as I've done my job properly), your eyes are actually taking in this text piecemeal – one jerky, momentary fixation at a time – and constantly hopping or saccading from one portion of the text to the next. Indeed it is during reading that our eye movements are at their fastest: on average, you'll shift along a line of text by roughly eight or nine characters at a time (often irrespective of the spaces between words), with your eyes taking scarcely one-fiftieth of a second to make the leap from one fixation to the next. How you're *actually* reading this text is not as a smooth stream of word-by-word information, but as a long chain of rando   m and se   parate sn   apshots, t   hat onl   y appea   r as a so   lid stre   am of inf   ormatio   n, becaus   the mov   ement of   your eyes f   rom one p   art of t   he text t   o the nex   t happens   so quickly. (And well done if you got through that in one piece.)

There are two further complications here. First, in order to speed up the reading process, our brain is also capable of skipping over any word or section of text it considers unimportant – like the repeated name of a character in a story, or even short function words, such as *a* and *the*. Although grammatically we might need these elements, mentally they're considered so throwaway that our eyes and brains scarcely bother to take them in at all. Missing them out accelerates our reading, allowing us to jump a little further along the line at the next saccade. But that time-saving comes at a cost.

With our eyes now leaping haphazardly around a text and routinely omitting things that our brain presumes we don't need to know, we become frustratingly susceptible to typos, errors and misinterpretations. Our brain can act overconfidently and presumptuously, and sometimes skip over a word it has in fact misidentified, or an error it has failed to see. It is this that makes us so vulnerable to glitchy sentences like *I love Paris in the the springtime*, in which it's easy to presume that all is well when it really isn't – especially when the the problem in question appears at a break in a line:

I
LOVE
PARIS IN THE
THE SPRINGTIME

A second complication comes from the anatomy of our eyes themselves.

The innermost layer of the eye, the retina, effectively works like the film inside a camera. An image is focused and projected onto it by the lens of the eye, before the tens of millions of light-sensitive photoreceptor cells that line it, called rods and cones, translate that information into electric impulses that can be sent to the brain for interpretation. Rods, which outnumber cones by almost 20 to 1, are best suited for low-light conditions; animals that have exceptional night vision have many more rod cells than us. Cones, though much less numerous overall (around 6–7 million per eye, compared to well over 100 million rods), are responsible for all our full-colour, high-acuity vision.

Despite their importance, our cone cells aren't arranged evenly across the inside of our eye but are much more tightly centred around a single tiny millimetre-wide pit on the back of the eye, the fovea, in which there are no rod cells at all. Slightly outside that, in an area called the parafovea, there are fewer cones and considerably more rods. And outside that, in the perifovea, the balance shifts again. It is in the cone-rich fovea that our vision is at its sharpest, while our less acute peripheral vision is governed by the rest of the eye.

This unevenness means that all the individual 'snapshots' we take when we read a line of text are themselves uneven too. As we read, the central point of each fixation – perhaps wide enough to take in around only three or four characters at a time – will be absolutely pin-sharp and perfectly clear. But each side of it, the surrounding letters and words will fade away into blurred obscurity, as more of our peripheral vision takes over. What we truly see as we scan a line of text is not a staggered series of flawless snapshots, but something far more chaotic:

What we actually see as we scan a line of text is something more like this.

But if a lot of what we read falls in this blurrier, less acute part of the eye – as it is estimated around half the letters that pass our eyes do – how are we still able to understand it?

Our peripheral vision might be blurred but, as we read, it is nevertheless capable of providing enough information to assess things like how long or short the upcoming words are, whether any of them might look as if we could miss them out, how far we can jump ahead next, or whether there's anything unfamiliar or unusual ahead that might require extra attention. If I, for instance, were suddenly to become stuck in a meaningless loop while writing this sentence like this and like this and like this and like this and like this and like this and like this and like this and like this and like this and like this and like this and like this and like this and like this and like this and like this, the ability of your peripheral vision to spot upcoming skippable content would save your eyes from having to labour onwards through every individual *and like this* until the end of the sentence. Instead, it will effectively raise the alarm, sense there's something afoot, and begin calculating how best to jump ahead. (And let's be honest – you skipped ahead to the comma at the end of all that, didn't you?)

That's an extreme example, of course, and in truth there's a little more going on in a longer pattern of text like that than meets the eye, so to speak. But the principle is the same: as we read, our eyes are stuttering along from one fixation to the next, not smoothly scanning the text all in one go, and while only one tiny part of our eyes is taking in everything in pin-sharp detail, another part is already looking and reading ahead, figuring out how far to jump onwards next time, and what, if anything, can be skipped over. With those two processes working in harmony, we can read fluently and swiftly.

Then what?

We know now how our eyes take in visual information, and what the effect of that mechanism is when what we're looking at is a line of text. But how do we transform all the squiggles and symbols on this page into recognisable, contentful language?

The cells in our retina certainly don't know that what they're looking at is language, as they can respond only to basic stimuli like sections of light and shade, and the outlines or borders between differently coloured areas. But this information is sent to our brain by so many millions of individual cells that, rather like putting together the pieces of a jigsaw or the individual pixels of a digital image, a complete image can easily be reassembled in our visual cortex, at the back of the head. Once that image is recognised as writing, it is sent across to a second region of the brain, called the angular gyrus, which essentially transforms it into an internal monologue – replacing the written text with a string of phonological material, so that the brain effectively reads out loud to itself. This stream of 'spoken' information is then sent to a third part of the brain called Wernicke's area (more on that later), which is responsible for language comprehension. Here, the words we have read are matched with the words that we know, and the meaning of the text is finally deciphered.

Precisely how our internal store of words is organised is debatable, but it's thought our brain relies more on the overall shape or outline of each word to identify it, rather than looking it up letter by letter in any kind of mental dictionary. So if you were to read the word *dog*, your brain wouldn't begin by searching through all its D-words and then its DO-words, but would instead scan its vocabulary for all those words that vaguely match the shape of *dog*. *Day*, *dig*, *dug*, *leg* and *log* might all be thrown forward by your brain's neural networks, before the shortlist is trimmed down – with a little help from the context in which the word appears – and the most precise match filters to the top. Once it knows for sure that the word is *dog*, the brain can then connect it to everything else it knows about the concept of *dog* and build its understanding of a sentence from there.

And all of this – from the firing of your rods and cones in response to the light and dark areas of a page to your brain recognising those areas as text and connecting its words to their meanings – happens unconsciously and instantaneously, in the milliseconds-long duration of a single fixation of your eyes. Then, as if nothing has happened at all, your eyes simply jump forward to a new set of light and dark areas, and the whole mechanism starts again. And that's happening right now, over and over again, multiple times a second, as you read these words, without you ever being aware of it. It sounds almost too extraordinary to be true – which raises one final question. How on earth are we even capable of this?

As we've already mentioned, language has been inherent to humankind in one form or another for tens if not hundreds of thousands of years. But written language is only a few thousand years old; before then, as odd as it might sound to us today, there would simply have been no concept of reading at all. So how have we managed to become so effortlessly proficient at so complex a skill in so brief an amount of time?

This is a long-standing linguistic enigma known as the paradox of reading. We humans have seemingly miraculously acquired the ability to read with remarkable speed, despite it being a relatively new phenomenon. According to one theory, however, no matter the newness of reading in human culture, the act of reading itself is not a new skill. Rather, we have come to adapt to it so rapidly because reading is a repurposing of a skill we have had and honed for millions of years.

Imagine if an abstract artist were to paint a picture of a landscape of rolling hills and mountains. What we would see as a complex and multilayered expanse of trees, fields, rocks, clouds, birds, roads and so on, might be recreated on their canvas as little more than a diagram-like network of basic shapes. A columnar tree here. A triangular hill there. A circular sun above. And wherever any of these basic shapes end or meet, an angle would be formed. A perpendicular T where a tree meets the horizon. A right-angled L where its trunk meets the ground. A pronged K, or V, or Y where its branches fork and split in two. At its simplest, absolutely everything we perceive can be boiled down to a rudimentary network of these shapes, lines, curves, corners, junctions, angles and edges. Importantly, all of these are non-accidental forms: if you were to randomly splatter paint on a canvas, Jackson Pollock-style, it's unlikely a perfect L-angle or a K-shaped meeting of three clear lines would ever appear. When something recognisably L-like or K-shaped *does* turn up in the world around us, ultimately, our brains and eyes are naturally drawn to it. In fact, our vision seems to be all but hardwired to seek out non-random shapes like these, because it is from them that everything in the perceptible world is fundamentally built.

In order to then understand what we're looking at, our brain has effectively amassed a library or 'alphabet' of these basic shapes. So when we look at something that comprises a lot of T, L, K, V and Y shapes, the neurons connected to those shapes in the brain's shape library leap into action. That pattern of signals is then recognised as matching our concept of a tree, and in that way our brain understands what we are seeing. That's a very facile summary of an enormously complex process, and our visual perception undoubtedly contains a much more complex library of shapes and forms than just the few we can easily reproduce here. But the mechanism is nevertheless the same: our eyes are fundamentally drawn to the shapes and angles that things form, rather than the things themselves, and it's through the unique combination of those shapes that we perceive things for what they are. And it's precisely this process of recognition that we have hijacked in order to learn how to read.

According to a theory called neuronal recycling, devised by the French neuroscientist Stanislas Dehaene, we humans have acquired our reading ability so rapidly because we now deal with the basic lines and shapes of our letters in exactly the same way that we were already dealing with the lines and shapes of everything else. Just as our brain recognises a mass of T, L, K, V and Y shapes as corresponding to its concept of *tree*, it has also learned to connect the combination of lines and angles in TREE with the same concept. What's more, as we have refined our writing systems over the past 5,000 years or so, we have naturally come to adopt letters and alphabets that play into our innate ability to perceive things. All the world's alphabets might be different, but think about all the things they have in common: clear repeated shapes and angles, letters built from interconnecting lines, curves and vertices, and a sharp contrast against their background. As we gradually simplified the cumbersome image-based writing systems of the past, like Egyptian hieroglyphs, we unwittingly built for ourselves a collection of shapes and symbols whose forms we can decode easily, and constructed alphabets and writing systems that exploited our natural perceptive processes. Consequently, we can now read – and read so quickly and effortlessly – because the means by which we do so is nothing more than a natural extension of how we have always taken in the world around us.

Q. 17

How Do We Speak?

A word is dead
When it is said,
Some say.

I say it just
Begins to live
That day.

Emily Dickinson,
A Word is Dead (1896)

In 1840, a thirty-year-old Frenchman named Louis Victor Leborgne was admitted to Bicêtre Hospital in Paris. Leborgne was epileptic, and over the previous three months his condition had mysteriously worsened, leaving him now largely unable to communicate. In fact, although he could still understand his doctors, Leborgne himself could produce only a single syllable, '*tan*' – the nickname by which he soon became known at the hospital.

Tan remained at Bicêtre for twenty-one years, during which time his condition continued to deteriorate. Initially taken to the hospital's psychiatric wing, on the assumption he was suffering only a short-term side-effect of his epilepsy, he later became paralysed down much of his right side and spent the final years of his life confined to his bed. In the spring of 1861, he was moved to a surgical ward for further treatment but died just a few days later at the age of fifty.

At the time of his death, Tan was in the care of a surgeon named Paul Broca. In an effort to understand more about his puzzling condition, Broca performed an autopsy and found an area of deeply damaged tissue on the left side of Tan's brain, slightly above his temple, in a region called the inferior frontal gyrus. Given the nature of his illness, Broca theorised this area of the brain must somehow control the production of speech, and hence the lesion that had developed there had robbed Tan of his ability to communicate. It was a controversial theory; at the time, it was largely believed that the brain as a whole was responsible for complex bodily processes, not just individual parts of it. But a few months later, in the autumn of 1861, Broca had the chance to test his hypothesis with the arrival of a second patient at the hospital, with symptoms all but identical to Tan's.

Lazare Lelong was an eighty-four-year-old Parisian groundskeeper who was suffering from an advanced form of dementia. Like Tan, his vocabulary was now severely limited, and at the time of his examination he was capable of saying only his own name, the number three (which he used for all numbers), and the isolated words 'yes', 'no' and 'always'. After Lelong's death, Broca once again performed an autopsy and found another lesion in precisely the same area of the brain as in Tan's. The two findings supported one another indisputably and, in 1865, Broca revolutionised our understanding of language by announcing he had identified the brain's 'centre of articulated speech'.

This region of the frontal lobe is now known as Broca's area. Just as he described, damage here tends not to affect a person's ability to interpret language, but greatly impairs their ability to produce it, giving rise to the condition he had seen among his patients, now called Broca's aphasia. Well over a century later, we now have a greater knowledge of the workings of the brain than ever before, and although much is still unknown, more recent experimentation has suggested Broca's area might also aid our verbal memory, the organisation of grammar and syntax, and even the interpretation of hand gestures and ambiguous language. But it is as the control room of speech that it remains best known to linguists and neuroscientists – so when it comes to explaining how we produce spoken language, it is here that this astonishingly complex process is organised.

Crucially, Broca's area is positioned beside the brain's motor cortex, the central part of the cerebral cortex responsible for all our body's voluntary motion. When we speak, Broca's area fires signals into specific parts of the motor cortex, and in doing so cues up the precise sequence of movements required for us to say what we want to say. Those cues are then relayed via the cranial nerves to all the body parts involved in speech production, including the larynx and vocal folds, the jaw, and the articulators of the mouth, the tongue and lips. From start to finish, these speech-producing signals engage more than a hundred different muscles in the head, neck and chest, yet our brain is capable of coordinating them so adeptly that we can easily produce 120–150 words per minute in the flow of a typical conversation.

But if that explains *how* we speak, how do we decide *what* to say in the first place? For that, we need another part of the brain entirely and the pioneering work of another nineteenth-century surgeon.

Carl Wernicke was a German neurologist who, inspired by Broca, a decade later carried out his own research into the brain's handling of language. While working in Vienna in 1873, Wernicke examined a stroke patient who was able to hear and produce speech perfectly well but could neither understand what was said to him nor read anything that was put down on paper. In essence, he was the direct opposite of Tan: his production of language was not impaired, but his comprehension of it was.

Like Broca before him, Wernicke performed an autopsy after the patient's death. Again he discovered an area of damaged tissue on the left side of the man's brain, though this time in a region much further back, above and behind the left ear. If Broca's area were responsible for the articulation of speech, he reasoned, then given this patient's symptoms, it must be in this more anterior region – now called Wernicke's area – that language is understood. Damage here doesn't affect a person's ability to produce language, but drastically impacts their ability to interpret it – a condition known as Wernicke's aphasia. Sufferers are ultimately capable of producing a perfectly fluent stream of speech, but one that is often riddled with errors, full of confused or invented words, and sometimes lacking any kind of sensible meaning altogether.

With two distinct regions of the brain now seemingly involved in speech production, Wernicke set about devising a model to explain how this two-part system might operate. As it was his newly discovered anterior region that apparently dealt with language comprehension, Wernicke theorised that it must be home to our vocabulary, from which the words we produce are chosen. From there, our words must be somehow communicated to Broca's area via a language 'pathway', so that it can then organise the motor movements necessary to verbalise them.

In the century after this model was first outlined, linguists and theorists continued to expand on it as more of the brain's functions were deciphered. We know now that Wernicke's and Broca's areas are indeed connected by a dense mass of white matter called the arcuate fasciculus, along which information from our vocabulary is sent to be arranged as speech. We know too that Wernicke's area is located beside the brain's auditory cortex – the region that receives aural information from the ears – so whenever we hear speech, that data can easily be passed to Wernicke's area for interpretation. And when we read, it is to Wernicke's area that the optical information from our eyes is sent by the visual cortex, so that we can understand written language too.

More recently, advances in medical neuroimaging technology have revealed the inner workings of the brain as never before. Real-time scanning techniques have shown that when we first prepare to speak, a number of different regions of the brain – including some once thought not to be involved in language production at all – flush into life before our established language pathways are activated. In preparation for speech, the brain appears to recruit several areas separate from those identified by Wernicke, and as a result his model (and those based on it) are now considered far too simplistic. In their place, more up-to-date speech production models have attempted to account for this early eruption of mental activity by taking this entire process back to its most fundamental stage: the point at which we first contemplate saying anything at all and begin to transform our thoughts into words.

This initial stage is known as conceptualisation, or conceptual preparation. It is here that we first realise our intention to communicate – either as a response to someone, or merely to articulate a thought or idea of our own – and our brain starts to arrange the central concepts and areas of meaning relating to whatever we want to talk about. No actual words are involved at this stage, and quite how this all takes place remains a mystery (not least because none of it is a conscious act). Some linguists have suggested the brain operates in its own system of 'mentalese', and our thoughts only become perceptible to us once they're arranged in more recognisable terms. Either way, the brain combines several different streams of information at this conceptual phase, mixing data from our inbuilt knowledge base (that is, our factual, encyclopedia-like understanding of the world) with the likes of our awareness of the current situation (what we know of the context in which we will be speaking), and the discourse we will be contributing to (what has already been said, how formal or informal it is, and so on). We use our memory to recall what, if anything, has already been said, and to adapt to recent conversation so as not to repeat ourselves. And we even take into account social and emotional cues from some of our more intuitive right-brain regions, reshaping what we intend to say based on more personal factors such as our conversation partner's emotional state (do they really want to hear what you need to tell them?), their understanding of a subject (how specific can you be?) and how well or how little you know them (can you be candid, or should you be more guarded?). The wholesale result of all this neural activity is a package of information called a preverbal message – essentially, an abstract summation of what we intend to say and how we intend to say it, from which our brain can construct a more meaningful statement.

At the next stage, known as formulation, this mental 'message' is handed over to our vocabulary. Here, all the words we will need to communicate it effectively are selected and attached to it, via a process called lexical selection. Essentially, this operates a little like a word-on-word popularity contest: our vocabulary throws forward all the terms it associates with the concepts in the preverbal message, and those that receive the greatest boost in neural activity – those that seem the most appropriate to express the idea – win the game and are selected for speech. The successful words then undergo grammatical and syntactic encoding (and so are placed in sentence order and receive all their appropriate endings and tense markers), followed by phonological encoding (which transforms them into a string of sounds or syllables). Newly repackaged, this information can finally be sent on one last time for articulation, and as our motor cortex is stimulated, it sends out the necessary signals to produce speech. As long-winded as all of this may seem, incredibly the journey from conceptualisation to articulated speech is over in as little as 600 milliseconds.

A simpler way of imagining this process is to think of our speech as the script of a play. At the conceptual stage, our playwright has only the vaguest idea of what they want to produce, and perhaps has just a sense of its genre, its setting, its principal characters, and its beginning, middle and end. Nothing has been put down on paper yet, however, and the entire production remains little more than an intended project or a work in progress. At the formulation stage, the play is written. Words are selected, lines and scenes are fleshed out and ordered, and the story as a whole takes shape. Lastly, at the articulation stage, the curtain goes up and the play debuts – with its lines at long last brought to life in a spoken performance.

This basic sequence of conceptualisation, formulation and articulation underpins several contemporary models of speech production, but many questions still remain unanswered. Some theorists see this as a one-way system, and believe the material generated at each stage cannot be fed back to any earlier stage for fact-checking or reassessment. Others disagree, and envisage a constant back-and-forth between the different stages, ensuring what we say is always optimally formed and worded. Some theorists sign up to a more 'modular' map of the brain, with each of these processes occurring in distinct regions, operating independently of the others. Alternatively, this could all be a much more fluid system, with different brain regions taking on elements of multiple roles, sparking intermittently, not sequentially, and playing off one another as our spoken statements are brought to life. In fact, for some linguists, the idea that language is chiefly restricted to Broca's and Wernicke's areas at all – and for that matter, what the precise location and extent of these areas even are – remains controversial.

Questions such as these will undoubtedly be resolved in the future as research continues to shed light on how our brain operates. But we don't need to rely on cutting-edge technology to test whether this more multilayered model is itself accurate. Just as many of us often don't appreciate the workings of our car until it starts to break down, we can take a tantalising glimpse under the bonnet of our language by examining not how this system works but what happens when it fails.

Considering how rapidly we're capable of talking, errors in spoken language are relatively rare: on average, a person will muddle or stumble their words only once or twice in every 1,000 words they say. When speech errors do occur, despite how haphazard they may seem to us, research has shown they tend to fall in predictable places and produce predictable outcomes. A core set of regularly encountered errors has been described by linguists and speech therapists for decades – and it is how, when and where these errors occur that can provide us with some unexpected insight into how our brain handles language.

Two common errors of pronunciation are known as perseveration and anticipation. In perseveration, a sound from a previous word accidentally 'perseveres', and ends up influencing the sound of a later one – giving us sentences like *I'm taking a tath*, instead of *I'm taking a bath*. In anticipation, conversely, a sound from a later word arrives too early, and trips up the pronunciation of a preceding one – producing something along the lines of *I'm baking a bath*. Mistakes such as these always tend to fall within the same grammatical or rhythmical unit, so that a word from one sentence will rarely influence a word in another. They also tend to occur symmetrically, so if it is the initial sound of one word that instigates the error, it will be the initial sound of the blundered word that will change as a result – giving us *baking a bath*, but never *taking a kath*, or *tabing a bath*. Unstressed words rarely influence stressed words too, and no matter which sounds are confused, less than 1 per cent of all recorded speech errors result in a sound combination not found elsewhere in the speaker's language. An English speaker would never come out with something like *I'm taking a ngath*, because the rules of our language simply don't allow the 'ng' sound at the beginning of words.

Many of these errors are caused by little more than the speed, quantity or complexity of free-flowing speech. As our brains and speech organs scramble to maintain an unbroken and fast-paced stream of language, it's only natural that something will eventually trip us up. That certainly explains why a sound from one word might accidentally reappear in a later one (*taking a tath*), but the fact that sounds can be anticipated (*baking a bath*), and thereby ruin a word even before we've produced them, hints at something more remarkable.

Anticipation errors prove our brain must pre-plan our spoken statements and is always a stage or two ahead of the words coming out of our mouth. The fact that these errors never tend to travel across grammatical or rhythmical boundaries, moreover, suggests our brain must itself have some sense of these breaks in pulse and scansion too. And the fact that the vast majority of all speech errors still follow the phonological rules of their language has been taken as proof that the brain constructs spoken words not from individual sounds but from syllables, and so simply cannot piece together a syllabic combination it has no use for elsewhere.

Another much less subtle type of speech blunder is a substitution error, in which an entire word is inadvertently exchanged for another. It's this that produces confused statements like *I'm going to take a tap* (instead of *bath*), or *My hair needs cutting, it's too short* (instead of *long*). As nonsensical as these errors can often be, even they tend to behave predictably. Words are typically swapped only for those of the same class – so a noun will always be swapped for a noun, an adjective for an adjective, and so on – and the exchanged words are also usually related, either in that they both belong to the same semantic category (both *bath* and *tap* are bathroom fixtures), or are synonyms or antonyms (*short* is the opposite of *long*). We therefore wouldn't expect to find a word replaced by something completely different, as in *I'm going to take a needs* or *My hair is too going*.

Errors of this kind prove our brain must organise its internal store of words around these considerations, and probably accesses the words we need based on similar semantic and syntactic grounds. The fact that an entirely incorrect word can make it through to articulated speech at all implies there really is little crosschecking or reassessment along the way here, and that the route from conceptualisation to articulation is a one-way street. And the fact that the incorrect word is still pronounced correctly proves our speech is a multilayered process: saying *tap* rather than *bath* is an error only at the level of lexical selection, with a momentary malfunction causing the wrong word to 'win' the selection process. This error doesn't break the entire system, however, nor necessarily spark any further errors. So *tap* may be the wrong word, but as it continues on through the different stages, it is nevertheless dealt with grammatically and phonologically as if it were the right one. In the end we say and use it perfectly well.

Even when our speech errors become so total that we fail to produce any word at all there is still something going on beneath the surface. In a 'tip-of-the-tongue' scenario – when a word simply cannot be called to mind – many people will feel they still have some mental concept of it and will be able to call up an image of it, come up with related words, or even provide an appropriate description of it. If you were to blank on the word *bath*, for instance, you might be still able to envisage a bathtub in your mind's eye, recall similar words such as *shower* or *sink*, or even begin describing something that is *white*, *shiny* or *enamel*. This ability to access the overall concept of the word we're blanking on is what sometimes causes us to come out with ludicrously long-winded synonyms, out of sheer desperation. Case in point, I once blanked on the word *pen*, and called it an 'ink pencil'. Case in another point, a friend of mine once referred to Starbucks as 'the coffee pub'.

Speech errors such as these are thought to be driven by a specific breakdown between the stages of conceptualisation and formulation. Because actual words are not involved at the conceptual stage, at this point our brain is able only to access the idea of a word (known as a lemma) rather than the word itself (known as a lexeme). A lemma is essentially an abstract tag, corresponding to the basic concept of a word, but offering no more detail about its phonological or grammatical content; it's a little like the index label on the drawer of a filing cabinet, locked inside of which is all the more precise information, or lexemes, we require. Ordinarily, as soon as the correct lemma has been identified, the lexeme we need would immediately follow; in other words, once we know we've found the right drawer, we'd open it and take out what we want. But in a tip-of-the-tongue situation, the connection between the lemma and lexeme fails, the drawer remains closed, and because the lemma alone doesn't carry enough content to be taken through to the next stage, our entire process of speech production stalls too.* We can still visualise and describe the word we want, because the conceptualisation stage has seen to that. And we can still recall related words, because although we can't open the drawer, we're certainly in the right part of the office (and can take a look around while we're there). To rectify things, we either have to start the process again and hope the glitch repairs itself second time around, or simply wait until the broken connection is restored and the lexeme can be accessed.

It might seem odd that we can learn anything at all from frustrating and embarrassing slip-ups like these, and given that our entire understanding of language in the brain started with speech defects in the nineteenth century, it's somewhat fitting that our breakdowns

---

* Research has also suggested that bilingual and multilingual people experience the tip-of-the-tongue sensation more frequently than monolinguals and will often end up exchanging a word from one language for one they find they cannot access in another (as in, *I'm going to take a bain*). This has been taken to suggest that our brain does not store lexical information from separate languages discretely, and is not able to 'switch off' a language in which a person is fluent, even in monolingual situations.

and lapses today are still revealing so much about how this all works. But there is a serious side to all this. The more we know about how our brain stores, accesses and produces language – no matter how that information is found out or confirmed to be true – the better equipped we can be to repair those processes when they are damaged or impeded by illness or trauma.

As recently as 2019, for instance, a team of neuroscientists at the University of California, San Francisco, developed an electronic speech decoder, roughly the size and shape of a postage stamp, that when placed directly onto a patient's brain could intercept the articulatory signals being sent from the motor cortex to the vocal tract and use them to produce a synthesised voice via a computer. For sufferers of paralysis and neurodegenerative disorders, the implications of technologies such as these are incalculable. Existing language-synthesis devices – many of which rely on patients laboriously spelling out words letter by letter, often by monitoring eye or finger movements – could potentially be replaced by newer neuroprostheses, capable of reproducing their speech as quickly as they can think of it. Two years after this technology was first announced, in fact, the device was implanted into the brain of a twenty-year-old man whose vocal tract had been paralysed by a childhood stroke; it allowed him to speak naturally and at an ordinary conversational pace for the first time for fifteen years. With advances like these on the horizon, how our understanding of speech and language in the brain will continue to evolve in the years ahead is surely one of the most exciting areas of twenty-first-century linguistic research.

Q. 18

How Do We Understand?

Our understanding is conducted solely by means of the word.
Michel de Montaigne, *On Giving the Lie* (c. 1580)

Let's recap. When we hear speech, our brain's auditory cortex sends the input from our ears to Wernicke's area, where it can be run past our internal store of words and interpreted. Similarly, when we read, our visual cortex sends its input to Wernicke's area, so we can understand written language too. Naturally, the same applies to other visual forms of language, such as sign; in fact, the connection between vision and communication is so strong that even reading Braille has been found to activate areas of the visual cortex (as well as those regions of the brain that deal with touch) before Wernicke's interpretive region takes over. But no matter the form of the input, as soon as our brain knows it is dealing with language, its language-processing areas are activated and we begin to understand it. However, as flawless as all this neural circuitry is, there is a missing piece of the puzzle.

Even if we were to learn every conceivable word in our language, we would still not be able to understand everything we heard, read or saw. That's because our language is not always word-for-word literal and logical, and often our understanding relies on a far subtler level of analysis: reading between the lines, and figuring out what has *not* been said, as opposed to what has.

Out of sight, below the surfaces of our conversations, are a number of unspoken rules and conventions that quietly dictate how we understand what is said to us, and how we in turn make ourselves understood to other people. We're never taught them, never consciously learn them, and would probably never even know they existed without being told about them. Yet they're there, forming an invisible basis on which every instance of communication we ever make or enter into is structured. Imagine, for instance, a conversation such as this:

A. *How many children do you have?*

B. *Three.*

A. *What are their names?*

B. *John, Paul, George, and Ringo.*

A. *I thought you said you had three children?*

B. *Yes, I do. I mean – I also have a fourth, but you can't have four children without having three, can you?*

Frankly, it's not the kind of conversation we would ever expect to hear (not least because surely no one would name their children that). But as ludicrous as that exchange is, it aptly demonstrates one of these unwritten rules: a curiosity of language called scalar implicature.

Whenever we quantify something in conversation, such as *three children*, it is naturally understood that the number we've used is the total – no more, no less. In other words, although it might be *logically* true that you can't have four of something without also having three of them (as well as two or one of them, for that matter), our use of a specific number is taken to mean *that* number only, and nothing more or less from further up or down the arithmetic scale. So the statement *I have three children* is understood to mean *I have three children in total*, even though the statement itself doesn't explicitly say so. That rule is broken in the exchange above, and so B's finicky response comes across as an utterly befuddling and unnatural thing to say.

Scalar implicature even applies to less specific quantifiers too, including *few, some* and *most*. If someone were to say, 'Most of the schools are closed today', for example, we'd naturally understand *most* to be the highest quantity they could specify, and thereby deduce that *not all* of the schools are closed, and some of them are open. We intuitively cancel out any quantities higher than the one that is explicitly used – by *most schools* we naturally understand that means *not all* schools, in precisely the same way that *three children* was assumed to cancel out the possibility of having *four children*.

The idea that words can be intuitively ranked like this doesn't end with numbers either. In more general terms, the words we use to grade all kinds of faculties are arranged this way, like admiration, excellence, chance, frequency and even temperature. We naturally know that to *love* something ranks higher than to *like* something. *Good* would come below *excellent*, which in turn might come below *outstanding*. *Likely* ranks above *possible*. *Rarely* is outranked by *occasionally*, then by *sometimes, often* and *always*. And *mild* would come below *warm*, with *hot* and perhaps then something even more expressive, like *scorching* or *boiling*, at the very top of the list. In conversation, selecting a scaled word is naturally assumed to be the furthest or most extreme that we're willing to go – so if you were to say you *like* a movie, it's understood that you didn't *love* it, because you would have said so if that were the case. Similarly, if you were to say the weather somewhere is *warm* and it *rarely* rains, it's assumed the weather isn't *boiling*, but at least it doesn't rain *often*.

Scales like these are known as Horn scales, after the linguist Laurence R. Horn who introduced the idea in the early 1970s. In technical terms, they're based on a broader concept from the philosophy of language called semantic entailment: words that rank higher up the scale are said to 'entail' those beneath them. So *excellent* entails *good*. *Often* entails *rarely*. *Most* entails *some*. But logically, this entailment creates an odd situation in which everything below what we specify in conversation is still technically true. Just as you cannot literally have *four* of something without also having *three* of them, it's only natural that something cannot be *excellent* without it at least being *good*. Something that happens *often* must also logically happen *occasionally*. And if *Most of the schools are closed*, then it stands to reason that *a few* of them are closed, *some* of them are closed, and *many* of them are closed too. In fact, the only words on a Horn scale that we can logically discount are those ranked higher than the one we use. So something that is only *good* cannot be *excellent*. Something that is *warm* cannot be *hot*. And by talking about *most* of the schools, you would be understood to mean not *all* of them.

Apply the same reasoning to our *How many children do you have?* conversation, however, and things become even more mind-bending. Just as *most* entails *some* but not *all*, *four* naturally entails *three*, *two* and *one*, but not any higher numbers, like *five* or *six*. So saying *I have three children* when you actually have four is indeed logically true: you cannot have four of something without also having three. Saying you have *five* or *six children*, by comparison, would be an outright lie: you literally cannot have five of something if you have only four. But that means the statement *I have three children* seems to occupy some kind of conversational grey area. It is logically true, but conversationally misleading – and yet we can't call it a lie, because it isn't factually untrue, as *five* or *six* would be. So what exactly is going on?

The answer concerns another of our invisible rules of language, known as the cooperative principle. Devised by the philosopher Paul Grice in 1975, the cooperative principle is effectively an undeclared mutual understanding between all the speakers in a conversation: when we talk to someone, we automatically assume they will be conversationally cooperative, and they assume the same of us in return. That cooperation is borne out by a shared assumption that everything we say will be truthful, relevant, unambiguous and informative. Essentially, it is a conversational do-as-you-would-be-done-by. We wouldn't want to be bored or confused, lied to, or told irrelevant or unhelpful information, and we rightly assume the people we're talking to wouldn't want that either. As a result, we all enter into our conversations with this understanding in mind, and tacitly agree to talk to one another as cooperatively as we can.

Grice expanded on this idea by outlining four of what he called conversational maxims: quantity, quality, relation and manner. As its name suggests, the maxim of quantity deals with the amount of information we contribute to a conversation. It is effectively the Goldilocks maxim – what we say should not be too much, nor too little, but just enough to get our message across. So if you were to ask someone for directions to the beach, an optimally cooperative answer might be something along the lines of, 'Turn left at the end of this street, then first right, and follow that road down to the seafront.' That provides a perfectly adequate amount of information, without any unnecessary details, and so meets Grice's notion of quantity admirably. Either of these, on the other hand, would not:

A. *Excuse me, how do I get to the beach?*
B. *Okay, so, you want to turn left at the end of this street here – where that house is on the corner with all the cherry-blossom trees in its front garden, though some of them haven't bloomed as well this year as last because of the late frost we had last month. Anyway, turn left at that house, and you'll pass by a lovely café round the corner on the next street. It usually has a little board outside advertising its afternoon teas, but I'm not sure they do them on a Saturday so you might have to come back another day. But from there . . .*

A. *Excuse me, how do I get to the beach?*
B. *That way.*

Grice's second maxim, the maxim of quality, concerns truthfulness. We shouldn't lie in conversation, nor say anything of which we have no proof or that we know to be false, unreliable or not entirely genuine. So if the person you ask for directions doesn't actually know the way to the beach, you would naturally expect them to tell you so, rather than make something up and send you off on a wild beach chase.

Thirdly, the maxim of relation deals with relevance, and requires everything we say to be as pertinent as possible to the thread of the conversation. The long-winded answer above certainly risks straying into more relevant territory, as would someone who answered your request for directions with a comment about how many schools were closed today, the number of children they have, or an unnecessary story about why they had named them after The Beatles.

Lastly, the maxim of manner concerns not what we say, but how we say it. Our conversational contributions should be fundamentally clear, and avoid vices like ambiguity, repetitiveness, disorderliness, repetitiveness and unnecessary wordiness. 'Pedestrianate sinistrally afore that demesne with the florigerous viridarium', for instance, would not be a particularly cooperative way of giving directions.

Grice's decision to call these 'maxims' rather than 'rules' was intentional. These are not dogmatic commands, meant to be learned and prescriptively adhered to, but rather established norms or guidelines that all of us, whether we realise it or not, already know to adhere to when we speak to someone. Unlike the laws of grammar or syntax – which, if broken, have the potential to alter or even destroy what we intend to say – breaking one of Grice's maxims simply makes what we're saying less optimal, or harder to interpret. The rambling answer to your request for directions above, for instance, might have broken Grice's maxim of quantity, but it was still perfectly accurate, and despite its long-windedness would still have taken you to the beach. Similarly, if someone were to use arcane vocabulary like 'florigerous viridarium', what they're saying still stands; they're just not making our interpretive task as easy as it could be, and thereby infringing on the maxim of manner. And if someone were to underspeak and use a word from lower down a Horn scale than they accurately should (claiming to have three children when they have four in total, for example), they're dodging Grice's maxim of quantity by not being optimally informative. What they've said might still be logically true, thanks to the rules of scalar implicature, but we recognise it as being misleading because it doesn't follow our mutually established rules of conversation.

Grice himself even provided an example of how it is sometimes necessary to break one maxim in order to uphold another. In his 1989 book *Studies in the Way of Words*, he outlined a scenario in which two people, A and B, are planning a holiday, during which A wants to visit their old friend C:

A. *Where does C live?*
B. *Somewhere in the south of France.*

B's response here does not fulfil the maxim of quantity, because it does not provide enough information to answer A's question. If we assume both A and B are adhering to the cooperative principle, however, A has to believe that B is providing as much information as they can. If they were to say any more, they might risk breaking the maxim of quality, and say something for which they have insufficient evidence. Although the maxim of quantity has not been met, A can therefore assume the maxim of quality has, and that B is being truthful and does not know exactly where C lives. There is, however, another possibility.

Imagine B really *does* know where C lives, but the two have fallen out and, unbeknownst to A, are no longer on good terms. Suddenly, B's response becomes a *deliberate* infringement of Grice's maxims, as they are now intentionally withholding information from A. Both the maxims of quantity and quality are now being broken purposefully, not for any wider conversational benefit, but a surreptitious one: B simply does not want A to know the truth. In Grice's terms, that makes their reply a conversational violation.

When we deliberately break a maxim of the cooperative principle – in order to lie, obscure reality, lead someone astray, deflect an accusation and so on – we are said to violate it. Deliberately failing to provide enough information, for example, would violate the maxim of quantity. Trying to outsmart someone by choosing words you know they won't understand would violate the maxim of manner. We can violate the maxim of relation by deliberately saying something unrelated to the thread of the conversation to avoid a subject. ('Who made all this mess?!' / 'Oh look, the sun's coming out.') And in the case of your request for directions, someone intentionally and maliciously sending you off the wrong way would violate of the maxim of quality. But then again, what if they were to respond like this:

A. *Excuse me, how do I get to the beach?*
B. *There's a bus coming.*

Taken literally and logically, B's response here does not answer A's question. On the surface, it is a violation of the maxim of relevance: the question is a request for directional information, but the response is an unrelated statement about something that's currently happening on the street. If our understanding of language were based on purely literal and logical terms, these two utterances could not be connected, and we might expect the next line here to be an increasingly bemused A repeating their question more forcefully: 'Okay, that's nice, but *how do I get to the beach?*' In reality, of course, we know that is not the case, and that B has given a perfectly adequate answer. It may seem logically unrelated, but their response clearly implies that the bus that's about to arrive will take A to the beach. This much subtler bending of Grice's maxims is what he called flouting.

When we flout a maxim, we break it in such a way that we intend the person to whom we're talking to notice, and read between the lines to extract our true meaning. There is no maliciousness here, no surreptitious obscuring of the truth, nor any attempt to deflect a question or change the subject. Instead, a flout is just a less explicit means of speaking that invites our conversation partner to seek information outside what has actually been communicated. But how can we possibly be capable of understanding something that – quite literally – hasn't been said?

Our natural assumption that everyone we talk to is abiding by the cooperative principle is so strong that when it appears the principle has been ignored, we're naturally attuned to hunt out meaning and relevance even when none seems evident. So as disconnected as B's answer might seem from A's question, based on the maxim of quantity A will still assume B is providing an adequate amount of information. Based on the maxim on quality, B's answer must also be truthful. The maxim of relation means it must be relevant to the current conversation. And, following the maxim of manner, B has rightly made what they have said clear and succinct. Through this series of inferences, A can reason that B's answer must still be pertinent to the question they posed, and join the intuitive dots to deduce that the arriving bus will take them to the beach – a conclusion not explicitly stated in anything B said.

This invisible, inferential information we're able to extract from a statement is called a conversational implicature. The literal, logical, word-for-word meaning of a statement, conversely, is its explicature. The border between the two matches that between a major pair of fields in the study of language: semantics, which effectively deals with the literal meaning of words and statements, and pragmatics, which looks at how our language is used and manipulated in real-world situations, and how those manipulations are then understood by other people. In essence, while semantics deals with explicit meaning, pragmatics concerns implicit meaning – that is, everything that is implied by our choice of words outside their literal meanings.

Admittedly, Grice's approach to all this is just one pragmatic theory, and in more recent decades alternatives to his cooperative principle have emerged that explain this inferential process from different perspectives. No matter the means by which this happens, however, our ability to pick up this invisible layer of meaning – and, in return, our ability to communicate pragmatically to other people – forms an enormously important aspect of how we use and understand our language. Without it, we would have to be purely logical and literal, and our language would be hugely uneconomical as a result, as we could no longer leave anything unsaid or implied. Moreover, it allows us to indulge in sarcasm and irony too by flouting the maxim of quality, safe in the knowledge that you'll be understood sardonically. Imagine leaving the cinema with a friend, having both sat through an absolutely atrocious movie. 'Well, that was the best film I've ever seen,' your friend says, knowing full well how what they have said will be interpreted. The same goes for metaphorical and expressive statements too. 'I died when I saw it!' clearly breaks the maxim of quality (not least because you wouldn't be able to tell someone you had died if you actually had), but it does it so blatantly that its figurative meaning becomes obvious. We can damn with faint praise this way too. 'Did you have a nice time at the beach?' someone might ask. 'The bus ride there was comfortable,' you might tactfully reply. Clearly, without nuances like these – or the subtle capacity to interpret them – the world in which our language operates would be a duller, more solemn and much more coldly logical place.

Q. 19

Why Is This a Question?

'Am I correctly informed?'

*It being one of the principles of the Circumlocution
Office never, on any account whatever, to give a
straightforward answer, Mr Barnacle said, 'Possibly.'*

Charles Dickens, *Little Dorrit* (1857)

Punctuation is important. A single omitted comma and suddenly *I love cooking, my family and my cat* becomes something far more sinister. But as necessary as punctuation is, it is a relatively recent idea. For centuries our writing had no punctuation at all, nor even spaces between words. In fact, while written texts date back some 6,000 years or so, it wasn't until around 2,000 years ago that the first markings resembling modern punctuation began to appear.

Although some earlier writers and speakers had used various handwritten symbols to annotate their texts oratorically, it is Aristophanes of Byzantium – he of our acute accents and circumflexes – who is popularly credited with the concept of standardised punctuation. At the time, Greek was typically written as ONELONG UNFORGIVINGLINEOFUNBROKENUNPUNCTUATEDUPPERCASE LETTERS, as its readability was much less of a concern than its spoken performance. In an effort to make this solid lettering more immediately accessible, Aristophanes championed a system of bottom (.), middle (·), and top-aligned (˙) dots to break it up into shorter sections, based on where someone reading it aloud would pause or take a breath. The idea was simple: the higher the dot, the longer the pause. This wasn't exactly punctuation as we know it, as Aristophanes' system was based on rhetorical not grammatical concerns, but the foundations were nevertheless there. Unfortunately, the idea failed to catch on, and much classical Greek and Roman writing continued for a time to be written as solid text – a style known as *scriptio continua*.

After the emergence of Christianity, written language became a powerful tool in spreading the word of God. Scholars and scribes – especially those in Britain and Ireland only just becoming familiar with the new Latin script – began to recognise the importance of spacing and punctuation as a means of clarifying their writing, and ensuring it was interpreted correctly. The older bias towards speech and oratory shifted, and as ever more techniques were adopted to make the written word easier to digest, European learning embraced reading and writing as never before.*

---

* As bizarre as it might seem to modern readers, the concept of silent reading reportedly did not appear until around this time too. In the fifth century, Augustine of Hippo wrote of the reading habits of St Ambrose, the bishop of Milan, that 'when Ambrose used to read, his eyes were drawn through the pages ... however, his voice and tongue were quiet. Often when we were present – for anyone could approach him and it was not his habit that visitors be announced to him – we saw him reading in this fashion, silently and never

It was around this time that another of our major players stepped back into the fray. In his *Etymologiae* in the early seventh century, Isidore of Seville provided a description of Aristophanes' system of dots and outlined how best they should be deployed. A low-lying dot, or *subdistinctio*, he explained, should be placed 'where the speech has begun, and the sense not yet complete' (where we would put a comma today). A middle dot, or *medius*, should be placed where 'the sentence now makes sense, but something still remains for completion' (where we might prefer a semicolon). And the upper dot, or *distinctio*, was used to show 'complete closure of the sentence' (where we would place a full stop). Isidore's arrangement was topsy-turvy compared with ours, as his equivalent of a full stop was written at the top of the line, not the bottom. Nevertheless, it is clear that punctuation was now being increasingly deployed in accordance with grammatical rules.

Over the centuries that followed, this bare system of dots was expanded and embellished, and all manner of dashes, slashes, stars, strokes, swirls and other flourishes were added to the scribal inventory. But their use remained haphazard, and the rules behind them varied from place to place, language to language, and even document to document. Individual writers adopted their own practices and opted for whatever symbols they personally preferred. And among them was one more of our familiar faces, Alcuin of York.

---

otherwise.' Although some historians have interpreted this as a comment on Ambrose's rudeness (reading was seen as a more social activity, with the wisdom of the text shared among a group), others see this as proof that the idea of reading in silence was clearly such a novel concept to Augustine that it demanded comment.

Around the time that he was busy devising our upper- and lowercase letters, Alcuin introduced a novel symbol to his writing called the *punctus interrogativus*. In effect, it looked a little something like a modern tilde (~) written above a full stop (˙), which Alcuin used to highlight any written statement that posed a question. The squiggling *interrogativus* soon caught on, and as its curve gradually rotated over time (perhaps to conserve writing space on the line), the modern question mark emerged. The printing press helped to standardise its use and appearance in the fifteenth and sixteenth centuries – along with much of the rest of our emerging punctuation system – and we've been using an upright version of Alciun's *interrogativus* (?) ever since.*

It's just as well too, as the question mark is now an important interpretive tool in how we understand written language. As soon as we see one tagged onto the end of a sentence, we know to take the words before it as a query, even if its grammatical structure belies that fact. *It's going to be sunny today*, for instance, is a simple statement of fact – in grammatical terms, a declarative. That contrasts with *Is it going to be sunny today?*, which acts as a request for information, and as such is flagged with a question mark – grammatically, an interrogative. But in between the two, we have *It's going to be sunny today?*

---

* Admittedly, there are alternative theories here. One long-standing titbit of etymological folklore claims the Egyptians used a curled cat's tail to mark questions in their hieroglyphic script, and our question mark is a simplified version of that. Another suggests the Latin word *quaestio* ('question, inquiry') came to be abbreviated to '*qo*' by space-saving scribes in the Middle Ages, and as the *q* drifted above the *o* to save even more space on the line, it morphed into our (?). As popular as these tales are, there is scant evidence to back them up, and Alcuin's invention is now the more widely accepted explanation.

That's structurally a declarative, yet functionally an interrogative, so despite how it is worded, it too is written with a question mark, and interpreted as such.

So what exactly is this unruly halfway point? We have no punctuation in speech, of course, so how would we be able to tell whether *It's going to be sunny today* is meant as a statement or a question when read aloud? For that matter, what exactly is it that makes something a question at all?

In simple terms, a question is an appeal for information. Want to know something you don't already? Ask a question and you'll get your answer.* In English, we can form questions in one of three ways. Firstly, we can add a question-asking word into a sentence – *who, what, where, when, why* or *how*. Although properly known as interrogative words, these are also more loosely known as '*wh–*' words, and the questions we create from them are '*wh–*' questions. In forming a *wh–* question, the *wh–* word undergoes a process known appropriately enough as *wh–* movement, or fronting, which places it at the start of the sentence. *We are going to the beach* therefore corresponds to the *wh–*-fronted question *Where are we going?* It is possible to have non-fronted questions too, in which case the *wh–* word simply

---

* As if this subject were not already complicated enough, not all answers are actually answers. In linguistics and the philosophy of language, an answer is, strictly speaking, a response that resolves the problem posed by the question. If we were to ask *Where is the beach?* an answer would give us directions to it. A reply, in contrast, is any statement made in response to a question. So if someone were to come back with something like *I'm not sure; he'll be able to tell you* or *I wouldn't go there today!*, they would be replies, not answers, because the question itself remains unresolved.

takes up the position of the part of the sentence that would serve as its answer: *We are going to the beach* becomes *We are going where?*

Secondly, we can also change the order of the words in a statement to turn it into a question, by switching around its subject and verb. *We are at the beach* – in which *we* is the subject and *are* is the verb – therefore becomes *Are we at the beach?*, with the subject knocked into second place. This syntactic reshuffling is known as subject–auxiliary inversion, as it works only with auxiliary or 'helper' verbs (for example *will*, *could*, and *shall*), and forms of the verb *be* (*am*, *are*, *is* or *were*). If a sentence doesn't contain either of those, we have to compensate for their absence with a phenomenon called *do*-support, which throws the relevant form of the verb *do* into the mix as well. *He knows how to swim* would therefore become *Does he know how to swim?* (The inverted alternative, *Knows he how to swim?*, sounds a little too archaic these days to slip into casual conversation.)

And we can also form a question by simply saying a declarative statement with the same pattern of intonation as that of a question. Straightforward yes–no questions are usually accompanied by a rising tone of voice (marked ↗ in writing). Apply that pattern to a declarative, and you'll end up with something called a rising declarative – just like the hybrid we had earlier, *It's going to be sunny today?* ↗.

Other languages have their own techniques. Some, such as Turkish, mark the difference between declaratives and interrogatives with an inflection – so *Mutlusun* ('You are happy') becomes *Mutlu musun* ('Are you happy?'). Others use so-called question particles – short tags added into a sentence to transform it into a question. In French, adding *est-ce que* changes *Vous êtes content* ('You are happy') into *Est-ce que vous êtes content?* ('Are you happy?'). Around the world, this is by far the most common question-forming method; by comparison, as we've already discovered, our syntax-shuffling method is found in less than 1 per cent of languages. The Chalcatongo Mixtec language of Mexico, meanwhile, is all but unique in marking no distinction at all between declarative statements and yes–no questions. The Chalcatongo word *xakúro*, for instance, could mean either 'You are laughing' or 'Are you laughing?', and only context alone would let you tell one from the other.

So not only are there are multiple ways of forming questions, not all languages use the same ones, and nor do they all recognise questions in the same way. Complicating things even further, however, is the fact that not all questions *themselves* are the same – and in fact, some of them are not even true questions at all.

Fundamentally, questions belong to one of two categories: verbal and non-verbal. Non-verbal questions include all those silent, self-directed musings we mentally pose ourselves (known as covert non-verbal questions), as well as the questioning glances and furrowed brows we use to communicate doubt or confusion (known as overt non-verbal questions). Verbal questions are all those we put into words and ask of other people, but it's entirely possible for the two types to co-occur. 'What do you mean?' you ask verbally, while non-verbally lowering your eyebrows.

Questions can also be either direct (*Where is the beach?*) or indirect (*I wonder where the beach is*), and they can be either open, in which case there are multiple possible answers (*What should we do at the beach?*), or closed, with only a limited set of answers (*Is the beach far?*). Open questions can then either be simple, if only one piece of information is sought (*Where is the beach?*), or complex, if multiple unknowns are involved (*Who said what at the beach when?*). And closed questions can be either polar, in which the potential answers are polar opposites (yes or no), or alternative, with a set of options often presented in the question itself (*Did you go to the beach or the park?*).

The difference between polar and alternative questions is sometimes quite subtle, and we need intonation on our side again to tell one from the other. *Did you swim or snorkel at the beach?*, for instance, could be interpreted either way. As an alternative question, it's outlining two possible answers – the person being addressed has either swum, or they have snorkelled. But as a polar question, it's effectively asking whether any activity, such as swimming or snorkelling, has been undertaken at all – in which case the answer is either yes or no. The only difference is that polar questions keep their rising pattern of intonation, while alternative questions take an either–or pattern, in which the pitch rises on the first option, and falls on the second.

POLAR QUESTION:	*Did you swim or snorkel ↗?*
POSSIBLE ANSWERS:	*Yes; no*
ALTERNATIVE QUESTION:	*Did you swim ↗ or snorkel ↘?*
POSSIBLE ANSWERS:	*Swim; snorkel*

Skirting around the edges of these are a handful of more wayward question types. Direction questions, for instance, are those in which the answer is an order (*How should I go to the beach? / Take the bus*). Echo questions are those mirrored replies we use to confirm something doubtful or surprising (*I'm going to the beach / You're going to the beach?!*), or something we've misheard (*You're going to the where?*). Tag questions are conversation markers – *isn't it?, aren't you?, didn't they?* – that instantly turn declarative statements into clarificatory questions. Structurally, tag questions are usually 'balanced', or are said to have 'reversed polarity', meaning that a positive statement (*You are going*) will be followed by a negative tag (*aren't you?*), or vice versa (*You aren't going, are you?*). That crisscross arrangement essentially creates the same scenario as in a polar or alternative question, offering up a dual set of possible answers. In an unbalanced tag, either a positive statement is followed by a positive tag (*I'm too late, am I?*), or a negative statement is given a negative tag (*I'm not too late, am I not?*). The resulting overlap works to reinforce the question rhetorically, and often produces sparky statements with an emphatic or sarcastic bite, like *Oh, I am, am I?*, or *You think you're right, do you?*

With the exception of rhetorical questions – the effectiveness of which rests on the fact they're not intended to be answered – all questions, regardless of their type, still have the same basic purpose: they are appeals for information and are structured in such a way as to elicit some manner of answering knowledge or confirmation from the person to whom they are directed. But the deeper we delve into how questions operate in our language, the less even that fundamental function remains clear.

Display questions are those we ask to assess or confirm someone's knowledge. It's these you'll hear at a pub quiz or on a television game show, and it's these a teacher might pose a student, or set in a school examination. When a display question is asked (*What's the capital of France?*), the information being sought is not the actual answer to the question itself (which will already be known to the questioner), but whether or not the person being asked knows it. Put another way, display questions are not seeking the unknown factual information that would answer them (*Paris*) but are looking to confirm the fact of *knowing* itself (*Does this person know Paris is the capital of France?*).

And as if that weren't complex enough, one final type of question here strays even further afield.

To illustrate it, the philosopher John Searle devised this simple scenario. Imagine a group of friends are sitting around a table in a restaurant eating a meal. One of them, A, turns to the friend beside them, B, and asks, 'Is there any salt?'

Based on the definitions above, *Is there any salt?* is a polar question – there either is salt on the table, or there isn't – in which case, the answer should either be yes or no. But in this context, we'd scarcely expect B to treat A's question this way, and simply answer 'yes' and continue eating. (They could be deliberately trying to wind A up, of course, which, knowing my group of friends, is a very viable option.) Instead, although it's posed as a question, we'd naturally interpret *Is there any salt?* as a veiled request *for* the salt, not for some kind of confirmation of the existence of salt. In fact, it's entirely feasible A may already have seen the salt on the table and knows it's there, in which case there is no new or unknown information to be gleaned by their question at all. Even though A might well know the answer, however, this is not a display question. The purpose of *Is there any salt?* is not for A to ascertain whether B has spotted the salt too, in the same way that the purpose of *What is the capital of France?* would be to discover whether B knows the answer or not. Instead, what is going on here leads us away from the grammar and structure of questions themselves, and into the true mechanics of how we utilise questions in our language.

In the mid-1950s, the philosopher J. L. Austin outlined a revolutionary new theory of communication. Austin recognised that when we talk, we often don't produce simple statements of fact (known as constatives) but say things that are intended to bring about some kind of change or action in the real world (known as performatives). Those changes might be subtle (having someone pass you the salt) or they might be of enormous importance (swearing an oath, quitting your job, declaring war). No matter how vast or insignificant they are, all performatives change something about the world into which they are uttered, while constatives do not. Saying 'Paris is the capital of France' does nothing to affect you nor to change the reality of that situation. Accepting a proposal of marriage below the Eiffel Tower, however, does.

Key to Austin's notion of performativeness were three further concepts: locution, illocution and perlocution. Whenever we say something, we produce a locutionary act – a spoken statement or utterance, consisting of a set of words that carry a meaning. The effect those words then have on the real world is an illocutionary act – the action or force that we intend to bring about by saying what we have said. The outcome of that, in terms of the effect it has on our audience, is a perlocutionary act. So when A says to B, 'Is there any salt?', that bare statement would be the locution; the request for the salt that those words imply is the illocution; and B then handing A the salt would be the perlocution. Altogether, these form a single 'speech act' – the basis of what is now known as speech act theory.

Given Austin's interest in the performativeness of what we say, the illocutionary act was the most important aspect of his theory as it is here that the real-world action or change we wish to happen is brought about. Several different types of illocutionary act have since been identified and categorised, including commissives (promises and commitments), declarations (formal pronouncements) and directives (requests and orders). But just like questions, all such acts can be expressed either directly or indirectly. A could simply have demanded B 'Pass the salt!', but instead they couched their demand as a question, 'Is there any salt?' Both utterances would have had the same perlocutionary effect (being handed the salt), and both would be classed as illocutionary directives (requests for action). But while *Pass the salt!* is direct, *Is there any salt?* is indirect – it disguises what A truly wants to happen. So why did A veil their request like this? In other words, why is this a question?

The answer here is rooted in something we might not even think of as a linguistic concept at all: politeness. When we imagine someone being polite, we conjure up images of them holding open doors, keeping their elbows off the table, and dutifully saying please and thank you. But in linguistic terms, politeness covers a lot more than the socially enforced behavioural adjustments we make in line with the rules of etiquette. When we talk to someone, we constantly monitor and change what we say and how we say it, in order not to annoy them, take up too much of their time, or impinge on them too greatly. But there is one enormous obstacle in achieving that: by its very nature, the act of communicating itself is impolite.

No matter what we say or how we say it, communication is fundamentally a demand for a person's time, attention, effort, interest, knowledge and cooperation. By simply starting a conversation, we are forcing ourselves into another person's world and interrupting their current state. And the longer we talk, the more that intrusion manifests itself, and the more disruptive and impositional we have the potential to be. If that sounds like a social minefield, remember communication is a two-way street. Just as we are impinging on other people, they and countless others will be impinging on us, and just as we change what we say in order to be not too overtly intrusive, they will be doing the same to ensure they come across equally personably to us.

In linguistics – and in the field of pragmatics, in particular – all of this comes down to the concept of face. In the 1970s, the linguists Penelope Brown and Stephen Levinson introduced what they called politeness theory, at the root of which is the notion that we all have an intangible positive social value – our sense of face – that we wish to maintain. We naturally wouldn't want to do anything that could damage another person's social face, nor come across to them in a way that might threaten our own face. So rather like Grice's cooperative principle, we all enter into our spoken interactions attempting not to tread on the toes of anyone else, while also wanting to maintain our own autonomy, and not be too overtly impinged on ourselves. In effect, we're all just constantly trying to save face.

Naturally, the easiest way to do that would be never to interact with anyone at all. If you don't speak to anyone and nobody speaks to you, you can project whatever version of yourself you wish to onto the world, and claim whatever 'face' value (so to speak) you want to. We can't go through life eternally divorced from the world around us, of course, and nor can we constantly pussyfoot around everyone, terrified of ever bothering or upsetting our delicate social balance. Yet if the act of communication is itself such a disruptive social impingement, how can we ever get anything done? The solution is politeness.

In an effort not to come across as blunderingly rude and demanding, we tend not to speak bluntly, but veil what we say behind layer on layer of linguistic courtesy. We could, of course, ignore this convention and treat everyone as our menial servants, sugar-coating nothing and speaking as curtly as necessary to get the job done. That might get us the salt faster at the dinner table, but it would damage our social face, and see us lose others' respect and future cooperation. Instead, pragmatic politeness allows us to act more coaxingly and respectfully, meeting our conversation partners on an equal standing so that neither of us loses face.

In conversation, this would manifest itself in innumerable ways far outside our usual understanding of 'being polite' and saying please and thank you. We might, *uh*, for instance, *uh*, hesitate before, *I guess*, revealing what we truly want to say. We might try to foster a friendly or respectful relationship with endearments such as *mate*, *buddy*, *dear*, *sir* or *madam*. We can, *kinda*, hedge what we say too, so it *sorta like* doesn't come across too forcefully. And we can fall back on tag questions to, *y'know*, instinctively invite the agreement of who we're talking to, or cushion their potential disagreement. A more modern manifestation of this is so-called 'upspeak' – the use of a rising tone of voice towards the end of every sentence? Like those rising declaratives before? That make everything sound like a question? Even though it isn't? Which leaves the conversation constantly open for other people to interject? As if they're answering a question even when they're not?

Back in the restaurant, A is still waiting for the salt. But the problem they have is that direct commands and demands are among the most potentially face-threatening speech acts we can produce. They are naturally hugely impositional – we are asking someone to take the time and effort to do something purely for us – so unless we're in a situation in which rank is socially predetermined, as with a teacher and a student or a boss and their employee, we are instantly and unavoidably straying into impolite territory. To get around that, we disguise what we truly wish to happen by dressing it up in often ludicrously convoluted words and structures that belie its true illocutionary purpose. *It would be great if you could pass the salt. I know you're eating, but would you mind passing the salt? I'm sorry to bother you, but can you pass the salt, please, only I can't reach from here, and I don't want to have to reach across your plate.* It may be long-winded, but the more we disguise our demand, the less of an imposition it appears to be, and the less of a risk there is of us damaging our social face.

By moving from a direct request to an indirect one, however, we run the risk of veiling our request so thickly that its actual purpose is no longer clear. *Is there any salt?* is a perfect example: what could have been nothing more than a direct request is now repackaged as a polar question and could easily be interpreted as such ('Yes'), leaving what we truly want out of it unfulfilled. But in terms of politeness theory, the risk entailed in this face-saving indirectness is worth it. With a little help from Grice's conversational maxims, it is unlikely B will not take the hint, and so A can naturally assume B will read between the lines and understand the true nature of their request. Not only that, but B will appreciate the fact A has *not* presented their request as a barked directive, and so has *not* treated them as a menial gofer, allowing them both to save face. And A *knows* they know that. And B *knows* they know they know that. And A *knows* they know they know they know that. And on and on it goes, through endless unspoken layers of understanding, all so that we can maintain face. It may seem circuitous, even unnecessarily so. But by manipulating our language this way, and by not asking for what we truly want, we can not only get it but maintain a friendly relationship, appear outwardly cooperative and well-meaning, treat others with respect, and thereby invite that respect in return – all by simply asking a question.

Q. 20

Why Do We Use Our Hands When We Talk?

As the tongue speaketh to the ear, so the
gesture speaketh to the eye.

Francis Bacon, *The Advancement of Learning* (1605)

A few years ago, I was in our local pub with my brother and two friends one busy Saturday night. The four of us were crammed together at the bar, surrounded by people, where my brother was telling a story. I forget now what it was about, but as his tale reached its conclusion his storytelling naturally became more animated, until finally, in a grand punchline-heralding gesture, he threw his hand back over his shoulder – only for it to collide with the head an old lady sitting behind him quietly sipping a glass of white wine.

Happily, there were no injuries to report (just a few awkward glances and an embarrassed apology or two). But this tale of attempted murd—, sorry, particularly animated conversation, raises an intriguing question. Why do we use our hands when we talk? We all do it, certainly, and it feels entirely natural to do so. But is there really any need for a physical aspect to our speech? Why don't we conserve energy, keep our hands out of harm's way, and let our words quite literally do the talking?

Many people will have you believe this kind of gesturing is about confidence, persuasiveness and commanding attention. A well-executed movement of the hands can make all the difference in coming across convincingly to an audience – while a failure to gesture effectively risks signalling you're not engaged with them, not convinced by what you're saying, or not even to be believed at all. There certainly seems to be some truth to this. The effectiveness of gesturing in public discourse has been known about since antiquity, and studies have shown time and again it plays a role not only in maintaining an audience's attention, but in making a speaker appear more credible. In an experiment at the University of Naples in 2009, a group of students was shown a recording of a staged speech advocating the university introduce a 20 per cent fee increase. A different group was shown the same speech, delivered by the same person – only this time, she intentionally made no hand gestures as she spoke. Quizzed on their opinions of the proposals afterwards, the first group was found to be almost three times more likely to support an increase in their fees than those who had been shown the less dynamic version of precisely the same argument. Clearly, there is more to gesturing than meets the eye.

We don't move or act in casual conversation the same way we do when delivering an impassioned speech, of course, and nor was my brother's inadvertent karate-chop driven by some grand oratorical desire to convince us his story was true. Our more natural, everyday conversational gestures are known as *co-speech gestures*, and have been found to be common to all languages, all cultures, all conversation topics, and all people of all ages. Proving just how innate these gestures truly are, even people who have been blind their entire lives will still gesture to one another when they talk.

According to many theories of the origin of language, innate really is the word here. Our ancestors might have communicated via hand and body movements long before they began vocalising language, and if this so-called gesture-primacy hypothesis were true, a connection between hand movements and communication would have been established in our brains long before that which now connects spoken words to their meanings. Little wonder we find ourselves gesturing in conversation if doing so is an older form of communication than spoken language itself.* We're some way on from our primordial ancestors now, of course, and have long since developed the power of speech and a robust vocabulary to furnish it. So if gesturing really is a relic from our wordless past, why do we maintain it? Oddly, at least part of the answer here concerns how relatively unimportant words actually are.

It has been estimated that only around one-third of what we *truly* communicate when we converse with someone is driven by our choice of words, with the remaining two-thirds conveyed by subtler factors like tone of voice, facial expression, hesitancy and body language. These are so expressive that even when we try to hide

---

* Some evolutionary biologists have taken the innateness of hand gestures even further down our family tree and suggested that the neural networks that now govern communication probably evolved from nerve bundles in the hindbrains of our aquatic ancestors that governed the movement of their bodily appendages, allowing them to signal to one another underwater. It's just that all those millions of years ago, the same nerve impulses that now prompt you to make hand gestures would have been sending messages to fins and flippers, not hands and arms.

our feelings by choosing our words more carefully, our bodies can still give us away through the nervous tapping of a foot, a half-suppressed smile, or an irritated drumming of our fingers. Put simply, you cannot *not* communicate.

In linguistic terms, all these subtle communication-shaping phenomena are known as paralanguage – an umbrella term for anything and everything that adds colour and meaning to our speech outside of the actual words we use. Beneath that heading we find subdisciplines such as proxemics, the study of how we use the space around us in conversation, and vocalics, the study of how our voices can alter what we mean – like talking slowly to show uncertainty, or using hushed tones to imply what we're saying is not to be repeated. Haptics deals with the use of touch in conversation, to convey factors such as friendliness or intimacy. Oculesics accounts for how our eyes modify what we say, by winking, rolling, frowning and making and breaking contact. And kinesics deals with the interpretation of bodily movements, including hand gestures. These phenomena might all have individual names, but we don't use them in isolation; instead, we combine them, interweaving their different implications to flesh out our bare words and forge the most meaningful statements possible.

Take a simple statement: *I'm not going*. In conversation with a good friend whose birthday party you can't attend, this would be an admission of regret, and accompanied by the likes of a gently tilted head, arching eyebrows, a downturned mouth, a conciliatory hand on an arm, and a soft, low tone of voice. In conversation with someone who has ordered you somewhere you really don't want to go, however, the same sentence becomes a defiant rejection, accompanied by folded arms, a furrowed brow, broken eye contact, and a much firmer, stronger tone of voice. Everything has changed – and yet nothing has changed, because if we were to transcribe those conversations, we would record the same three words both times. By altering *how* we communicate rather than *what* we communicate, paralanguage lets us craft two completely different scenarios from the same raw materials: *I'm not going*.

So hand gestures are part of paralanguage, and paralanguage works to embellish our words to convey our feelings more precisely. But that's not all that's going on. Pay close attention to someone's hand movements as they talk, and you'll soon see not all of them are the same. Some are small and subtle, while others are grand and dramatic. Their overall shape and form will differ too, as will their pacing and timing. Linguists and gesture analysts use these criteria to classify gestures into categories, and in doing so can further explore how and why each type of gesture is deployed.

The simplest form of hand gesture is the so-called deictic gesture – that is, any movement that merely involves pointing. Deixis is the earliest form of gesturing human beings adopt, with most babies learning to point to the things that interest them before their first birthday. Our index finger typically takes the lead here, but deixis can be no less effectively led by another finger or thumb, a hand or arm, our head, a leg, a foot or even something that's being held, like a pen, a key or a phone. No matter their form, the purpose here remains the same: deictic gestures provide clarity and disambiguation, often in a much more economical way than speech alone ever could. When giving orders or directions, for instance, it's often easier just to point than expend time and effort describing something in detail. So 'Give me that!' exclaimed alongside a pointed finger is much more efficient than keeping our hands uncommunicatively by our sides and stating, 'Give me that pen next to the book on the table in the corner of the room.'

As helpful as these gestures are though, we don't feel the need to use them all the time, or else we'd be forever pointing out anything and everything around us like excited tourists (and there'd be a lot more dazed old ladies wandering around as a result). Instead, we call on deixis only when there's something to be gained by doing so – whether it be time or effort saved on our behalf, or enhanced clarification for our audience. We wouldn't point to the sky when chatting about the weather on a sunny day, for example, as there's a reasonable chance your conversation partner will know that happens to be where the sun is. But when offering someone a drink, we might point towards a boiling kettle or a freshly brewed pot of tea to communicate (*a*) tea is one of the drinks on offer; (*b*) that tea is now, or soon will be, ready; and (*c*) pouring a cup will not take long, nor be an imposition. None of those finer details is encoded in the question 'Would you like a drink?', but they can nevertheless be wordlessly communicated via an accompanying gesture. Some deictic gestures are so efficient, in fact, that they can stand alone without any verbal content at all. Silently gesture towards a drafty window or a ringing telephone and the person to whom you're communicating will doubtless understand.

Another fundamental gesture is the so-called motor gesture or beat. The appearance of a co-speech beat is unimportant – it could be as subtle as a wagging finger, or as dramatic as a fist banging on a table. What matters instead, as its name suggests, is its rhythm. Beats are all those gestures that follow the natural stress patterns of spoken language, metrically tapping along with the inbuilt ups and downs of what we say. This makes them a favoured ploy of public speakers, as their regular movement helps to hold an audience's attention visually, while allowing speakers to reinforce what they're saying by synchronising their hands to their most meaningful words. In essence, beats are the co-speech equivalent of *this* kind of *writing*, which ensures our *most important points* can be *visibly* HIGHLIGHTED.

Not all gestures are as simple as tapping or pointing, however. Often people will use their hands to mime or replicate what they're talking about, roughly recreating its size, shape or layout. These are called iconic gestures, or kinetographs, and act almost like conversational charades: we might make a sinuous movement with a hand while talking about a snake, or raise and tilt an arm to replicate the angle of a ladder or the steepness of a flight of stairs. Not everything is as tangible as snakes and ladders, of course, so where iconic gestures end is where metaphoric gestures, or ideographs, take over. Essentially, these are gestures that accompany abstract concepts with no physical, mimicable form. We can't easily mime a concept such as the past or the future, for instance, but in conversation we might nevertheless produce what feels like a relevant gesture when mentioning them – moving our hands from one side to the other perhaps, to imply the passing of time.

The purpose of these more figurative gestures is puzzling. It's certainly true they make us more visually engaging than remaining motionless, so it's likely they at least play some part in maintaining attention. But they certainly don't bring anything essential to the conversation, and nor are they meaningful enough to survive out of context. If I couldn't hear what you were saying while you mimed a snake, for instance, I might watch your hands and presume you're talking about a river, a winding country lane or a car weaving through traffic. So what are these movements actually achieving?

Recent neurological experiments are at long last beginning to shed light on this bewildering aspect of our language. Using real-time brain scanning techniques, studies have already established a linguistic element to hand gestures, as the language-processing areas of our brains can be seen to flush into life not only when we hear someone speak, but when we see them gesture too. But in one study in particular, seeing someone gesture was also found to trigger a 'pre-auditory' response – an electrical signal sent to the sound-receiving part of our brain, preparing it to receive speech. This preparatory effect was so potent that merely seeing someone *gesture* stirring a cup of tea was found to spark a greater pre-auditory response than seeing someone stir an *actual* cup of tea. Essentially, the gesture acted as a conversational cue – an unspoken, subconscious equivalent of telling someone to listen to what you're about to say. By gesturing as we talk, ultimately, perhaps we're retaining a cycle of auditory preparedness that ensures our audience's attention is maintained until we've finished speaking.

There is even evidence to suggest our brains can anticipate the importance of what we have to say and increase our rate of gesturing to ensure our audience pays closer attention. In an experiment at New York's Colgate University in 2011, volunteers were asked to read a short wilderness survival guide and then record an explanatory video outlining what they had learned. But while half the participants were told their videos were merely to be shown to college freshmen as part of a light-hearted team-building exercise, the other half were told theirs was for a group of advanced students enrolled on an outdoor education programme preparing for a midwinter excursion to the Adirondack Mountains. Those who believed their video was for this second considerably higher-stakes group were found to make three times more hand gestures in their explanations than those whose videos were intended for the freshmen. When we really need people to listen, it seems, our brains instinctively redouble our gesturing efforts to stimulate a stronger listening response in our audience. But oddly, our audience is not the only beneficiary here.

In another experiment at the University of Wisconsin–Madison in 2004, participants were asked to describe an arrangement of dots on a computer screen, set out in such a way that they formed the corners of simple shapes, like triangles and stars. But some people were shown the dots linked together by lines, thereby forming the outlines of the shapes more clearly, and making the entire task much simpler. Those given this version of the test made fewer gestures in their descriptions than those left to imagine the outlines of the shapes themselves – yet in both versions, the person to whom the subjects were speaking was sitting behind a screen. Not one of the gestures made during either test, regardless of difficulty, could possibly have been intended to benefit the listener. So why were the test subjects bothering to gesture at all when nobody could see them? And why did those given the harder exercise still feel the need to gesture more frequently?

Far from merely being a means of clarifying or elaborating verbal information, experiments such as this one suggest that gesturing might in fact aid our brain's processing and visualisation of spatial information itself, allowing us to talk more fluently about it. When you instinctively form the shape of something with your hands, you're not just mimicking its appearance for the benefit of the person you're talking to, but creating a robust, almost tactile version of it for your own benefit too. Imagine, for instance, that someone were to ask you your usual route to work, or the layout of your house, or your local pub or coffee shop. How quickly would you start using your hands to supplement your answer, marking out the arrangement of the roads or walls you're talking about? Consider this too: who do you think would most benefit from that? Are the shapes you make with your hands meant to give your audience a visible framework, so they can watch what you're doing and map the route out in their minds? Or do they provide you with a more solid reference point, so you can word a more accurate and fluent description of it?

As odd as it may seem for the gesturer rather than the gesturee to be the greatest beneficiary here, surely one of the most bizarre studies ever conducted in this field suggested the mental connection between the gesturer and their gestures might run even deeper. In 1996, researchers at Columbia University carried out a remarkable experiment in which a modified armchair was used to immobilise participants' heads and limbs during a conversation, making it impossible for them to gesture at all. For the period they were restrained, participants were found not only to compensate for this lack of mobility by exaggerating their facial movements and expressions but were found to pause and stumble on their words more frequently, suggesting gesturing really does help us to talk more fluently. Closer analysis of the actual words the participants stumbled on, however, suggested something even more profound was going on: most were words associated with physical activity, spatial information and bodily movements. Not only that, but when all the words used under restraint were analysed together, the participants were found to have used more basic, less imaginative vocabulary than when their movements were unrestricted. These two extraordinary findings suggest that far from simply helping us conceptualise what we're talking about, hand gestures might be overtly involved in our brains' accessing of their linguistic databanks. Being free to form the shape of something with our hands could ultimately be a means of facilitating our brains' retrieval of the words we associate with that movement, and so when that process is disrupted our ability to access those words – and think and speak freely about them – is impaired.

You can test just how potent this mental connection is (mercifully, without the need for a self-restraining armchair) by asking someone to describe somewhere they know well – their kitchen, their bedroom, or their favourite shop or bar, for instance. Then have them describe somewhere equally familiar, only this time remaining as still as possible, with their head forward and their hands kept behind their back or in their pockets. The description they come up with will still be accurate, but many people will find themselves unable to speak as fluently or in as much detail in this semi-restrained state, and will talk more carefully, pause and stumble more frequently, and struggle to find the words they need. Allow them to relax and the system will reopen, returning their language prowess to normal.

The more we find out about how gesturing is entwined with language in this way, the more we can aid our brains' ability to build and access its language store, and repair those connections when they are damaged. Recent studies of second-language learners, for instance, have found people are better able to retain new words when they're encouraged to memorise them alongside an accompanying gesture. Studies of child language have found babies who gesture frequently in their early years go on to develop larger vocabularies in childhood – as do the children of parents who gestured more to them during their development. And in a long-term investigation at the University of Chicago, a group of five-year-old children was asked to watch a cartoon and then explain what had happened in it. When this test was repeated with the same children at ages six, seven, and eight, those who had used more hand gestures when they were five were found to provide better-structured descriptions when they were eight than those who had used fewer. Encouraging children, parents and learners to gesture might therefore prove beneficial not just to our acquisition of language, but to our ability to use and remember it effectively.

It has even been suggested the gestures we make when our words fail us altogether could still play a role in language production. Some linguists identify a fifth and final type of co-speech gesture called a speech failure – or, in honour of one of the first linguists to identify and study it, a Butterworth. These are all those automatic, impatient hand movements we make when our language breaks down and we're left struggling to recall the word we want or were about to say. It was once presumed these movements were little more than visual cues, used to signal to an audience that although you had stopped talking, you still wanted to hold the conversational floor and would resume speaking as soon as you had regathered your thoughts. But it has since been suggested Butterworths might be our bodies' way of expelling the tension that naturally builds when we become frustrated. By effectively burning off this excess energy, these movements help to defog our minds, and thereby hasten our ability to access the words we need. Our inbuilt, long-established system of hand gestures, it seems, might even be helping us communicate when we stop talking altogether.

Q. 14 Puzzles: The Solutions

Words ending –*amt*

The only familiar dictionary words that typically fit this pattern are the past-tense forms of *dream*, and its derivatives: *dreamt, undreamt, daydreamt*, and *pipedreamt*.

Words ending –*cion*

'There are three common English words that end –*cion*,' this puzzle often reads, 'two of which are *suspicion* and *coercion*. What is the third?'

When put like that, the answer here is usually said to be *scion* – but extend this search slightly and more than a dozen words fit the bill, including *antiscion* (a sign of the zodiac as equidistant from one of the tropics as another), *bocion* (a glandular swelling in the neck), *contrantiscion* (the opposite of the antiscion), *epenicion* (an Ancient Greek ode of triumph), *internecion* (mutual destruction), *ostracion* (the boxfish), *pernicion* (total destruction) and *reminiscion* (the act of reminiscing).

Adjectives ending in –*dous*

'There are four English adjectives ending in the letters –*dous*. Two of them are positive, two of them are negative. What are they?'

For some reason, popular history has come to credit this particular puzzle to the author Isaac Asimov, but various iterations of this question have been around since the 1880s. Back then, the four correct answers were said to be *stupendous* and *tremendous* (the positives), and *horrendous* and *jeopardous* (meaning 'causing jeopardy'). Our language has moved on a great deal since the Victorian period, of course, and as *jeopardous* has largely fallen out of use, *hazardous* has stepped in to take its place.

Elsewhere in the dictionary, however, you'll find such suitable answers as *blizzardous* (snowing heavily), *enodous* (untangled, free from knots), *infandous* (unspeakable), *lagopodous* (fleet-footed), *lapidous* (stony), omnimodous (existing in many forms), *pudendous* (causing shame), *repandous* (bending upwards) and *surquidous* (very arrogant). If scientific terms are included, this can be expanded further to include *acanthocladous* (having spiny branches), *apodous* (having no feet), *molybdous* (containing molybdenum), *nodous* (covered in nodules), *ornithopodous* (having feet like a bird), *rubicundous* (intensely red-coloured) and *viverridous* (relating to the civet cat).

Words containing –*nkst*–

There's a popular myth that claims *inkstand* is the only English word to contain the string –*nkst*–. It certainly seems an unlikely mishmash of letters, but it's by no means rare: *bankster* (a profiteering banker), *clinkstone* (a type of feldspar), *funkster* (a 1960s term for a fan of funk music), *funkstick* (a timid horse rider), *junkstore*, *pinkster* (the pink azalea), *prankster* and *sinkstone* (a weight for submerging a fishing line) are all suitable matches.

Words containing *–shion–*

'*Cushion* and *fashion* end in the letters *–shion*. Name a word that contains that string of letters somewhere in the middle of it' is how this puzzle was often posed in the nineteenth century. The missing answer is *parishioner*.

Words ending in *–gry*

It's not the case, no matter how many times this claim is repeated, that *hungry* and *angry* are the only English words that end *–gry*. Shakespeare used *anhungry* to mean 'afflicted by hunger' in *Coriolanus*, and a standard dictionary will typically list the likes of *aggry* (a West African glass bead), *puggry* (a type of turban or head-scarf), *podagry* (an old name for *podagra*, a gout-like condition of the foot) and *shiggry* (an old word for being drunk). Even *gry* itself is a permissible word (used since the seventeenth century as the name of a unit of measurement equal to one-hundredth of an inch) while the word *hangry*, meaning 'angered by hunger', has found its way into the language ever since this puzzle was first posed in the 1800s. Despite its contemporary slanginess, *hangry* was first used by the author Arthur Ransome to describe an elephant in 1913.

References

Q. 2

Lameira, A. R., Call, J. (2018) 'Time-space–displaced responses in the orangutan vocal system', *Science Advances*, 4 (11)

Jusczyk, P. W., Friederici, A. D., Wessels, J. M. I., Svenkerud, V. Y., Jusczyk A. M. (1993) 'Infants' sensitivity to the sound patterns of native language words', *Journal of Memory and Language*, 32 (3)

Q. 3

Harrington, J., Gubian, M., Stevens, M., Schiel, F. (2019) 'Phonetic change in an Antarctic winter', *Journal of the Acoustical Society of America* 146 (3327)

Everett, C. (2013) 'Evidence for direct geographic influences on linguistic sounds: The case of ejectives', *PLOS ONE, Public Library of Science* 8 (6)

Maddieson, I., Coupé, C. (2015) 'Human language diversity and the acoustic adaptation hypothesis', *Proceedings of Meetings on Acoustics, the Acoustical Society of America* 25

Sonderegger, M., Bane, M., Graff, P. (2017) 'The medium-term dynamics of accents on reality television', *Language* 93 (3)

Blasi, D. E., Moran, S., Moisik, S. R., Widmer, P., Dediu, D., Bickel, B. (2019) 'Human sound systems are shaped by post-Neolithic changes in bite configuration', *Science* 363 (6432)

Bakker, P. (1987) 'A Basque nautical pidgin: A missing link in the history of FU', *Journal of Pidgin and Creole Languages* 2 (1)

Miglio, V. G. (2008) "'Go shag a horse!'": The 17th–18th century Basque–Icelandic glossaries revisited', *Journal of the North Atlantic* I (25–36)

Falk, D. (2004) 'Prelinguistic evolution in early hominins: Whence motherese?', *Behavioral and Brain Sciences* 27 (491–503)

Krause, J., Lalueza-Fox, C., Orlando, L., Enard, W., Green, R. E., Burbano, H. A., Hublin, J. J., Hänni, C., Fortea, J., de la Rasilla, M., Bertranpetit, J., Rosas, A., Pääbo, S. (2007) 'The derived FOXP2 variant of modern humans was shared with Neandertals', *Current Biology* 17 (21)

De Boer, B. (2012) 'Loss of air sacs improved hominin speech abilities', *Journal of Human Evolution* 62 (1)

Q.4

Jurado, A. B. (2019) 'A study on the "wordgasm": the nature of blends' splinters', *Lexis: Journal in English Lexicography* 14

Pagel, M., Atkinson, Q. D., Calude, A. S., Meade, A. (2013) 'Ultraconserved words point to deep language ancestry across Eurasia', *PNAS, Proceedings of the National Academy of Sciences* 110 (21)

Q. 5

MacIntyre, P. D., Gardner, R. C. (1994). 'The subtle effects of language anxiety on cognitive processing in the second language', *Language Learning* 44 (2)

Horwitz, E. K., Horwitz, M. B., Cope, J. (1986) 'Foreign language classroom anxiety', *Modern Language Journal* 70 (2)

Shahsavari, M. (2012) 'Relationship between anxiety and achievement motivation among male and female students', *Journal of American Science* 8 (11)

Pellegrino, F., Coupé, C., Marsico, E. (2011) 'Across-language perspective on speech information rate', *Language* 87 (3)

References

Haviland, J. B. (1998) 'Guugu Yimithirr cardinal directions',
   Ethos 26 (1)

Q. 6

Lew-Williams, C., Fernald, A. (2007) 'Young children learning
   Spanish make rapid use of grammatical gender in spoken word
   recognition', *Psychological Science* 18 (3)
Luraghi, S. (2011) 'The origin of the Proto-Indo-European gender
   system: Typological considerations', *Folia Linguistica* 45 (2)
Boroditsky, L., Schmidt, L. (2003) 'Sex, syntax, and semantics', in
   Gentner, D., Goldin-Meadow, S. (eds.) *Language in Mind: Advances
   in the Study of Language and Thought* (Cambridge University Press)
Prewitt-Freilino, J., Caswell, T. A., Laakso, E. (2011) 'The gendering
   of language: A comparison of gender equality in countries with
   gendered, natural gender, and genderless languages', *Sex Roles* 66

Q. 7

Saxe, G. (2012) 'Cultural forms of number representation used in
   Oksapmin communities', in *Cultural Development of Mathematical
   Ideas: Papua New Guinea Studies* (Cambridge University Press)
Wolfers, E. P. (1971) 'The original counting systems of Papua and
   New Guinea', *Arithmetic Teacher* 18 (2)
Franklin, K. & J. (1962) 'The Kewa counting systems', *Journal of the
   Polynesian Society* 71 (2)
Wassmann, J., Dasen, P. R. (1994) 'Yupno number system and
   counting', *Journal of Cross-Cultural Psychology* 25 (1)

Q. 15

Goldin-Meadow, S., So, W. C., Ozyurek, A., Mylander, C. (2008)
   'The natural order of events: How speakers of different languages
   represent events nonverbally', *PNAS, Proceedings of the National
   Academy of Sciences* 105 (27)

Sandler W., Meir I., Padden C., Aronoff, M. (2005) 'The emergence of grammar: systematic structure in a new language', *PNAS, Proceedings of the National Academy of Sciences* 102 (7)

Q. 17

Gollan, T. H., Bonanni, M. P., Montoya, R. I. (2005) 'Proper names get stuck on bilingual and monolingual speakers' tip of the tongue equally often', *Neuropsychology* 19 (3)

Q. 20

Maricchiolo, F., Gnisci, A., Bonaiuto, M., Ficca, G. (2009) 'Effects of different types of hand gestures in persuasive speech on receivers' evaluations', *Language and Cognitive Processes* 24 (2)

Bass, A. H., Chagnaud, B. P. (2012) 'Shared developmental and evolutionary origins for neural basis of vocal acoustic and pectoral-gestural signaling', *PNAS, Proceedings of the National Academy of Sciences* 109 (1)

Kelly, S., Byrne, K., Holler, J. (2011) 'Raising the Ante of Communication: Evidence for Enhanced Gesture Use in High Stakes Situations', *Information* 2 (4)

Hostetter, A., Alibali, M. (2004) 'On the tip of the mind: Gesture as a key to conceptualization', *Proceedings of the Twenty-Sixth Annual Conference of the Cognitive Science Society*

Rauscher, F. H., Krauss, R. M., Chen, Y. (1996) 'Gesture, speech, and lexical access: The role of lexical movements in speech production', *Psychological Science* 7 (4)

Butterworth, B., Beattie, G. (1978) 'Gesture and silence as indicators of planning in speech', in Smith, P. T., Campbell, R. (eds.) *Recent Advances in the Psychology of Language: Formal and Experimental Approaches* (New York: Plenum)

Acknowledgements

As always, I cannot thank the exceptional team at Elliott & Thompson enough for their limitless ideas, assistance, encouragement and, above all, patience in hauling this book out of my imagination and onto the page. They are truly the alphabet of publishers: a small team that together works wonders.

Many thanks too to my agent Andrew Lownie for his hard work and peerless advice, as always.

Special thanks to Danny Bate and Calvin Dreher for linguistic counsel and input.

Dr Matthew Edmundson: an expert in the world of decoding biological research papers that were beyond my unscientific brain. Your knowledge of gills was more necessary than I knew.

Thanks to Shane Telford for reminding me that the chameleon effect existed (and for your not so thinly veiled constructive criticism).

A great many people helped to keep both me and this idea heading in the right direction while it was still a work in progress, either through their constant reassurance or inspiration, or by quite rightly hurling things at me when I told them it still wasn't finished.

Team 7am: Mark Anderson, Mark Findlay, Oliver James, Matt McGeary and Pete Tuddenham.

Mark Faircloth – see, I told you I'd get this finished one day.

James Bell, your excellent flat whites kept me going.

Expert encourager, Neetika Dang.

Ideas man, Graham Snelson.

Happy birthday, 2015 FA Vase winner Gaz Bainbridge.

Matt Norris, who inspired the preface without even knowing about it. I think I still owe you that drink.

Andy Smyth ('superfluous', I believe you said).

Gavin Howard, for no reason.

Thanks too to Elizabeth Hanks for reminding me never to underestimate the Dutch.

Lastly, this book is for my mam and dad. I held on to this idea too long; I so much wanted them to see it, but life had other plans. It's theirs all the same.

Index

Index

Index

Index

Index

About the author

Paul Anthony Jones is something of a linguistic phenomenon. He runs the popular @HaggardHawks Twitter feed, blog and YouTube channel, revealing daily word facts to 90,000 engaged followers. His books include: *The Cabinet of Calm*, *Word Drops*, *The Accidental Dictionary*, *The Cabinet of Linguistic Curiosities*, *Around the World in 80 Words*, as well as several other books on trivia and language. He appears regularly in the media and has contributed to the Oxford and Cambridge dictionaries online. He lives in Newcastle upon Tyne.